TRADE MAKES STATES

T0386233

/ AFRICAN
/ ARGUMENTS

African Arguments is a series of short books about contemporary Africa and the critical issues and debates surrounding the continent. The books are scholarly and engaged, substantive and topical. They focus on questions of justice, rights and citizenship; politics, protests and revolutions; the environment, land, oil and other resources; health and disease; economy: growth, aid, taxation, debt and capital flight; and both Africa's international relations and country case studies.

Managing Editor, Stephanie Kitchen

Series editors

Adam Branch
Alex de Waal
Alcinda Honwana
Ebenezer Obadare
Carlos Oya
Nicholas Westcott

Additional longer monographs and edited volumes are published in association with the series, under the auspices of the International African Institute.

Associate editors

Eyob Gebremariam
Elliott D. Green
Jon Schubert

TOBIAS HAGMANN
FINN STEPPUTAT

(*Editors*)

Trade Makes States

Governing the Greater Somali Economy

HURST & COMPANY, LONDON

IAI   International African Institute

Published in collaboration with the International African Institute.
First published in the United Kingdom in 2023 by
C. Hurst & Co. (Publishers) Ltd.,
New Wing, Somerset House, Strand, London, WC2R 1LA
Copyright © Tobias Hagmann, Finn Stepputat and the Contributors, 2023
All rights reserved.

A Cataloguing-in-Publication data record for this book
is available from the British Library.

ISBN: 9781787387058

This book is printed using paper from registered sustainable
and managed sources.

www.hurstpublishers.com

CONTENTS

CONTENTS

PREFACE AND ACKNOWLEDGEMENTS

This book is the outcome of a collective research endeavour aiming to understand the relationship between everyday trading and state-formation dynamics across the Somali territories. The bulk of the empirical material, analysis and theorising was developed as part of a six-year interdisciplinary research project entitled 'Governing economic hubs and flows in Somali East Africa' (GOVSEA). GOVSEA involved over a dozen Somali, Kenyan, Ethiopian and Danish scholars and ran between 2014 and 2019. *Trade Makes States* synthesises more than a dozen peer-reviewed articles, three doctoral dissertations, several MA theses as well as fourteen GOVSEA working papers that came out of this project. The working paper series was published by the Danish Institute for International Studies (DIIS) between 2016 and 2019. It featured a number of authors who were not part of the GOVSEA project, but who share our enthusiasm for studying Somali political economies. The authors of Chapters 2 and 3 and of the afterword of this book fall into this category.

We owe a debt of gratitude to our fellow GOVSEA researchers for their hard work, patience and enthusiasm in seeing our project through in spite of numerous challenges faced along the way. We are thankful to the Danish International Development Agency (DANIDA) and Denmark's Consultative Research Committee for Development Research (FFU) for funding our research and providing support during critical moments of the project. A particular thanks is due to the leaders, administrators and finance officers at Roskilde University, DIIS, Forum for Social Studies (FSS),

PREFACE AND ACKNOWLEDGEMENTS

University of Nairobi and University of Hargeisa who made up the GOVSEA research consortium.

Numerous colleagues have accompanied and enriched our research, thinking and writing over the past decade. They include Emma Lochery, Kate Meagher, Markus V. Hoehne, Hannah Elliott, Neil Carrier, Peter D. Little, Deborah James, Luca Ciabarri, Nauja Kleist and Gregor Dobler, all of whom provided detailed and constructive feedback on various GOVSEA working papers. The book manuscript benefited greatly from critiques by two anonymous reviewers as well as incisive comments from Peer Schouten, Claire Elder, Jethro Norman, Vanessa van den Boogaard, Mark Bradbury, Warsame M. Ahmed, Rens van Munster, Helene Kyed and Dominik Balthasar. All of them deserve our thanks. None of them bear any responsibility for the remaining omissions and errors of interpretation in this book.

We are also indebted to Hussein Mohamoud, Jatin Dua, Gianluca Iazzolino, Nicole Stremlau, Lars Buur, Lindsay Whitfield, Peter Kragelund, Amanda Hammar, Christian Lund, Brenda Chalfin, Hannah Stogdon, Mustafe M. Abdi, Ken Menkhaus, Kristof Titeca and Tom de Herdt for their support and intellectual companionship, and to Rune Korgaard and Hannah Arndal Rasmussen for their invaluable editorial assistance.

A particular thanks is reserved for Professor Jesse T. Njoka from the University of Nairobi who played an important role in doctoral supervision, as well as for Stephanie Kitchen from the International African Institute and Hurst's publication management team.

Finally, all of us owe a debt of gratitude to the many men and women who took time to share their experiences, views and analyses during interviews and encounters with GOVSEA team members. Receiving their insights has been a truly rewarding experience.

Trade Makes States is dedicated to the memory of Kassahun Berhanu Alemu and Warsame M. Ahmed, both former GOVSEA team members. Kassahun was a professor in the Department of Political Science and International Relations at Addis Ababa University, a prolific intellectual and student of politics. He passed away on 22 February 2022. Warsame was the Director of Research and Community Services at University of Hargeisa, an economist and researcher driven by curiosity. He passed away on 16 January 2023. We are thankful for their friendship, collegiality and contributions to this book.

Tobias Hagmann and Finn Stepputat, January 2023

LIST OF CONTRIBUTORS

Note: Names are listed alphabetically following the names of the book's editors; the author of the Afterword completes the list. As is customary, the first names of Ethiopian authors are used in the list as well as in citations and references.

Tobias Hagmann is a Senior Program Officer at Swisspeace and a fellow at the Rift Valley Institute and Somali Public Agenda. He was Associate Professor in International Development and Comparative Politics at Roskilde University in Denmark where he directed the Governing Economic Hubs and Flows in Somali East Africa (GOVSEA) research project between 2014 and 2019. His research interests include the sociology of the state, peace and conflict studies and international development. He is the co-editor of *Aid and Authoritarianism in Africa: Development Without Democracy* (Zed Books, 2016).

Finn Stepputat is a senior researcher at the Danish Institute for International Studies. He has published extensively on forced migration, post-conflict issues, peace and conflict, logistics and the state in Latin America and Africa, including theoretical and ethnographic approaches to state and sovereignty. He is (co-)editor of various volumes and special issues, such as *States of Imagination* (Duke University Press, 2001), *Sovereign Bodies* (Princeton University Press, 2005), *Governing the Dead* (Manchester University Press, 2014), and *States of Circulation* (Environment & Planning D, 2019).

LIST OF CONTRIBUTORS

Warsame M. Ahmed was Director of Research and Community Service at the University of Hargeisa. He was an economist and former Head of Research of the Somaliland Economic Association. He was also Senior Lecturer at the Hargeisa School of Economics. Warsame's research interests included the Berbera corridor, informal economics, transportation, taxation and finance. He sadly passed away on 16 January 2023.

Asnake Kefale is Associate Professor of Political Science and International Relations at Addis Ababa University. Formerly, he was Director of Research and Publication at the Forum for Social Studies, a policy think tank in Addis Ababa. Asnake's research interests include politics of development, governance, federalism and migration. He is the author of *Federalism and Ethnic Conflict in Ethiopia: A Comparative Regional Study* (Routledge, 2013).

Neil Carrier is Associate Professor in Social Anthropology at the University of Bristol. His research interests encompass drugs, photography, transnational trade, migration and urban transformation, with a regional focus on Kenya and East Africa more broadly. His recent books include *Little Mogadishu: Eastleigh, Nairobi's Global Somali Hub* (Hurst, 2016) and (as co-editor) *Mobile Urbanity: Somali Presence in Urban East Africa* (Berghahn, 2019).

Hannah Elliott is Assistant Professor at the Copenhagen Business School. She holds Bachelor's and Master's degrees in Anthropology from the University of Manchester and SOAS University of London, and a PhD in African Studies from the University of Copenhagen. Her research focuses on the anthropology of diverse economies, in particular in Kenya, where she has been conducting research since 2009.

Fana Gebresenbet is Director of the Institute for Peace and Security Studies at Addis Ababa University. His research focuses on politics of development, state developmentalism, pastoralism and migration. He co-edited *Lands of the Future: Anthropological Perspectives on Pastoralism, Land Deals and Tropes of Modernity in Eastern*

Africa (Berghahn, 2021) and *Youth on the Move: Views from Below on Ethiopian International Migration* (Hurst, 2021).

Gianluca Iazzolino is Lecturer in Digital Development at the Global Development Institute at the University of Manchester. Before, he held research positions at the Centre for Socio-Legal Studies, University of Oxford, and the Firoz Lalji Institute for Africa, London School of Economics. He is a fellow of the Institute of Money, Technology and Financial Inclusion, University of California Irvine. His research interests lie at the intersection of political economy, socio-legal studies and digital geography, with a geographic focus on East Africa. Before completing a PhD at the University of Edinburgh, he worked as a consultant for NGOs and aid organisations in Senegal, Burkina Faso and Niger, and as a journalist in Central and South America, the Middle East, Russia and India.

Ahmed M. Musa is a postdoctoral research fellow at the Peace Research Institute Oslo and the Institute of Development Studies at the University of Nairobi. He is also a research fellow at Somali Public Agenda and the Centre for Public Authority and International Development at the London School of Economics and Political Science. His research interests include political economy, institutions, humanitarianism and trade.

Philemon Ong'ao Ng'asike is a researcher at the African Drylands Institute for Sustainability at the University of Nairobi. Formerly a part-time lecturer at the University of Nairobi, he obtained his doctoral degree in Drylands Resource Management studying the governance of livestock value chains in the Kenyan–Somali borderlands. His articles have appeared in *Pastoralism: Research, Policy and Practice* and the *Journal of Eastern African Studies*. Philemon consults for various humanitarian NGOs in South Sudan.

Omer Qualonbi is Executive Director of the Civil Service Institute (CSI) of Somaliland. He holds an MA in Public Sector Management, a BA in Economics and an LLB in Law, and has worked as an independent researcher with the University of Hargeisa and University College London. Omer has also worked as a public sector reform specialist with different Somaliland government institutions and served as an expert and advisor for international organisations and companies such as UNDP and Oxford Policy Management.

Jacob Rasmussen is Associate Professor in International Development Studies at Roskilde University. His research interests include political mobilisation, social movements and vigilantism, urban governance and development, youth and generational politics.

Nicole Stremlau is Head of the Programme in Comparative Media Law and Policy at the University of Oxford's Centre for Socio-Legal Studies and Research Professor at the University of Johannesburg. Her research focuses on media and conflict, particularly in the Horn of Africa. Recent books include *Media, Conflict and the State in Africa* (Cambridge University Press, 2018) and the (co-)edited volumes *Speech and Society in Turbulent Times* (Cambridge University Press, 2018) and *World Trends in Freedom of Expression and Media Development* (UNESCO, 2018).

Kirstine Strøh Varming is an independent researcher and consultant, who completed her PhD at Roskilde University in 2020 as part of the 'Governing Hubs and Flows in Somali East Africa' (GOVSEA) research programme. Her research interests include the anthropology of the state, migration studies and minority advocacy.

Simon Wallisch is a consultant in Germany, with a focus on international development, development finance and climate change. He concluded his MSc in Human Security at Aarhus University with fieldwork in Somaliland, where he conducted research on the emergence of logistic service providers and their utilisation of humanitarian actors.

Mahad Wasuge is Executive Director of Somali Public Agenda. Mahad holds a Master of Public Administration (MPA) from the

University of Roehampton in London. Prior to that, he earned a Bachelor's degree in public administration from Mogadishu University and diplomas in Law and English. Mahad's research interests focus broadly on governance, democratisation, civil service reform, public finance, constitutional development, post-conflict justice and migration.

Peter D. Little is the Samuel Candler Dobbs Professor of Anthropology and Director of the Global Development Studies Program, Emory University, USA. He has conducted studies of political ecology, pastoralism, poverty and inequality, informality, contract farming, and development in Africa, especially Kenya, Somalia, and Ethiopia. Little is the author of *Economic and Political Reform in Africa: Anthropological Perspectives* (Indiana University Press), *The Elusive Granary: Herder, Farmer, and State in Northern Kenya* (Cambridge University Press), and *Somalia: Economy Without State* (Indiana/James Currey), as well as the co-editor of seven other books.

LIST OF MAPS, TABLES AND FIGURES

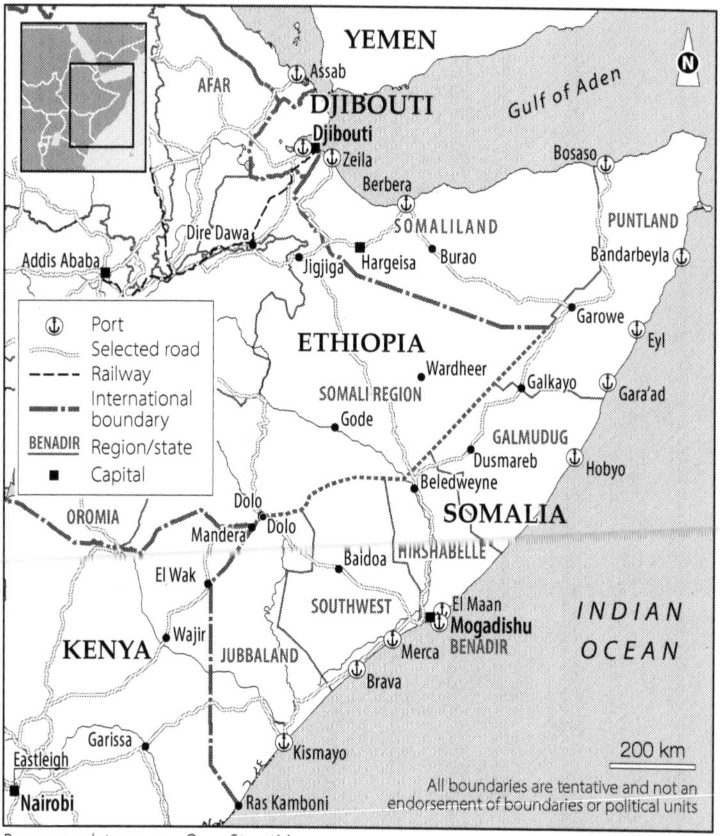

YEMEN
Assab
AFAR
DJIBOUTI
Djibouti
Zeila
Gulf of Aden
Bosaso
Berbera
SOMALILAND
PUNTLAND
Dire Dawa
Addis Ababa
Jigjiga
Hargeisa
Burao
Bandarbeyla
Garowe
Eyl
Port
Selected road
Railway
International boundary
BENADIR Region/state
Capital
ETHIOPIA
Wardheer
SOMALI REGION
Galkayo
Gara'ad
Gode
GALMUDUG
Dusmareb
Hobyo
Beledweyne
Dolo
SOMALIA
OROMIA
Mandera
Dolo
HIRSHABELLE
Baidoa
El Wak
SOUTHWEST
El Maan
Mogadishu
BENADIR
INDIAN OCEAN
KENYA
Wajir
JUBBALAND
Merca
Brava
Garissa
Kismayo
200 km
Eastleigh
Nairobi
Ras Kamboni
All boundaries are tentative and not an endorsement of boundaries or political units

Base map data source: OpenStreetMap

© **MAP***grafix* 2022

Map 1: The Horn of Africa

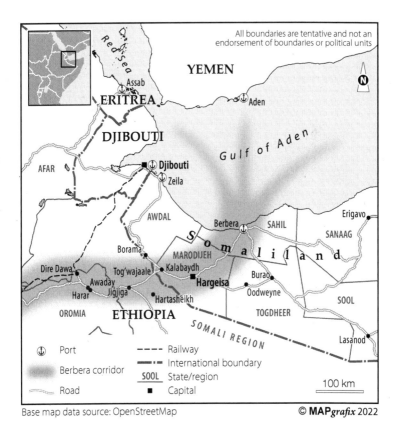

All boundaries are tentative and not an endorsement of boundaries or political units

YEMEN

Assab

ERITREA

Aden

DJIBOUTI

Gulf of Aden

AFAR

Djibouti

Zeila

AWDAL

Berbera

SAHIL

Erigavo

Somaliland

SANAAG

Borama

MARODIJEH

Dire Dawa

Tog'wajaale

Kalabaydh

Hargeisa

Burao

Awaday

Jigjiga

Oodweyne

SOOL

Harar

Hartasheikh

OROMIA

ETHIOPIA

TOGDHEER

SOMALI REGION

Lasanod

⚓ Port — — — Railway

Berbera corridor ▪▪▪ International boundary

SOOL State/region

Road ▪ Capital

100 km

Base map data source: OpenStreetMap

© **MAP**grafix 2022

Map 2: The 'Berbera corridor'

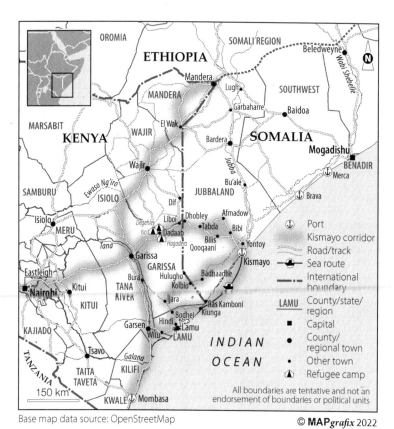

Base map data source: OpenStreetMap

© **MAP***grafix* 2022

Map 3: The 'Kismayo corridor'

INTRODUCTION

TRADE AND STATE FORMATION IN
SOMALI EAST AFRICA AND BEYOND

Finn Stepputat and *Tobias Hagmann*

Introduction

One hot day in 2015, we met with Ali Mohamed Omar 'Horhor', the general manager of Berbera Port on the Somali coast on the Gulf of Aden. The port didn't seem too busy. Some dhows and two smaller cargo ships were at berth. Piles of tyres, wooden planks, bags of cement and grain, containers and second-hand Japanese cars sat sprawled across the wharf, and a few trucks were being unloaded by the ships' cranes, as the port didn't have any. Customs officers brought stacks of Somaliland Shilling to the customs building, which was teeming with people yelling, waiting, negotiating and filling in forms by hand. Yet, despite the inauspiciousness of the port and routines that seemed archaic in a time of mega-ports, terminal operating systems and online customs procedures, Berbera Port has been a key actor in the formation of the de facto state of Somaliland.

Ali 'Horhor' had been in charge of the port for most of the time since 1993, when President Mohammed Ibrahim Egal first appointed him as port manager. There had been attempts to put him out of office, but given his political clout in Berbera and beyond it would take a top international port company to end his reign. That's what happened in 2017, when Dubai-based DP World won a 30-year concession to operate and upgrade Berbera Port. When we met Horhor in his office, he was busy multitasking: signing off letters and invoices, negotiating contracts, mediating a brawl between men who had burst into the office, talking with the vice-president in the capital city of Hargeisa, watching the news on Al Jazeera and talking with us. He told us about the early days of Berbera Port, which he remembered as being 'a very difficult period': 'People with guns controlled the port, people who didn't know anything.'[1]

Yet despite political strife and clan conflict in north-west Somalia, where Somaliland had declared its independence in 1991, Horhor and his colleagues managed to keep the port running as ships from Djibouti and Adan called at Berbera's docks with humanitarian aid and imported goods. Meanwhile, the multiple roadblocks between Berbera Port and the Ethiopian border were brought under control by government forces. This allowed live-stock exports to the Middle East to resume, and trade intensified along what would later become known as the Berbera corridor. The corridor provided a lifeline to local communities on both sides of the border and a small but steady stream of revenue for the security forces and emerging public administration of Somaliland.[2] Twenty-five years after Horhor's appointment and the humble beginnings of the de facto Islamic Republic of Somaliland, DP World was investing in Berbera Port and corridor, leading maritime experts to speculate that Berbera Port might become a competitor to Djibouti, the Horn of Africa's main logistics hub.[3]

The story of Somaliland and its main port raises questions about the political significance of trade and transport when state institutions are weak or absent; about how trade and transport—and economic life more broadly—is regulated under such circumstances; and about what institutional consequences these forms of regulation have. In short, what kind of lessons does Somali economic life—and commodity trading in particular—offer for our understanding of contemporary politics and capitalism at the global margins three decades after the breakdown of central state institutions in Somalia?

These are some of the key questions that this book addresses by looking at the politics of trade networks and commodity flows across the Somali territories. Drawing on multi-sited research across this greater Somali economic space (see Little 2014)—meaning the entirety of the Somali inhabited parts of East Africa, including some of its diaspora hubs like Dubai or Nairobi's Somali-dominated Eastleigh—this book analyses the variegated ways in which trade and state formation interact, in short how trade makes states.[4] The chapters provide fascinating insights into the everyday governance of commodity trading, marketplaces and cross-border commerce.

Somalia's state collapse in 1991 has resulted in considerable human suffering, displacement and destruction. The repercussions of these have earned Somalia the, often repeated, label of the most 'failed' or 'fragile' state in the world.[5] But, unknown to many, the disintegration of the former Somali regime has been enormously productive in reordering the economy, rerouting trade flows and unleashing the private sector. This book thus highlights how trade and the circulation of goods are central to Somali societies, economies and politics. Moreover, we demonstrate how the facilitation and capture of trade flows have been instrumental in institutionalising polities across the Somali territories.

The Somali territories have historically been characterised by pastoral mobility and long-distance trade between Somali ports and the interior of the Horn of Africa (Cassanelli 1982; Lewis 1999 [1961]; Little 2003). In the wake of the civil war and state collapse, this economic space has expanded as commercial linkages intensified with the displacement of people and capital into Ethiopia, Kenya and beyond. Furthermore, with economic growth in these two countries and increasing demand for imports, trade and transport, the Somali territories have become more integrated into global logistical networks. Concomitantly, new sub-national state entities were formed across Somalia, ranging from short-lived 'mini-states'[6] to more durable administrations such as Somaliland or Puntland. In the process, interactions between 'state' and 'economy' have become more complex. Federalism and competing state-building projects—many of which occurred in resistance to the Federal Government of Somalia (FGS) in Mogadishu—have led to a fragmentation of territory along clan and political lines (Hoehne 2016). Additionally, the insurgent Islamists of Harakat al-Shabaab al-Mujahideen, popularly known as al-Shabaab, continue to control important parts of south-central Somalia, defying the Somali government and its international backers (Hansen 2013; Maruf and Joseph 2018). Despite these divisions, Somalis are connected across boundaries by genealogical descent, religion, language, culture and, importantly, cross-border trade.

Economic and liberal theory has long suggested that trade and interdependent markets pacify relations between states and people (for example, see Dorussen and Ward 2010). But the stories and arguments in our book go beyond an uncritical celebration of a 'stateless economy' (Mubarak 1997), which US libertarians detected in Somalia following the disintegration of government institutions (Leeson 2007). The Somali economy provides incisive insights for students of economic sociology because it shows how the absence of a state does not mean that there are no rules or institutions governing economic transactions. The contrary is the case, as everyday trading—both small scale and large scale—in the Somali territories is governed by a myriad of rules, norms and routinised practices.

Since 1991, many sectors of the Somali economy have thrived and proved remarkably resilient despite violent conflict, droughts and very limited state regulation and support. Commodity trading has produced substantial financial resources for aspiring state-builders, whether formal government institutions or competing non-state groups. Somali merchants and members of the business class have played crucial roles in shaping political dynamics (Marchal 1996; Meester et al. 2019; Musa and Horst 2019). They draw our attention to historical and quasi-universal questions of how economic and political elites relate to each other when new states are being built (Spruyt 2011), as we discuss in Chapter 8.

Three contributions

The insights garnered in this book travel far beyond the dusty marketplaces, bumpy roads, local checkpoints or mushrooming seaports of the Somali Horn of Africa. The authors provide original insights into how states are being formed beyond technocratic state building blueprints proposed by the international community. Understanding the real economy of Somali areas and its 'state-building' (Mitchell 1999) requires a disciplinary openness that enables the study of trade politics, markets and governments both from 'below' and from 'above', as well as across 'local', 'national' and 'global' scales. Hence, our accounts of how trade makes states in the Somali territories are inspired by and speak to political and economic sociology, geography and anthropology. Our book makes three main contributions.

First, we contribute to theory building by asking what the post-1991 Somali experience teaches us about state formation. Understanding state formation to be 'a cultural process, rooted in violence, that seeks to normalize and legitimize the organized political subjection of large-scale societies' (Krupa and Nugent 2015: 4), we see the state as an idea about ultimate authority within a given territory as well as a system of practices and institutions (based on Abrams 1988; Hansen and Stepputat 2001; Migdal and Schlichte 2005). We highlight the centrality of commodity trading and the logistics underpinning it in the establishment of state and state-like entities. We pay particular attention to the circulation of goods in the transnational Somali economy and the everyday practices and politics that accompany this circulation. Based on the premise that the shifting flow of goods can underpin, change or undermine political orders and therefore change relations between competing political elites, we propose a theoretical framework of 'trade makes states'. At the core of this proposal sits what we call a 'politics of circulation' (Stepputat and Hagmann

2019), meaning struggles over the power to influence the movement of commodities, finance and people as well as the revenues that derive from these movements.

As will be spelled out in the next section, state-builders are confronted with the challenge of organising and managing the circulation of commodities in a manner that allows them to capture revenue and, in the longer term, to be recognised as legitimate regulatory authorities. Circulation involves both coercion and capital (Cowen 2014) and depends on supply chains, infrastructures and logistics that are often beyond the control of states. As the chapters in this book illustrate, the governance of circulation is a key political technology. The ability to influence and manage the flow of goods is one factor that distinguishes successful from less successful state-builders. This ability to govern goods—rather than people or land—has been under-appreciated by state-building interventions focusing on institution building, good governance and public finance reform. What the Somali example demonstrates is that political orders and states, whether weak or strong, are based on particular logistics and infrastructures which co-create each other (Schouten et al. 2019).

Second, our book offers a particular methodological vantage point to study dynamic transnational economies and their political entanglements. We propose a 'corridor approach' to study these politics of circulation, which in the Somali case mostly revolve around the governance of trade and transport corridors connecting seaports and hinterlands (Hagmann and Stepputat 2016). Our understanding of a trade or transport corridor is thus not a purely technical one, as is the case in the applied literature on trade facilitation (Lakshmanan et al. 2001). When economists and logistics experts discuss 'corridors', they tend to focus on transnational infrastructural assemblages—of ports, roads and railroads—and their assumed economic effects. But they usually ignore social and geopolitical aspects, perspectives relating to local governments and informal cross-border trade (Fau 2019). Putting more emphasis on networks and connectivity rather than on the infrastructure as such (Nugent and Lamarque 2022), we understand a corridor as a transboundary geographic space of economic, political and social relations which facilitates the conveyance of commodities between economic hubs such as (sea-, air- and dry-) ports, entrepôts and marketplaces. While facilitating circulation, corridors also concentrate 'friction' (Tsing 2005) in the form of checkpoints, transport congestion, taxation, border-posts and so on.

More than an analytical concept, 'corridors' provide a methodological vehicle that helps us choose sites for studying everyday economic transactions, commodity flows and the performance of various forms of public authority in a transnational economy. But at the same time, it allows us to analyse economic and political dynamics associated with 'corridors', which have become the 'main intellectual construct through which roads, ports and railways are conceived by development actors in Africa' (Cissokho 2022). As Cissokho shows, the early belief in transport infrastructure as inducing development was reinvented by a group of World Bank experts who, from the late 1980s, connected this belief to the free trade ideals of the new Washington Consensus, now promoting different kinds of 'corridors'. Hence, the corridor approach adds an ideological aspect to the analysis of the politics of circulation and the competition over and between different corridors in Somali East Africa.

Third, our book provides novel insights into the political economies of Somali East Africa and Sahelian Africa more broadly. Rather than an 'economy without a state' (Little 2003), the Somali territories have seen the emergence of a complex patchwork of 'trading states' (Hagmann 2021) since state collapse in 1991. Among them are de facto states, de jure states, national—including Ethiopia, Kenya and Djibouti—and sub-national state entities. All of them are involved in governing and taxing commodity flows, whether livestock exported from Ethiopia's Somali Regional State via Berbera Port, the import of rice and pasta from Bosaso Port to central Somalia or the re-export of sugar from Kismayo Port to Kenya. The Somali territories have seen a proliferation of nested, overlapping and competing public administrations that have made multiple tax claims on trading and transport of commodities since 1991 (Musa et al. 2021). This observation contradicts, or rather adds nuance to, earlier accounts of Somalia

TRADE MAKES STATES

as a post-conflict 'duty free shop' (Menkhaus 2004a). Traders and
transporters pay a sizable amount of taxes and fees to officials,
security forces, militias and armed groups like al-Shabaab to move
their goods across clan, local and international boundaries. They
play important roles not only in providing livelihoods to local
populations but also in co-producing 'empirical statehood'
(Jackson and Rosberg 1982) in the Somali territories.

Three arguments

Commodity trading and state formation are co-produced as trade
makes states and vice versa. The chapters in this book demonstrate
how everyday trading and the facilitation and capture of trade
flows have been instrumental in institutionalising polities in the
greater Somali economic space. The 'trade makes states' framework proposes three basic arguments. These are interrelated, and
they bring to the fore different, yet complementary, aspects of the
nexus between the governance of economic hubs and flows and
state-formation dynamics. These arguments highlight how the
governance of goods is not a technical or apolitical process but is
situated at the core of state building, public revenues and state–
society relations,

Argument 1: Effective state building requires that public administrations and state-like entities balance between the circulation and
the capture of commodity flows.

Whether nascent public administration or rebel group, state-
builders need to strike a balance between promoting the circulation of commodities within and across their territories on the one
hand, and capturing revenue from these goods to fund their state-
level activities on the other. There is thus a fundamental tension at
play as state-builders must both facilitate and capture commodity
flows. Without circulation the volume of traded goods remains
low, and local populations will lack foodstuffs and other consumer
items while business groups—traders in particular—will be
unhappy. But in the absence of commodity capture, states and
state-like entities will lack financial means. As a result, aspiring

political rulers have an interest in doing two things. First, they need to eliminate competitors who are also in the business of taxing and regulating commodity flows. These competitors are what Olson (1993: 567) famously described as 'stationary bandits', i.e., other proto-state actors who 'monopolize ... and rationalize ... theft in the form of taxes'. Second, aspiring political rulers will seek to standardise and routinise the terms of circulation and friction (or capture) of commodity flows within their territory. Standardisation creates predictability and reduces giving off the impression of arbitrariness. More importantly, it increases the 'authority' of state officials to tax and regulate goods when traders and merchants recognise, submit to or even accept state taxation. Our argument about the imperative for states to balance between the circulation and the capture of commodity flows translates into the following hypotheses.

First, states and state-like entities that are unable to organise or maintain circulation in their territory will lack trade-derived revenues. They will have to seek other sources of funding for their expenses. The inability to effectively organise circulation could be the result of incomplete territorial control due to the presence of competing state-builders, a lack of administrative and enforcement capacity or policies and market dynamics beyond the border,[7] all of which can hamper the volume of goods traded. Alternative sources of revenue which do not derive from trade are, for example, foreign aid, remittances, rents based on economic licensing and income from illicit business. These too, however, often rely on various forms of circulation.

Second, states and other public administrations are differently endowed in terms of their ability to capture revenue from commodity flows even without facilitating these. Such states typically generate revenue through 'gatekeeping' (Cooper 2002, 2018), meaning they control a chokepoint—a port, a strait or a particular road—that allows them to impose fees on passing goods. This is notably the case when they are endowed with 'judicial statehood' (Jackson and Rosberg 1982), which allows them to practise 'chokepoint sovereignty' (Dua 2018). Without doing much in terms of facilitating flows or providing services for the private sector or society at large, such states can make a rent[8] from selling their judicial statehood—turning their right to tax and set rules into revenue—in exchange for passage. Coercive capacity and the disciplining of economic operators who do not comply with trade and customs rules also contribute to capturing trade-based revenues.

Third, from the above follows that—barred these cases of chokepoint sovereignty—the better an aspiring state or state-like entity can balance 'circulation' and 'capture' of commodity flows, the more revenue it can generate and the more 'state-like' it can appear. This balancing act is at the heart of what we refer to as politics of circulation. As the Somali territories after 1991 demonstrate, this is a contested process fraught with uncertainties and unpredictable outcomes. In civil war and post-conflict situations, territory is usually fragmented as (central) state authority is limited or has vanished entirely. The main challenge for state-builders then is to reopen transport routes, to re-establish the circulation of goods by demobilising, co-opting or displacing competing 'stationary bandits' (Olson 1993) who interrupt the flow of goods. As Olson (1993) and Tilly (1992) famously argued in their accounts of state formation, this requires military capacity and, ultimately, financial resources, which emerging administrations typically lack, precisely because they struggle to capture revenue from existing trade flows. The main challenge is thus to mobilise capital to re-establish circulation, which may then produce more permanent revenue streams in the future.

Argument 2: The fragmentation and multiplication of state(-like) entities increase friction in commodity flows but allow trade operators to hedge different custom and taxation regimes against each other.

Once state entities are able to tax and regulate commodity flows, they have to deal with, negotiate or accommodate the trade policies of their neighbouring states. These can be a foreign country—Djibouti, Ethiopia or Kenya in the Somali case—or sub-national entities such as one of the Federal Member States, a region or a district within Somalia or Somaliland. The Somali inhabited territories have seen a proliferation of local administrations over the past three decades. This was the combined result of federalisation—i.e., the creation of the Federal Member States—in Somalia, 'ethnic-based' decentralisation in Ethiopia and, more recently, devolution in Kenya (Ng'asike et al. 2021). With each new administrative unit created, new claims to trade-derived revenue emerged. As can be seen in north-eastern Kenya, but also on the Somaliland–Puntland trade border (Musa 2021), newly created local governments seek to obtain a piece of the trade revenue pie as they collect small fees for 'security' or 'development', thus increasing traders' cost of doing business (see Chapter 7).

If the multiplication of political authorities increases competition over trade-derived revenue, it leads traders to reconsider trading routes and to re-channel goods along different networks. The choice of a trade route is influenced by several factors. Among the most important are transport costs, taxation and security. Many commodity traders in the Somali territories rely on cross-border kin relations to move their goods (see Chapters 2 and 6). Sharing genealogical descent with a majority population in a market or coastal town facilitates credit. The collective 'liability' afforded by the clan system insures commodities and therefore improves their safety. But if the circulation of goods is faced with too much friction—for example, because multiple unpredictable state actors tax or otherwise seek to control commodity flows—traders will choose alternative trading routes to evade regulation and taxation.

Argument 3: The materiality of traded commodities shapes their 'state effects' as well as their governance.

All goods are not created equal. They have different values and, importantly, different materialities. As suggested by Fana Gebresenbet (2018), a useful distinction of the materiality of commodities considers their value on the one hand, and their durability on the other. Schematically, traded goods can be either low or high value, and they can be either durable or perishable. From this results a basic matrix of four types of materialities that apply to commodity trading. Each of these types relates in a particular manner to state intervention and capture as well as the kind of attention that political entities give to a specific commodity (see Table 1.1 below).

Low-value commodities which are perishable are typically ignored by state officials. Vegetable trading in the Somali territories is a case in point. As Fana Gebresenbet (2018: 27) highlights, 'Trade in bulky perishable items that have low value for volume such as vegetables, is less rewarding for state institutions and officials that seek to regulate, control or seize.' This is not the case for perishable commodities that have a high value. In Somali East Africa, this is best exemplified by *khat*, a mildly stimulating narcotic leaf that is mostly chewed by men. *Khat*, or *miraa*, is exported daily from the Ethiopian and Kenyan highlands to the Somali inhabited lowlands (Carrier 2007; Ezekiel Gebissa 2004). *Khat* trading is a lucrative business built on elaborate supply and distribution networks, reaching nearly every town and village in the Somali territories. Because it is expensive, state officials 'tailor regulations and control' (Fana Gebresenbet 2018: 27) of *khat*. It is taxed both officially and unofficially, and both governments and state-like entities have at some point banned its export and sale, either for public health reasons or to exert political pressure on Somali consumers and, indirectly, administrations.

More durable commodities fare differently regarding the kind of state regulation that they provoke. Low-value but durable produce such as grain is 'more "worthy" of being regulated' (ibid.) by government actors. As its value does not decrease quickly, these commodities are more easily taxed in kind, or confiscated and resold. Finally, high-value commodities that are not perishable are a main target of state regulation. In the Somali territories, electronics in particular fit this bill, as they involve major profits, but small electronics such as mobile phones are relatively easy to smuggle due to their size. Livestock are somewhat durable when there is access to water and feed, and while they are attractive for taxation due to their high value, they are hard to capture in the borderlands when trekked 'on the hoof'. However, when trucked, traded in markets and subjected to veterinary controls before export via a port, they are amenable to sales taxes in marketplaces as well as fees and custom duties along the way to terminal markets.

Table 1.1: Materiality of commodities and state regulation

	Durability	
	Low	**High**
Low	*Ignored by state officials* e.g., vegetables, petty trading	*Low state attention* e.g., grains
High	*State capture and regulation* e.g., *khat*, trucked livestock	*Difficult to capture* e.g., livestock on the hoof, electronics

Source: Fana Gebresenbet 2018.

All these politics of circulation are not new to the region. There are colonial and pre-colonial precedents, and examples abound in Somali East Africa. Many of these politics revolve around issues of taxation and economic development, but military and security issues are also at play. The Siad Barre government saw to the construction of Bosaso Port in an attempt to undermine the rebel Somali National Movement (SNM) in Somaliland, who partially controlled the Berbera corridor, by diverting the flow of livestock for export through Bosaso instead of Berbera (see Chapter 4). In today's south-central Somalia, al-Shabaab thrives on taxing vehicles at checkpoints on roads under its control. To increase this revenue, al-Shabaab forces nudge truckers to use 'their' roads by attacking alternative routes to increase insecurity (Schouten 2022). Meanwhile, in disputed territories around Lasanod in the West of Somaliland, transit is taxed by both Somaliland and Puntland authorities as a way of claiming sovereignty over the territory (Musa 2021).

Arguably, stronger state polities can reorient economic flows to their advantage by constructing infrastructure themselves, mainly roads and ports in the case of Somali territories. Colonial powers, and Italy in particular (Bertazzini 2018), left a road network to provide conduits for trucking and hubs for markets, and which still marks the orientation of economic flows. As the export of livestock to the Middle East picked up from the 1950s onwards, the trekking of animals was increasingly substituted by motorised transport, which made it easier for authorities to siphon off revenues from these flows. In the 2010s, the infrastructure–circulation nexus took on new life as economic growth in Ethiopia provided more opportunities for transit trade. This brought in new transnational interests as capital was needed for major infrastructure development of ports—such as Berbera, Bosaso and Mogadishu—as well as the corresponding trade corridors, and demand increased for the technology and knowledge necessary for the integration into global logistical networks. As we show in Chapter 4, these changes have increased the presence and influence of powers such as the United Arab Emirates and Turkey, but the investments also seem to strengthen the (sub-)national authorities that sign the contracts with investors and their home states.

Key themes

Our analysis of the relationships between state formation and trade in the greater Somali economic space engages the three complementary bodies of literature on logistics and circulation; state formation; and borderlands. They cover vast amounts of scholarly work, and therefore we pinpoint which particular insights and concepts we make use of, how these relate to our 'trade makes states' framework and how they play out in our geographical area of study.

Logistics and circulation in fragile states

With our focus on the governance and circulation of tradable goods, logistics are important to understand. They can be defined as the art and knowledge of organising circulation (Cowen 2014). Thrift (2004: 589) famously described logistics as 'perhaps the central discipline of the contemporary world'. Pointing to the increasing importance of logistics in a world in which industrial production has migrated towards Asia, where supply chains spread and intensify across the globe and where neoliberal policies have smoothed commodity flows within and across borders, in 2007 the

World Bank started publishing a Logistics Performance Index (LPI). The emergence of a logistics sector specialising in the management of entire supply chains resulted in a 'dramatic recasting of the relationship between making and moving', between production and circulation (Cowen 2014: 103; Bonacich and Wilson 2008). Far from viewing logistics as a field of private enterprise only, many states, including Ethiopia, have followed China's example in developing parastatal logistics operators and long-term strategies for logistical development (Coe 2012).[9] The rise of Asian and Middle Eastern logistics companies to the top of global rankings and the pervasive development of ports and transport corridors in Africa are indicative of the prominence of global logistics (Coe 2012; Dahou and Chalfin 2019; Enns 2019; Nugent and Lamarque 2022).

The logistics literature has been dominated by technical studies which aim at reducing transport time and costs or improving the organisation of supply chains through automation, inter-operability, standards, business alliances and other fixes. Since the 2010s, a scholarly field of 'critical logistics' has emerged, exploring the political and social effects of an ever-expanding logistics sector and the rationalities and spatial practices that characterise it (Chalfin 2010; Cowen 2014; Toscano 2014; Chua et al. 2018). While logistics scholars demonstrate how operators seek to forge the smooth, seamless and cheap conveyance of goods—often at the cost of logistics workers—this new literature harbours an ethnographically inclined interest in 'logistics at work' (Gregson 2017). Studying 'logistics at work' breaks with technocratic projections of circulation without friction. Instead, it brings out the messiness and contested nature of logistics, infrastructure and strategically important but vulnerable 'chokepoints' (Stenmanns 2019; Carse et al. 2020).

Most of the logistics literature has focused on the heartlands of logistical networks. Only recently have scholars started considering other regions—like the Horn of Africa—'where Amazon doesn't deliver at the doorstep' (Schouten et al. 2019: 780). In the Somali parts of East Africa, containers are still a rare sight on the dilapidated roads. In the World Bank's Logistics Performance

Index, both Ethiopia and Somalia rank very low—at number 131 and 167 respectively—out of 167 countries in the aggregate index for 2012–18.[10] But this measurement does not give credit to the existing art and expertise of managing circulation across the challenging and vast terrains of Somali East Africa. Historically, a social infrastructure of personal relations, clan alliances and common norms have ensured the protection, conveyance and exchange of goods between the sea and the hinterlands (see Chapter 6). Still, today, Somali brokers, trekkers, traders and transporters are skilled logistical entrepreneurs who manage shifting market conditions and conduits of circulation based on contextual, flexible and practical knowledge and skills, best described by Scott (1998) as 'metis'. In the 2020s, they will increasingly have to deal with the shifts introduced by global logistical networks, which are advancing in Somali East Africa with current investments in port and road infrastructure. These investments come primarily from Gulf countries, Turkey and China (Meester et al. 2019), but they resonate with strong political and business interest from the various states and sub-states in the region.

Against this background we consider Somali East Africa as a 'logistics frontier' as global logistical networks are expanding into the region. A frontier involves the discovery or invention of new resources, which in this case is the circulation of commodities between Somali ports and the Ethiopian and Kenyan hinterlands. Frontier spaces have been defined as 'transitional, liminal spaces in which existing regimes of resource control are suspended' (Rasmussen and Lund 2018: 388). But as Tsing (2009; 2015) suggested, the suspension of existing regimes of resource control is neither straightforward nor complete. Under 'supply chain capitalism'—a late-modern form of commodity chains in which lead firms shape networks and chains of subcontractors and subsidiaries across the globe—these firms do not necessarily control the conditions, infrastructural conduits and institutional environments of circulation. Tsing showed how supply chain capitalism works very well with—and in fact thrives on—the incorporation of difference, heterogeneity and disorder. Indeed, supply chains work as 'a mechanism of making and preserving difference within connection', forging 'a political economy of articulated heterogeneity' (Tsing 2016: 338). The supply chains of Somali livestock for the Saudi or Kenyan markets, for example, snake in and out of zones of partly controlled circulation—at marketplaces, quarantine stations and ports—while beyond the control of states and firms, livestock flows are managed by a host of logistical operators. However, these still contribute to the revenues and profits of the institutions they stand in for (Little 2003; Mahmoud 2010; Ng'asike 2019; Musa et al. 2021).

Infrastructure, gatekeeping and state formation

This book provides empirical insights not only from a global 'logistics frontier'—i.e., the Somali territories—but also from a context in which logistics and infrastructure evolve in areas of limited, or fragile, statehood. An obvious starting point here is Mann (1984; 2008), who identified the logistics of states' power as an important source of the (relative) autonomy of the state vis-à-vis other social forces. He coined the concept 'infrastructural power', which is 'the capacity of the state to actually penetrate civil society and implement logistically political decisions throughout the realm' (1984: 189). States that lack infrastructural power must rely on less effective 'despotic' forms of power. Having limited infrastructural power also rules out administratively demanding forms of (direct) taxation, as discussed in Chapter 8. Historically, before the twentieth century, Mann (2008: 356) explains, states were largely confined to taxing 'things that visibly moved around—a much weaker form of infrastructural power'.

The projection of power over distance relies on physical, legal and administrative infrastructures that facilitate centralised control over the circulation of goods, people, armies, ideas and intelligence. Roads and railroads have been essential infrastructures for state making, not least by facilitating the taxation of circulating goods. Making the same point, Shell (2015) talks about the 'road-based state' while looking at the subversive potentials where road-resistant materials such as sand and mud slow down road- and hence state making (see also Scott 1998).

In the Horn of Africa, Italian colonialism left a network of now dilapidated roads (see Ciabarri 2017), which states, local militias, soldiers and al-Shabaab have used for setting up roadblocks and harvesting substantial revenues from passing trucks and commodities (UNSC 2018). The Italian presence was not quite the 'infrastructural empire' that was built in the Belgian Congo (Schouten 2022), but the deterioration of its infrastructure following state collapse has resulted in similar conditions in Somalia as in the Democratic Republic of Congo. In Schouten's analysis, when 'value is concentrated in long-distance trade and the conditions to conduct this trade are not controlled by overarching political authority', it is possible for 'roadblock politics' to thrive (ibid.: 218). In Somalia after 1991, roadblocks have provided sub-national states and administrations with the means of collecting revenue (see Chapter 7). But, as Schouten reminds us, we should not project the desire of forging territorial states onto all political–military actors that siphon off revenues from circulating commodities. In fact, these actors can create nodal and networked polities that, lacking an ambition of controlling population or territory, use long-distance trade and lack of central control to keep centralising state-projects at bay. In other words, not every roadblock operator is a state-builder.

In Somaliland in the early 1990s, 'you couldn't move from one place to another' because of the armed factions, and 'every day there was a new roadblock', as President Egal's (1993–2002) former office manager told us.[11] But the President managed to gather sufficient support to free circulation from the multitude of roadblocks in the young Republic in the early 1990s and negotiate some control with important customs points (Balthasar 2013). Somaliland's promotion of trade circulation reached new heights with the current upgrading of Berbera Port and corridor (Ahmed and Stepputat 2019). The idea of the upgraded port and corridor is associated with strong images of development and progress, borrowed not least from Dubai's transformation to a global logistics hub. This is common for large infrastructure projects, which conceptually are linked to Enlightenment ideas of a world where free circulation of goods, ideas and people forged the possibility of progress (Mattelart 2000). Infrastructure, then, has strong affective dimensions in addition to the more obvious political–economic effects. In Somaliland, the Berbera corridor has had an almost mythological presence, linked even to hopes for international recognition of Somaliland (Stepputat and Hagmann 2019). But while infrastructure promises progress as well as economic growth, it is also vulnerable to delay, breakdown, contestation and congestion, making infrastructure a productive entry point for political analysis (Anand et al. 2018).

Mann (2008) revisited his own concept of 'infrastructural power', recognising that infrastructure does not necessarily translate into territorial control. He highlights Cooper's work (2002) to argue how selectively infrastructural power has been developed across Africa. Cooper emphasised the extent to which the infrastructures and institutions of colonial states had been designed to maximise and control resource flows in and out of the territories, and that these patterns were rarely transformed after independence (see also Dorman 2018). In these 'gatekeeper states', strategic control over the 'gate' at the intersection between national territory and the wider world, as well as the narrow 'pathways' between the gate and nodes of extraction, allowed gatekeepers to harvest revenues from the flows passing through the gate.[12] In many ways, the concepts of gates and pathways translate into what we call 'logistical space'—the narrow conduits of commodity circulation, such as rail or roads, ports and free-trade zones—which exist in tension with national territory. Yet, traditional gatekeeping can also include the administrative control of import and export licences, Letters of Credit, and where and by whom marketplaces can be set up (Cooper 2002; Hönke 2018).

Critics of the 'gatekeeper-state' concept emphasise that it has been overgeneralised, and that it gives too much prominence to the state—as opposed to other actors—as the main gatekeeper (Dorman 2018; Hönke 2018). Rather than characterising a political system or a type of African state, Hönke (2018: 348) argues, gatekeeping should be considered a government practice or technology that involves multiple actors and types of sovereignty. With the current availability of capital for infrastructure investments, expanding volumes of resource extraction and growing import of consumer goods to African countries, gates have proliferated. Gatekeepers increasingly include private and transnational actors, which is also the case with Turkish and Dubai-based companies investing in Somali ports.

Whereas Italian and post-1960 independent Somalia were fitted with gatekeeper-state characteristics, British Somaliland has been described as the least 'gate-keeping' among African colonies, as it was exempt from taxation (Young 1994). After 1991, the various incarnations of a central government lost control over Somali ports, including Mogadishu Port, part of the road network and various border posts to clan-militias, al-Shabaab, Somaliland, Puntland and other sub-national administrations who appropriated gatekeeper privileges (see Chapter 4).[13] State-makers in Somaliland—and to a lesser degree Puntland—have gained control over their gate with the import–export infrastructure, first together with oligarchic business interests and later involving Dubai-based companies. The Jubbaland administration, together with the Kenyan Armed Forces, has controlled Kismayo Port since 2013, and the FMS of Galmudug has signed a contract to develop Hobyo Port.[14]

Undoubtedly, 'gatekeeping' continues to be a key mechanism that produces political revenues in the Somali territories (see Chapters 7 and 8). It has been used both 'by the state'—in the case of the central state of Somalia or of Somaliland—as well as 'against the state', for example by al-Shabaab or independence-seeking Somaliland. As we point out in Chapter 4, the involvement of transnational investors and operators may well have the effect of strengthening a central authority's hold of the gate vis-à-vis local authorities around the gate. In the process, national revenues increase even though the role of gatekeeping is, as in the case of Somaliland, shared with the investors.

Borderlands

Our book draws on and contributes to the study of African borderlands. The concept of 'borderland' refers to the region on both sides of a state border (Asiwaju 1993) and focuses on social, economic and political dynamics in these areas as well as the 'intense interconnectivity' (Meehan and Plonsky 2017: 4) which they are often characterised by.[15] The concept gives a transnational perspective and de-centred look at states from the borders and not least from the populations that are both divided and connected by the borders (Barth 2000). We approach borderlands primarily from the vantage point of commodity trading and the 'arbitrage economies' whose raison d'être are the different regulatory regimes that the borders separate—including taxation and pricing, for example (Anderson and O'Dowd 1999: 597). However, borderlands provide a wider 'opportunity structure' (Feyissa and Hoehne 2010: 12–13), which factors in security, infrastructure, services and refugee regimes. The Horn of Africa shows how these factors intertwine, as was the case in the 1990s when insecurity and refugee movements provided conditions for the deepening and extension of Somali commercial activities across the Somali borderlands. This process created a 'de facto ethnic Somali run special economic zone' around refugee camps in East Ethiopia, making Garissa the largest market for cattle in East Africa (Stepputat and Hagmann 2019; Ng'asike 2019). These borderlands form important pillars of the greater Somali economic space.

Borderlanders must deal with two or more states and insurgent movements, such as ONLF in Ethiopia's Somali Regional State in the 2000s or al-Shabaab in the 2010s who claim sovereignty over areas and corridors in the Somali–Kenyan borderlands. Given the often-contested nature of borderlands, their political marginality, the pervasive perceptions of borderland communities as savage and backward and states' preference for increased security and militarisation of borderlands, scholars tend to see state making in the borderlands as following a 'coercive' rather than a 'capital-intensive' path (Tilly 1992). States have tended to focus on governing by exceptional rules rather than safeguarding the interests of borderlanders (Korf et al. 2013), which squares with Baud and van Schendel's (1997: 215) observation that 'the confrontation between "state" and "people" is particularly salient in borderlands'. But, while they are often on the receiving end of state-building projects, borderlands can be central to these processes in terms of resources generated (Goodhand 2009), identities produced (Sahlins 1989) and the images of otherness and disorder against which states legitimise their rule (Hansen and Stepputat 2001).

Spanning across Somalia (and Somaliland), Kenya, Ethiopia and Djibouti, the Somali borderlands vary greatly in terms of their geography, political stability, economic importance and national attachments. Cross-border trading is shaped by a multitude of dissimilar national regulations pertaining to trade, customs and security. However, despite their differences, Somali borderlands share several generalities. First, they are what Martinez (1994) describes as 'interdependent borderlands', in which societies on both sides of the border are closely interlinked. On both sides of the extensive borders, the Somali borderlands are predominantly inhabited by Somalis and are profoundly connected by kin relations, cross-border trade, capital and information flows. As a livestock exporter based in Hargeisa explained when asked about the border between Somaliland and Ethiopia's Somali Regional State, formerly known as Region 5: 'Region 5 and us are the same thing.'[16]

Second, borderlands are politically contested, and policies from the capitals have been dominated by security considerations. Historically, rulers in Nairobi and Addis Ababa focused on armed trade posts like Moyale or garrison towns like Jigjiga that made up the bridgeheads of an otherwise episodic state presence in the borderlands. Rulers have tended to consider these as buffer zones vis-à-vis neighbouring Somalia and its potential irredentist claims. They have treated Somali subjects with considerable suspicion, and both the Ogaden—today's Somali Regional State of Ethiopia—as well as the former Northern Frontier District (NFD)—today's North Eastern Province—have a long history of recurrent state-sponsored violence and popular resistance (Weitzberg 2017; Hagmann 2014).

While exceptional rule and militarisation still characterise these borderlands, formal and informal exceptions from national laws have favoured cross-border trade, with some commodities being exempt from customs. For example, Somali–Ethiopian borderlanders within a certain distance from the border have been allowed to import minor quantities of goods. IGAD[17] trade ministers have agreed to allow and support local cross-border trade.[18] Furthermore, the 2010s have seen a 'Somalisation' of regional government in Ethiopia's Somali Regional State (Thompson 2021). With devolution in Kenya, a similar dynamic has taken place in the North Eastern Province (see Chapters 5 and 6). Powerful Somali political brokers head regional governments, and they have been increasingly appropriating gatekeeping privileges by managing import licences and tightening control of circulating commodities in the borderland.

Making the 'greater Somali economy'

Amidst decades of violent conflict and the breakdown of state institutions, Somalia has evolved into 'an entrepôt economy for large parts of the Horn of Africa and beyond' (Little et al. 2015: 410). Trade has centred on the export of livestock to the Middle East and Kenya, as well as the import of consumer goods from the Arab Gulf to be subsequently exported—without adding value— to consumers in East Africa. In economic and social terms, a 'greater Somalia' (Little 2014: 177) exists, characterised by dependence on finance, trade and migration, with traders and transporters operating in Eastern and Central Africa, the Middle East, Europe, the United States and Asia. It consists of 'fragmented political and economic spaces' that are nonetheless 'interconnected and integrated into a globalized economy' (Carrier and Lochery 2013: 335).

Somalia's trading economy consists of a multitude of trade and transport corridors that are connected through the Somali ports to major international hubs outside of East Africa, notably Dubai and Abu Dhabi (UAE) and Aden in Yemen. They are also linked to global networks spanning the Somali diaspora in the United States, Europe and Asia, and they facilitate financial transactions including remittance transfers through the *hawala* system (Hammond et al. 2011). Over time, a transnational Somali business class and conglomerates have developed, and many of these large companies have set up headquarters in neighbouring countries (Dubai, Djibouti, Nairobi) where they access services that are not available in the Somali territories.

As the following summary overview highlights, over time the Somali trading economy has evolved from being radically decentralised to encompassing more integrated markets; from a reliance on clan protection and coercion to the establishment of multi-clan shareholder and decentralised franchise companies; from short-term capital accumulation to more strategic and long-term business expansions; from a low-tech and low-skill economy to one of more sophisticated skills and technologies; and from an avoidance of state regulation to increasing compliance with international rules and standards. However, to understand these processes, it is necessary to briefly consider the turbulent evolution of the Somali economy, from Somali independence via 'scientific socialism' and 'hyper-liberalism' to state collapse in 1991.[19]

From independence to state collapse

At the time of independence in the 1960s, the Somali economy was at near subsistence level. The new state lacked the administrative capacity to collect taxes, and during its first years Somalia relied on Italian and British subsidies. Under 'scientific socialism', introduced by Siad Barre who came to power in 1969, the Somali government exerted state control over the economy. Contracts for commodity exports and import/export licensing were given to loyal and select state patrons, often from Barre's own clan or a limited Majeerteen–Ogaden–Dhulbahante alliance (Marchal 1996). Barre curtailed easy access to foreign capital and hard currency, nationalised the economy and created a series of parastatal organisations. The adoption of a state-controlled economy proved economically disastrous (Samatar 1989), and by the late 1970s the economy had all but collapsed. This process was also affected by the global oil crisis, a crash in livestock prices, subsequent droughts and Somalia's 1977–78 Ogaden war against Ethiopia (Lewis 1989).

Budget deficits, inflation and external debt figures continued to grow steadily under the Barre regime (Mubarak 1997). The government eventually adopted structural adjustment programmes, dismantling public enterprises and loosening restrictions on the private sector. It also unleashed economic informality amidst liberalisation, including rapid rent-seeking among a class of new powerbrokers—what Elder (2022) calls *dilaal* ('deal') capitalism, *dilaal* being used to mean 'broker'—as businesses withdrew into social and kinship networks to mediate economic scarcity, formal financial markets and predatory state policies. *Dilaal* capitalism was embedded in the *franco valuta* system, or what Jamal (1988: 233) aptly named a 'Saudi wage—repatriated money—exchange rate—price spiral' that facilitated trade relations, offered critical access to foreign exchange and bound migrant workers, livestock exporters and importers of foodstuffs in critical relations of reciprocity (Jamal 1988; Mubarak 1996). Thus, during the 1980s, the private sector 'expanded largely in the informal sector', which, by the end of the decade, had become 'the largest employer in the urban labour sector and among low-skilled rural migrants' (Jamal 1988: 213, 126).

In the 1980s, transportation, health, education and financial services were largely outside the state's remit and shouldered by the private sector (ibid.: 127). As such, the actual Somali economy was larger than reported at the time (Mubarak 1996) and made up of a 'vast subsistence sector', urban incomes were determined by repatriated money, a rural economy worked in parallel to state regulation and livestock exports operated 'in an essentially free-market setting' (ibid.: 246). This large-scale 'informalisation' of the economy became both a product and cause of state failure and its 'hyper-liberalized economy' (Little 2014), creating resentment, uncertainty and unregulated competition for territorial and economic control as well as access to business opportunities.

From violent markets to shareholder firms

The repressive and divisive Barre regime was ultimately brought down in 1991 by 'political-military entrepreneurship' that drew on clan mobilisation and was embedded in networks of protection, security and territorial control, specifically in South and Central Somalia (de Waal 2015: 117). The war economy of the 1990s was characterised by an economy of plunder and widespread violent resource capture that echoed Elwert's (1997) accounts of markets in which profit-making essentially relies on physical force. This was a period of violent redistribution, during which those accused of collaborating with the ancién regime, as well as traders and businesspeople who lacked protection from powerful armed clans, were the ones targeted (Marchal 1996: 53). Most of the fighting revolved around control of ports and key corridors, as for example the 'banana wars' of 1995–96 over Merca Port (see also Chapter 4).[20] Most of Somalia's public infrastructure—including state buildings, small industries, parastatals and public utilities such as electricity, water or telephone lines—were ransacked and destroyed in this period (Mubarak 1997). Similar looting and targeting of former government supporters occurred in Somaliland. But, significantly, most of the stolen property was returned as a series of peace conferences managed to mend inter-clan relations in the breakaway republic (Bradbury 2008).

Rampant insecurity, violent crime and theft gave rise to a war economy dependent on 'protection payments' and the collusion of warlords, businesspeople and international actors in delivering aid and circumventing multiple taxation rackets (Hansen 2007). The 'business–warlord power alliance', that was largely created by the United Nations Operation in Somalia (UNOSOM) mission based on over-profits in the aid sector (Marchal 1996), extended the cost and timeline of the civil war. The withdrawal of UNOSOM and foreign aid weakened the warlord economy (Hansen 2007). The cessation of deadly clan violence between 1994 and 1999 was a period of re-establishment of businesses, as local enterprises gradually broke with the warlords (Menkhaus 2003; Hansen 2007). The money transfer company Dahaabshiil, for instance, which had its headquarters in Hargeisa, opened its Mogadishu office in 1995 (Marchal 2002: 22). Cross-clan business arrangements and decentralised multi-clan franchises increasingly replaced an economic logic in which military protection derived from one's clan lineage.

In the early 2000s, Somalia still constituted the 'largest duty-free shop in the world' (Menkhaus 2004a: 51). Merchants formed

INTRODUCTION

intricate networks across clan territories to move goods, capital and personnel, paying taxes and protection money to checkpoints and local authorities (Carrier and Lochery 2013). But the growing emancipation of the business class from the warlords allowed enterprises to expand. Inter-company solidarity within the business community was strengthened with the emergence of the Bakara Market and Hormuud Telecom in Mogadishu, and a new manufacturing sector developed, which included pasta and candy factories. Still, businesses suffered from inefficiency, coordination failures and risk aversion, which is consistent with how economic development has progressed in similar contexts with weak or absent state institutions (Nenova 2004; Hoffman and Lange 2016). Somali business was confronted with multiple authorities who sought to control capital and violence, including the resurrected central authority under the Transitional National Government (TNG) that emerged in 2000 from the Djibouti (or Arta) peace process. Businesses reacted by throwing their support behind the Islamic Courts Union (ICU), which protected a thriving economy. However, this economy was damaged by renewed fighting after the Ethiopian military intervened in December 2006 to take down the ICU, followed by retaliation involving al-Shabaab and the African Union (Ahmad 2014; Elder 2022).

Despite setbacks, which included major Somali business companies becoming targets of counter-terrorism policies, new economic opportunities came with the reopening of Mogadishu Port in 2006; investment from the Somali diaspora; and the lifting of the Saudi livestock ban in 2009. Some of the large companies, financial companies in particular, started to professionalise their workforce and business practices by adopting and integrating international standards and certificates in production and trade (see also Chapters 3 and 4). The Somali economy was no longer an ungoverned war economy, relying on remittances, the diversion of aid resources and the smuggling of goods. Firms increasingly broke with the parochial paradigm, prevalent in the early 1990s, of single-clan business and its reliance on physical force. The large telecommunication and finance corporations created shareholder and decentralised franchise schemes, bringing together capital and investors from within Somali East Africa as well as the global diaspora (Lindley 2009; Lochery 2015). Other smaller firms (including in construction and import/export) remained more reliant on kinship ties even when developing larger business networks based on religious and old student networks (Hansen 2007; Hoffman et al. 2017).

Yet, by the end of the 2010s, the lucrative domestic market still relied heavily on social institutions such as trust, kinship relations and reciprocal debt and credit relations as state-sponsored security, taxation and property rights continued to be subpar (Elder 2022; Hoffman et al. 2017; Hansen 2007; Carrier and Lochery 2013). Large businesses continued to depend on products and services provided by informal cross-border trading, particularly through the unregulated import of construction materials and foodstuffs. Banking still relied predominantly on the *hawala* system of money transfer and mobile banking that sent considerable financial resources out of the country. Moreover, the formalisation of many businesses—increasingly multinational, which registered offices in multiple countries, acquired international licenses and adopted global standards—did not necessarily translate into greater economic development or competition. Many sectors of the Somali economy—including electricity and utilities; finance and telecommunications; and even trading—have seen the development of monopolies, oligopolies and cartels, some of which masquerade as associations and cooperatives (Hoffman et al. 2017; Meester et al. 2019; Hagmann et al. 2022).

Studying trade and state formation in Somali East Africa

This book owes its existence to a collaborative research programme which asked how the governance of economic hubs and flows has influenced state-formation dynamics in Somali East Africa since 1991. Programme and associated researchers addressed this question through an interdisciplinary and multi-sited research strategy. The bulk of field research was concentrated in Addis Ababa, Berbera, Burao, Garissa, Garowe, Hargeisa, Jigjiga and Nairobi. Even though the research programme did not focus on South-

Central Somalia or areas controlled by al-Shabaab, the corridor approach allowed researchers to obtain select information from trade operators who passed through these areas.

Authors relied predominantly on qualitative research methods, including semi-structured interviews with traders and officials, focus group discussions, participant observation and a few surveys. We documented the experiences and conceptions of livestock traders, brokers, trekkers, transporters, shop owners, customs and revenue officials, elders and a broad range of community actors involved in or knowledgeable about trading in the Somali territories. Secondary data in the form of existing academic literature and grey literature, as well as government reports and data, complemented primary data. In light of this, several methodological, geographic and thematic gaps need to be highlighted.

First, reliable series of annual statistics on trade, taxation and related topics are missing in the Somali context. The Somaliland government publishes an annual trade statistics bulletin, but few Federal Member States provide reliable information on trading or trade-derived revenues. While *Trade Makes States* provides evidence of how public authorities collect revenues, this lack of comparable figures is partly the reason why our book does not look into how revenues are being spent on security, administration, education and other public tasks. A study of the expenditure side of revenues collected in the Somali territories, including the viewpoints of taxpayers, thus remains a task for future researchers.

Second, because of security concerns we did not conduct fieldwork in southern Somalia, including Mogadishu and Kismayo. All data collected on the southern trade corridor connecting Nairobi to Kismayo Port was carried out on the Kenyan side, i.e., either in Garissa or Nairobi. We have sought to bridge this gap by relying on existing secondary and grey literature on southern Somalia.

Third, while a good part of petty trading and marketing— including for camel milk, *khat* and textiles—is done by women, most of the long-distance trading involving traders, brokers, drivers and officials is shouldered by men. With the exception of Varming's (2021) study on female hawkers in Nairobi's Eastleigh market and Ng'asike's (2019) research on female livestock traders in the Garissa market, most of our studies thus documented the practices and life worlds of men.

Fourth, the GOVSEA programme did not focus on major Somali firms and companies, whether their evolution, internal organisation or business practices. But in Chapter 3, Iazzolino and Stremlau address some of the major mobile money and telecom companies in Somali East Africa. Other scholars have recently added incisive analyses on the formation and transformation of major Somali firms. Jaspars et al. (2020) analysed the crucial importance that food aid contracts and logistics had for the formation of oligopolistic business capital. Elder (2022: 395) has explored the same theme, theorising how the logistics economy 'as a system of "graft" endogenous to state building, has contributed to empirical state failure'.

Finally, this book is exploratory and deliberately situated at an aggregate level. There are a lot of empirical complexities and dynamics in specific economic sectors, corridors and business networks that we cannot do justice to in our analyses. Our individual studies published in the DIIS GOVSEA working paper series cover more—but nowhere near all—of these empirical complexities.

Chapters preview

The chapters in this book provide complementary analysis of how the 'greater Somali economy' is governed and how trade and state formation interact through politics of circulation across the Somali territories. Chapters 2, 3 and 4 provide accounts of key 'infrastructures' that undergird and facilitate the circulation of commodities in Somali East Africa. Chapter 2, 'Trust as social infrastructure in Somali trading networks', scrutinises the everyday functioning of trust in business transactions at the interface between kinship and religion. Trust, Carrier and Elliot explain, is a normative discourse that promotes mutuality in trade between fellow Somalis or adherents to Islam. These discourses lubricate the flow of capital and goods and create affirmative counter-narratives to common negative depictions of Somali society. Where insurance, Letters of Credit, bank loans, identity cards and licenses for trade and transport are lacking, acts of trusting help circumvent such limitations, even though trusting is always a risky business.

In Chapter 3, 'War, peace and the circulation of mobile money across the Somali territories', Iazzolino and Stremlau chart the development of the Somali digital financial and telecommunication industries, of which mobile money is the most visible manifestation. With its rapid and surprising development, this sector has provided a de facto financial infrastructure for the circulation of capital and commodities—as well as the physical infrastructure for telecommunication—across borders in the greater Somali economy. Due to their size, strategic importance and political versatility, these conglomerates are key actors in the politics of circulation. While there are cases of direct support to state making (in Somaliland), financial and telecommunication firms are generally averse to taxation and regulation and have managed to keep international competitors out of the Somali territories.

Chapter 4, 'The revival and re-embedding of Somali ports', suggests that the control and development of port infrastructures has been a key strategy in the sometimes-violent politics of circulation after Somali state collapse, a strategy that had a decisive influence on the making and eroding of Somali state entities. The chapter provides an overview of the conflictive history and recent revival of four major seaports on the Somali coast before focusing on the changes that DP World's investments brought to Berbera Port. It shows how this port has been dis-embedded from its previous social, political and economic moorings in Berbera town only to be re-embedded in new relations, which has increased the control of both DP World and the Somaliland government over the port's governance and revenue compared to before the upgrading.

The next three chapters look at the everyday governance of trade from complementary vantage points. Chapter 5, 'Governing marketplaces: Self-regulation, stateness and materialities', is based on studies of a handful of Somali-dominated markets in Kenya, Ethiopia, Somalia and Somaliland. The authors, Fana Gebresenbet, Varming and Ng'asike, focus on how hybrid governance arrangements have evolved since 1991, how ethnic and social differences characterise these markets and how the materiality of goods influ-

ence the intensity of regulation by public authorities. It also shows
how 'stateness' is being projected in marketplaces somewhat independently of the actual presence of state institutions. The trade
operators that animate these marketplaces partake in the politics of
circulation in various ways: first, by choosing to which market they
take their business, and second, through the various market organisations that try to influence the conditions of marketplaces.

In Chapter 6, 'Governing commodity flows in the Somali borderlands', Asnake Kefale and Rasmussen scrutinise the processes
and practices that shape the governance of cross-border trading
within Somali East Africa. Focusing on livestock, sugar, charcoal,
electronics and other goods traded across the Somali–Ethiopian
and Somali–Kenyan borders, the authors discuss the shifting roles
of state and state-like authorities in regulating, facilitating and
interrupting the circulation of goods. They highlight how Somali
traders and a host of other actors along the Berbera and Kismayo
corridors have specialised in maintaining the flow of goods,
releasing them back into circulation when they (inevitably)
encounter friction.

Musa, Varming and Stepputat take a somewhat broader view in
Chapter 7, 'Raising fiscal revenues: The political economy of
Somali trade taxation', which analyses formal and informal taxation
by a host of state, state-like and non-state authorities in Somali
territories. Taxation is at the heart of state making, but Somali
state(s) don't have a monopoly on taxation. The chapter focuses
on revenues from the taxation of commodity flows, on the politics
of circulation that evolve as different authorities compete over
revenue from different hubs and routes in the region and on various 'tax games' playing out between traders and taxing authorities,
which range from tax bargaining to avoidance of heavily taxed
routes. Finally, the chapter considers the effects of trade taxation
on fiscal social contracts, state (un-)making and inequality among
large and smaller trade operators.

In the last chapter 'Tilly in the tropics: Trade and Somali state
making', the editors discuss the book's overall trade-makes-state
framework in light of the state-formation experiences of different
(sub-)national Somali political entities. While sociologist Charles

INTRODUCTION

Tilly is famous for his idea that 'war made states', this chapter builds on Tilly's lesser-known work on merchants and traders vis-à-vis emerging states. Thus, we set 'Tilly in motion' by exploring politics of circulation involving nascent and aspiring state administrations in the Somali territories who seek balance between capture and facilitation of commodity flows. In this optic, and contrary to the assumptions commonly held of internationally supported state building, statehood in the Somali areas resembles a federation of cities and trading states of multifarious sizes. With the prevailing prominence of revenues from transnational commodity circulation and the continued fragmentation of Somali territories, Somali state entities are likely to remain at the mercy of global terms of trade, of various policies of states in the region and abroad and of external aid flows.

Since Peter D. Little's work has inspired much of this book, we asked him to write an afterword, which he generously agreed to do. In 'Somalia, an economy with "stateness"', he critically reflects on the strengths and weaknesses of our arguments, the wider applicability of the trade-makes-state arguments, and the gaps that future researchers must give attention to.

2

TRUST AS SOCIAL INFRASTRUCTURE IN SOMALI TRADING NETWORKS

Neil Carrier and *Hannah Elliott*

Introduction

'Trust' is a key concept through which social scientists seek to understand how 'informal' economies, operating in large part outside of formal state regulation, are governed and sustained. Somali trade provides a pertinent case. In Somalia, across Somali East Africa and beyond, business has continued, and in some cases thrived, in spite of—and sometimes partially because of—the statelessness of the homeland (Mubarak 1997; Little 2003; Leeson 2007). This chapter asks what the concept of 'trust' reveals and conceals about Somali economic life and the circulation of goods in the region. It draws primarily on ethnographic fieldwork in Eastleigh, an estate in Nairobi's Eastlands, whose booming economy is in many ways exemplarily 'informal' and driven in large part by Somali enterprise and capital investments (Carrier 2017). It is a hub through which many Somali trade networks are threaded, and as such a prime location for observing the social infrastructure supporting the circulation of goods and capital through these networks. In addition, we draw from studies of Somali trade in Somali East Africa and the diaspora.

The role of 'trust' in Somali trade and business has provoked widespread interest but received little scholarly attention (an exception is Mahmoud 2008). In Kenya, there has been popular speculation as to what lies behind Somali entrepreneurial success in Eastleigh which, since the early 1990s and the arrival of large numbers of Somali refugees, has transformed from a quiet residential neighbourhood into a global economic hub. Some commentators have glibly linked Eastleigh's transformation with the laundering of 'dirty' money and spoils made through Indian Ocean piracy or have perceived the estate as a terrorist hideout. But another popular, and more positive, explanation for Eastleigh's burgeoning economy is that Somalis make successful entrepreneurs because they trust one another. One article in Kenya's newspaper *The Standard*, for example, proclaimed that 'the driving force behind Somali traders' success was "trust"' (Masese 2013). Somalis themselves often emphasise and embrace analyses of Somali trade that put trust and social solidarity to the fore. Indeed, 'trust', or *aammin* in Somali, is not only an etic term used by scholars to understand Somali trade, but also a key emic term — that is, a term used by Somalis themselves to explain their entrepreneurial success.

In what follows, we examine the potentials and limits of 'trust' in elucidating Somali economic life, considering the term in both its etic and emic uses. We argue that while 'trust' can help explain the social relations underpinning trade, and in particular the provision of credit, trust is not a prerequisite for trusting behaviour or acts of trusting in business. Rather, acts of trusting themselves work to produce trust, even as they can also come to implicate deceit and mistrust. Trust in its emic usage creates a moral impetus for acts of trusting, even as 'trusters' may not necessarily fully trust those they do business with. In Eastleigh, an important driver of this discourse is the demand for credit, which itself plays a crucial role in driving the estate's economy.

Our analytical approach to trust draws inspiration from a wealth of social science work on trust, in particular Broch-Due and

Ystannes' (2016) edited volume and its emphasis on the importance of examining acts of trusting rather than tracking 'trust' as an 'affective attitude' (Jones 1996), orientation or disposition, which is something difficult to measure or pin down. We build on studies among transnational trading communities, which have found that such communities are characterised by a normative obligation to behave in trusting ways towards each other, often in the absence of solidarities with other groups or support from state institutions (Rosenfeld 2012; Whitehouse 2012; Portes and Sensenbrenner 1993). Rosenfeld (2012: 76), for example, describes what he calls 'enforceable trust' among Lebanese and Beninese transnational entrepreneurs, a mechanism that 'discourages wrongdoing by network members, who as part of a tightly bounded group must rely on one another for their mutual support and livelihoods'. This brings to the fore the social obligations, pressures and forms of control, such as social sanctions, surrounding trust that exist not only at the community or societal level but also between individuals. As Carey notes, 'trust' can be seen as a form of social control, since by trusting others, we attempt to extend control over them by rendering their behaviour towards us knowable and predictable (2017: 7). This echoes familiar ideas from classical Maussian approaches to gift-giving (Mauss 2001 [1923]), whereby the gift bestows the obligation of reciprocity onto the receiver, even as reciprocation may not be precisely equivalent to what was given in the first place or even occur within a specified temporal frame.

Rather than seeing trust as a prerequisite of trusting behaviour or acts of trusting, we instead see acts of trusting as themselves generative of trust or what Piotr Sztompka (1999: 28) calls 'evocative trust'. This argument is central to Parker Shipton's (2007) work on entrustment among the Luo in western Kenya, which argues that acts of entrusting objects, money and people do not necessarily hinge on trust, but rather produce trust over time. At the same time, one risks being deceived if the trusted party breaches the trust bestowed upon them and does not fulfil the social obligation to reciprocate. As will become clear in the following sections, trusting, in this sense, is also risking. Ultimately, we argue that 'trust' is key to enabling the

TRADE MAKES STATES

circulation of goods in the greater Somali economy, in particular through the provision of credit. Encompassing different nation-states, maritime networks and hinterlands along with multiple frictions and uncertainties regarding how goods should move—including those linked to state and state-like authorities—'trust' provides the social infrastructure which allows traders to circumvent these frictions and move goods transnationally.[1] In elucidating 'trust' as social infrastructure, the chapter provides an important backdrop to understanding the trading relations across Somali East Africa described in the chapters that follow.

Trust, clan and business

Trust has proved an enduring theme in Somali studies, particularly in the wake of the collapse of the Somali state in the early 1990s. In a context of heightened uncertainty, kin and lineage networks have become not just providers of social support and security but also conduits for trade. Unsurprisingly, many analyses of Somali social and economic life have emphasised trust emanating from kinship.

The classic Somali segmentary lineage model, as described by I. M. Lewis, looms large in these studies of trust. Trade is seen to operate within structures that emerged out of a nomadic pastoralist context as 'a continuation of the collective economic interests of agnates' (1994: 126). Goldsmith notes that 'members of the same *jilib*, subclan or sublineage units, retain especially strong reciprocal obligations to relatives, even if they are complete strangers who might share a common ancestor five or six generations removed' (1997: 469). Such reciprocal obligations allow strong trade networks to form by providing a framework in which trade flourishes. Clan networks constituted a key social infrastructure for cross-border livestock trade between Somalia, Ethiopia and Kenya already before the fall of Somalia's Siyad Barre regime (Mahmoud 2010), as well as for the transnational trade that followed with the Somali diaspora (Bjork 2007). As a result of state collapse in Somalia and liberalisation in Kenya, Somali trade networks have expanded and intensified considerably in the past three decades, with Eastleigh and Dubai being the most important southern and

38

northern hubs (Little 2014). Bjork (2007: 152) emphasises that the clan networks that Somalis rely upon for managing transnational capital should not be viewed as primordial or as essentially enduring, noting that in a context of transnational trade (as indeed in any context) they require constant work, being produced and reproduced in discourse and practice.

In line with our emphasis on acts of trusting, knowability and social control are important elements when considering the significance of lineage in enabling trust among Somalis. According to Simons (1995: 139), genealogy provides a sort of information system through which Somalis can quickly gauge the trustworthiness of individuals and whether to enter into business with them. Genealogy charts 'who has trusted whom in the past and where this has led in terms of thicker or thinner, and sustained or broken relationships'. Failing to be trustworthy has far-reaching implications, not only in terms of future relationships between the 'trusted' and the 'truster' but also within the wider family lineage as word spreads about an individual's untrustworthy behaviour and the wider social unit's inability to ensure their proper behaviour. This highlights the ways in which, contrary to much of the (Western) theorising on trust, trusting and being trusted are not limited to autonomous individuals but are situated within broader social configurations (cf. Broch-Due and Ystanes 2016).

Trust also features in analyses of some of the key infrastructures that have evolved since Somalis migrated across the globe, namely *hawala* money transfer companies which have facilitated the reproduction of social as well as trading networks (see Chapter 3). The *hawala* system has evolved through relations of trust, whereby one agent could accept money for a client in one location and trust that another agent would release the remitted money in another, the remittee often being identified through their place in the lineage structure (Cockayne and Shetret 2012). Even today, with many *hawala* being multinational companies with franchises around the world, they often recruit agents through clan networks. As Lindley (2009: 525) describes:

> Money transmitters tend initially to recruit agents through their clan networks, which helps ensure loyalty among staff and custom-

ers. As a former employee in Nairobi put it: 'If you go to Kaah, who are working there? The Ogaden. And who is working for Amal? The majority is Majerteen. And who is working for Dahabshiil … If you have your own business, you bring your cousin, your uncle … members of my family first, and then my community. That's our way of helping each other.'

In Eastleigh at the time of Carrier's research in 2011, money was said to be handed over at branches to customers who identified themselves not with ID documents but through lineage. This may be deemed a more effective way of eliciting information about somebody, especially where official documents are unreliable or unobtainable. In Kenya, Somali refugees often live precarious lives without ID documents, as do some Kenyan Somalis, ID cards notoriously being more difficult to obtain for Kenyans from northern regions, which include Kenya's Somali regions (KHRC 2009: 33–4). Furthermore, ID documents may be fake (see Rasmussen and Wafer 2019; Cockayne and Shetret 2012: 13). Somalis' 'who's who' knowledge derived through their recalling of lineage and family connections often proves a more pragmatic means of identification. However, pressures to implement formal customer identification measures have been felt across the global remittances sector since the post-9/11 crack-down on financial remittances. And in the wake of the insecurity in Kenya that followed the Kenya Defence Forces' intervention in Somalia in 2011, hawala services have been targeted by the government as potential sources of terrorist funding (Mohamed 2015), which has further increased the pressure on remittance companies to strengthen compliance systems.

Between April and June 2015, the Kenyan government banned Somali hawala services, claiming that there were links between money transfer companies and heightened terrorist activity plaguing the country (see Harding 2015). Many companies continued operations in spite of the ban, sending money received from abroad to receivers via M-Pesa. Elliott's experience of sending money to two friends in Kenya—one Somali and one non-Somali—via the Somali money transfer company fittingly named Amaana Express (amana means 'trust' in Arabic) during the ban suggests the continued importance of ethnic identity to trust in money transfer. The Somali friend picked up her money on the same day that it was sent from Copenhagen, receiving it from a local Amaana agent via M-Pesa. There were, however, complications with the transfer of the non-Somali friend's money, which a Somali friend assisting Elliott with the transaction in Copenhagen believed was due to their mistrusting her non-Somali and non-Muslim name in the context of the ban. It was only after Elliott followed up on the transfer with the Amaana agent in Copenhagen that the money reached its recipient.

'Trust' also features in accounts by both scholars and Somalis of the lack of formal contracts in Somali business dealings, especially when it comes to the provision of credit. In Eastleigh, doing business without formal contracts is commonplace, though this does vary. Some of Eastleigh's businesses are more intertwined with formal systems than others. Banks and larger businesses, for example, are integrated into the formal legal system. In some cases, Eastleigh's economy has pushed state institutions into the margins. For example, the demand for real estate led to the displacement of the chief's camp in the estate: the site had been bought from the government and used to erect a mall, and his office was relocated to a converted shipping container (Carrier and Lochery 2013: 346). Despite this, Kenyan law permeates Eastleigh, and Somalis living there sometimes refer to it when seeking redress, even if they prefer to turn to sheikhs, elders or the Eastleigh Business Association when it comes to business disputes. *Mu'salaha*—an informal institution of dispute resolution whereby members of the community help redress any complaints—is also used in Eastleigh between Somalis, similarly to how it is used by livestock traders and businesspeople in Somaliland as described by Musa (2019: 20). Most credit-based transactions taking place between wholesalers and retailers are informal and operate without written contracts. A wholesalers' notebook documenting who has taken what advances of stock is often the closest thing one sees to a legally binding record of debt.

Personalised relations dominate, and many businesses are connected through kin and lineage. Notably, clans of significant

strength in Eastleigh such as Ogaden and Garre are strongly represented in Kenya and elsewhere in the diaspora, which provides
opportunities for lineages within them to access capital, goods and
credit. As with Rosenfeld's (2012) study of the Lebanese diaspora,
Eastleigh Somalis have a network of people across the world who
can generally be trusted to meet obligations and who are aware of
the consequences for their reputation should they prove untrustworthy. In this regard, Somalis who build up debts are keen to pay
them back before their reputation suffers. For some traders who
have struggled to build successful enterprises in Eastleigh, unpaid
debts and the negative reputation accompanying them can push
them to leave the estate for new pastures. This was the case with a
trader who left his debt-ridden shop behind in an Eastleigh mall
and moved to South Africa. However, his reputation—tarnished
by widespread knowledge among Somalis in South Africa of the
debts he still owed in Kenya—compelled him to return to Nairobi
to repay these debts.

Given the emphasis on knowability through clan among Somalis,
formal written contracts may seem inappropriate, based as they are
on agreements between autonomous individuals or firms. As noted
above, trust tends to hinge on much more extensive social configurations. Moreover, contracts can also be negatively associated with
mistrust; as one young Somali businessman in Eastleigh described
it, 'educated folks' would 'accept formality', but older people
would be more likely to emphasise 'trust' and might accuse a
potential partner of not trusting them if they were to propose a
more formal way of doing business, such as through written contracts. His comments also point to the association—especially by
some younger people with business qualifications—of personalised
trust based in clan and familial connections with 'backward',
uneducated behaviour in business. The emphasis on trust in Somali
business is not always seen as a boon.

Diaspora Somalis who have become accustomed to business in
the West can find it hard to navigate the more informal business
environment of places like Eastleigh. The young Somali businessman quoted above had established a consultancy company for such
diaspora investors to help them adjust to working without con-

tracts. However, it is important to note that even in the West Somali business can also be guided by informal relations of trust. Samatar (2008), for example, writes about a Somali restaurant established in Minneapolis by three partners who each put in 35,000 USD and raised 300,000 USD from other investors. None of the investors signed any document stating the nature of their investment or its expected return: 'The investors completely trusted the three partners and believed that they would get their money back with a decent return at some point in the future' (ibid.: 80). No written partnership or agreement was made between the three partners either: 'Nothing was agreed on paper except to form a partnership and manage a restaurant' (ibid.).

The risk of spoiling reputation through a breach of trust links to the 'enforceable trust' discussed above. People can be pressured through family networks to behave appropriately and fulfil obligations, and family members may sometimes step in to resolve, for example, an unpaid debt to save the reputation of the wider social unit. This is particularly important in an economy such as Eastleigh's, as participation in it is often dependent on accessing credit. Should one family member renege on a debt, this could mark the family as untrustworthy and jeopardise another family member's chances of getting credit. Being barred from credit could restrict one's possibilities for trade and have serious consequences for the well-being of the family in question, thus raising the stakes of trust.

Trust beyond clan

I. M. Lewis argued that the effectiveness of lineage for creating trust had a negative effect on trusting beyond the kin network, making it hard for Somalis to trust non-kin (1999 [1961]: 30). Relations through the patriline—and relations managed through socio-legal institutions such as the payment of *diya* (compensation) between corporate groups—took centre stage in his structural-functionalist analysis, so that clan and lineage assumed a problematic primordialist importance. Yet this emphasis on trust within clan does not capture more inclusive or far-reaching networks through which Somalis conduct trade in Eastleigh and elsewhere. Furthermore, classic accounts of lineage networks tend to emphasise their patriarchal nature, paying little attention to women's more flexible clan identities which facilitate their reciprocal relationships beyond the clan of their fathers and husbands (Nori et al. 2006).

In Eastleigh, trust networks often stretch across clan boundaries, and the estate's boom would not have been possible were enterprise restricted solely to lineage and family ties. Ties beyond the lineage and family are, furthermore, created by trusting others in trade, including through the entrustment of credit. This is evident in the workings of Eastleigh's camel milk market. At the time of the authors' research, Kenyan Somali middlewomen operating in pastoralist, camel milk-producing areas of Kenya such as Isiolo would send milk on credit to other Somali women based in Eastleigh, who were often kin but could also be people they met during visits to the estate. These Eastleigh-based women operated as wholesalers, in turn entrusting milk on credit to women with whom they did not have a family relationship, including newly arrived refugees from Somalia. These wholesalers claimed that they knew little about aspiring milk traders other than that they were Somalis and Muslims. Trade networks thus expanded beyond the realm of family (cf. Nori et al. 2006), and trust between traders was also garnered through commercial relationships (Elliott 2014), echoing Shipton's (2007) point that trust may be created through acts of entrustment.

Larger business enterprises in Eastleigh also transcend clan, including some malls that have multi-clan ownership, often based on shareholder models. Beyond Eastleigh, Lindley also writes how *hawala* companies must move beyond narrow clan lines in expanding business, especially in offering services to different parts of the Somali regions (2009: 526). They have become multi-clan shareholder companies in the process. Lochery (2015) similarly shows that private companies operating in the provision of electricity services in Somaliland have moved towards establishing multi-clan shareholder companies to broaden market access and interconnect power grids. Mahmoud's study of livestock trade in the Somalia–

Kenya–Ethiopia borderlands shows that clan networks that had been prescient prior to the collapse of the Barre state gave way to multi-clan networks under Islamist rule as a 'risk mitigation strategy' (2010: 10). Entrepreneurs in Eastleigh frame transcending clan affiliations as making business sense in terms of efficiency, competitiveness, and quality. As a young entrepreneur involved in numerous projects in Eastleigh put it, choosing business partners on the basis of clan rather than their 'competitiveness or qualification' is what 'kills' business.

Furthermore, business networks in Eastleigh encompass non-Somalis. In some cases, these relationships are facilitated by particular goods. Many Meru living there, for example, are involved in the trade in *miraa* (or *khat*, the green leaf stimulant popular among Somalis and across the Horn of Africa and Yemen), and they talked about the opportunities that opened up to them through their forming friendships with Somalis in Eastleigh and beyond who might be able to open up trading outlets for them elsewhere (Carrier 2017: 177). It is also common to hear it said by people of other ethnic origins in Kenya that Somalis are especially trustworthy in business, thus rendering Somalis attractive business partners. The discourse claiming that Somalis are people to be trusted is thus not only spread by Somalis.

It is often high demand for credit that compels Somali wholesalers to entrust goods to non-Somali retailers, who can hail from as far away as Tanzania. Giving out credit is a way through which wholesalers can keep retailers happy and ensure their custom. This logic stretches beyond Somali wholesalers, and those importing goods also report receiving large quantities of goods on credit from Chinese firms keen to find an outlet for their stock. Credit is also crucial to Somali trade in other contexts. Livestock trading between Somaliland and the Gulf, for example, depends heavily on credit arrangements between producers, middlemen and exporters (Musa 2019: 13). Credit enables goods to move quickly, which is particularly important when it comes to perishables like *khat* and milk.

Fast movement is also a principle underpinning the circulation of other goods, such as the vast quantities of cheap clothing in the estate (see Carrier and Elliott 2019). Many talk about the principle of keeping goods moving through the ready provision of credit as one that differentiates a Somali business model from, say, a Kenyan Asian one, and they point to this as an explanation of the success of Somali business. 'Trust' is particularly important for this business model in terms of the provision of credit. Indeed, 'trust' could be criticised for disguising the impetus for both giving and receiving credit in Eastleigh and the role it plays in oiling the estate's economy.

However, 'trust' should not be seen as merely a cover or disguise for credit. As with Luo entrustment (Shipton 2007), a Somali model of entrusting credit generates trust and builds social relations as opposed to those relations being a precursor or determinant of credit. Sztompka (1999) writes about this as 'evocative trust': by trusting someone, we create trust. A similar point is made by Haas (2016), whose research among Barga Mongols shows that trust is considered a sign that one is trying to produce positive effects in the world. Even when dealing with people who are known to be untrustworthy, Haas found that her informants endeavoured to behave in trusting ways towards them.

In Eastleigh, acts of trusting are propelled by a moral economic principle: in addition to promoting trade and generating wealth for individual entrepreneurs, trusting ensures that trade and profit opportunities circulate and are inclusive, allowing diverse actors to participate in Eastleigh's economy. This was expressed by camel milk wholesalers, who explained that it was a social responsibility to give milk on credit to poor refugee women to enable them to find their feet in Eastleigh's economy. This principle of participation also has a 'what goes around comes around' logic. As one member of the Eastleigh Business Association put it, as a wholesaler, entrusting credit to a new retailer not only promotes their wealth and success but also one's own. After some time, that customer may be wealthy, and every week will pay you good money. Through that initial act of trusting, he went on, the customer may even become wealthier than the wholesaler.

Thus, it is not only kinship and lineage but also the mutuality that emerges from other kinds of relationships, often facilitated by acts of entrusting credit, which incubates trust in Eastleigh. This echoes the strong Maussian legacy running through the anthropology of credit and debt which has shown that credit/debt, an 'indissoluble dyad', generates social relations (Peebles 2010).

More mundanely, trusting is also encouraged by very concrete conditions; for Mohaa, a Kenyan Somali from Isiolo, it was renting a shop in a large Eastleigh shopping mall from which to do his retail business in men's clothing that meant that wholesalers began to be more confident and generous in their credit provisions. Still, Mohaa's path to obtaining the shop was initially carved out through his family connections:

> After earlier attempts at making a living in Nairobi had met with little success, a relative helped him settle in Eastleigh, providing him with accommodation and 100 shillings each day. Mohaa describes how he impressed the relative one time when he was left in charge of his shop. In his absence, Mohaa's sales charisma led to many sales, and he was given 300 shillings, and, more importantly, a job in the shop in 2006. He worked there until 2008 when his relative moved to Norway. In showing that he can be trusted both to be honest and effective in sales, Mohaa built up networks capable of advancing him goods on credit, essential when an opportunity came for him and his business partner—whom he had befriended as they worked in neighbouring shops—to obtain their own shop in the same mall when its previous occupier moved to South Africa in 2008. They still needed to raise the capital for the 'goodwill' payment to secure the shop, however, and had to raise 100,000 shillings each. Here, their experience of working in the malls no doubt loosened the purse strings of their relatives who could see they would work hard in the business. They both were loaned money by family, Mohaa by his father (a man of some means and influence in Isiolo), and his business partner by a brother, allowing them to start their shop.

While it was trust garnered through Mohaa's and his partner's family relations that led them to obtain the shop, the shop itself further generated trusting relations between them and those wholesalers with whom he did not have a familial relation. Having a shop in Eastleigh is a sign of permanence and means, and a material sign of trustworthiness. Indeed, without successful navigation of informal relations of credit and debt—themselves generative of trust, as we have argued—it would be very hard to have a shop, and these relations come to be symbolised by the shop itself.

Trust and Islam: Halal *and* haram *business*

A different dimension of trusting upon which Somalis place particular emphasis is Islam. Both the Kiswahili and Somali words for 'trust' derive from the Arabic *amana*, which refers to the fulfilment of trust. The term connects with wider Islamic values, which have long been present in Eastleigh but appear to be getting stronger with the global spread of popular Islam. Many of our informants spoke about the importance not so much of a shared Somali identity in generating trust in business relations but of shared Muslim faith.

Islam has long featured prominently in trade. The spread of Islam across Africa and elsewhere can be linked to the spread of commercial networks through Muslim traders (Chaudhuri 1985), and Cohen long ago emphasised the link between Hausa trade and Islam in West Africa (1969). More recent historical, anthropological and archaeological work explores the links between Islam and trade, particularly in the way long-distance trade networks operate, including trans-Saharan routes (Lydon 2009; Scheele 2012). Trust is a key theme in this literature (Forrest and Haour 2018), although archaeological work on the pre-Islamic forms of such trade networks raises questions about how dependent such trade was on Islam (Haour 2017). However, there is much resonance between Islam and trade. The Prophet Mohamed himself engaged in trade, and the morality of Islam links to the morality of business and making money. In Kenya, where Islamic influences are dominant, people debate what are *halal* and *haram* ways of making money. Economic success and religious piety are considered to be mutually reinforcing, so that those who make money through *halal* means will be successful, whereas wealth generated through *haram* practices will be fragile and short-lived (see Elliott 2018).

Debates on *halal* and *haram* wealth are well-rehearsed in Eastleigh and guide its economy. Mosques can refuse donations of money believed to be ill-gotten: for example, stories circulate of mosques refusing donations from prominent *khat* traders. Religious authorities have also criticised the financing model through which malls in the estate have been built: that is, requiring upfront payments of large sums to reserve shops, as described in the story of Mohaa's pathway to renting a shop above. Paying such sums is known as 'buying the key', and such payments are known as 'goodwill'. 'Goodwill' is a well-known business term for the intangible assets of a going concern, but in Kenya it refers to money paid on top of rent to gain the rights to run a business in the shop.

In Eastleigh, malls are often funded through such payments: after obtaining the rights to develop a plot, a company advertises retail space within the future mall and has those who are interested reserve shops through such payments. As a mall might have hundreds of such shops, and goodwill fees can be from 5,000–50,000 USD, depending on the size of the shop, huge sums can be raised to pay for construction with whatever is leftover constituting an early profit. Those who obtain rights to shops in this way often in future sublet to others, charging their own goodwill in the process. There is considerable resentment and bitterness surrounding such payments in Eastleigh and in the wider Kenyan economy, as they are often seen as additional barriers to entering shop-based trade (Carrier and Lochery 2013: 338). In Eastleigh, some see these payments as immoral and un-Islamic, believing them to be similar to charging interest (*riba* in Arabic), in that they make money out of the exploitation of others.

While goodwill has been a key business model for financing mall construction projects, some proprietors of Eastleigh's more recent malls have rejected it. Traders in one of the larger malls, built initially through such payments, talked of their expectations (and hopes) that in the future the mall's management would do away with goodwill payments under the influence of Islamic preachers. The names of some of Eastleigh's more recently built malls—Madina Mall, Mecca Plaza—attest to this championing of Islamic values in business, and the owners of these malls (built through a shareholder rather than the goodwill model) were keen to differentiate them from the latter through their Islamic business credentials. A revitalised commitment to *halal* methods of conducting business has also led to the promotion of Islamic financial products in Eastleigh; the Islamic insurance company, Takaful, for example, has established a branch in the estate. While insurance, seen as akin to gambling, is considered *haram* in Islamic teachings, with Takaful losses and gains are said to be shared equally between company and client. Many in Eastleigh prefer to bank with *hawala* money agents rather than banks, but a growing number of *shari'a*-compliant financial products promoted by banks such as the Gulf African Bank provide a more formal institutional basis for trusting.

Islam also underpins more personalised trade relations, particularly with the spread of Salafist forms which owe much to influences from abroad. Aisha Ahmad's (2012) work on Islam and trade in Mogadishu throws light on the shift from trade based on clan and lineage to trade based on Islamic principles. In the wake of state collapse, businesses came to depend on tight, clan-based networks as trust between clans and sub-clans disintegrated and numerous businesspeople were able to do well by taking advantage of clan conflict, especially with the flow of aid money into the country. When aid money dried up in the mid-1990s with the withdrawal of AMISOM, Mogadishu's business community grew increasingly sensitive to the negative impact of tribalism on businesses. Increasingly, businesspeople turned to Islamic principles. This discursive shift followed the more pragmatic solutions offered by the Islamic courts: they promised an overarching security provision, where clan warlords and militias, in contrast, were fragmented, predatory and unreliable, not to say expensive (Ahmad 2014).

Emphasising the importance of Islam to business in this context became a means of bolstering a more universal Islamic identity over more limiting clan identities which had begun to have negative connotations in local discourse. A similar discursive shift has been noted among Somalis in the diaspora. Tiilikainen, for example, writes that 'if Somalia carries an image of continuous war, refugees, misery, and the haven of terrorists, Islam as a global religion instead represents dignity, respect and morality' (2003: 65). Of course, both Salafi attitudes and lineage networks go together and indeed overlap. One could even argue that—when faced with the question with whom to cooperate within a family—piety might be a good selection criterion for choosing one's business partners (Marchal and Sheikh 2015).

In networks running through Eastleigh, too, Islamic identity garners trust, and Somalis there often more readily refer to Islamic faith than to ethnicity and clan as a basis for trust. Companies often look to reputed sheikhs to promote their businesses and give them the seal of approval. The manager of Takaful's Eastleigh branch, for example, talked about looking to sheikhs to promote their service and thus recruit clients. Shared Islamic identity has likewise promoted the extension of Eastleigh Somalis' trading relations, enabling links between Somalis and Gulf traders, as Ahmad (2012) finds is the case for traders in Mogadishu. Dubai has for decades been a crucial source of goods for Eastleigh, and Eastleigh traders rely on the strong relations Somalis have built up with Dubai's business community (who often sponsor permits for Somalis [Abdi 2015: 74ff]).

Kenyan Somalis also depend on Gulf contacts as buyers for Kenyan and Somali livestock. In all this trade, having Islam in common no doubt helps evoke trust. Some Meru in Eastleigh, who converted from Christianity to Islam, talked about the ways this improved prospects of trade with Somalis. This is not to conclude that people choose their religious affiliation solely to accomplish material ends, but rather to note the intertwining of economic and religious life. Ahmad (2012) points to the way the enactment of religious piety among businesspeople in Mogadishu becomes internalised, so that performing piety produces piety. Following the notion of 'evocative trust' cited above (Sztompka 1999), performing trust through acts of trusting or entrustment has a similar effect, producing substantive trust over time.

The risks of trusting

While Mahmoud (2008) demonstrated how Somali livestock traders in northern Kenya made use of 'trust' and social relations to reduce risks, entrusting is not without risk. Somalis' claims that they trust one another stand in stark contrast to the suspicion, mistrust and conflict that have pervaded everyday life in Somalia's recent history. Eastleigh itself is hardly free from deceit, and those navigating its economy must be savvy and alert to scams. Indeed, many in Eastleigh emphasise that the need to show oneself as trustworthy relates to the fact that there are many who are not (cf. Shipton 2007). In this context, maintaining a good reputation becomes ever more important. This is exemplified in one story told by Mohaa, the Kenyan Somali shopkeeper whom we met earlier. Mohaa recounted an incident that he and his friends refer to as 'Operation Linda Duka' ('Operation Protect the Shop'), named after 'Operation Linda Nchi' ('Operation Protect the Nation'), the name for the Kenya Defence Force's 2011 military incursion into Somalia (see Crisis Group 2012):

> A young man and acquaintance of Mohaa's from his hometown had moved to Eastleigh in search of work, and Mohaa had given him some work at his shop. He worked hard initially, bringing in good profits, but then started giving Mohaa less money, and Mohaa began to suspect that he was keeping some of the proceeds. The young man's explanation for the decline in profits was that he was only able to sell items at the lowest price. Thus, Mohaa set up a 'sting' operation to catch his assistant out should he be up to no good. He gave a Sudanese woman 10,000 shillings and told her to buy shirts and trousers. When she had done her 'shopping' and Mohaa returned and asked his assistant how much he had sold that day, he was told that he had only made a small profit. Mohaa then revealed that he knew how much he had in fact made, and the young man was given the sack.

There are many other such examples of deceit in Eastleigh and beyond. For all the talk of Somalis fearing loss of reputation and thus being compelled to be trustworthy, it is not hard to find stories of those who attract investors in business schemes only to 'take the money and run'. One camel milk trader, Saida, who was based in the estate, formerly operated from Isiolo, sending milk to trading partners in the city. She described an experience in which a trading partner, whom she had initially met while visiting Eastleigh and to whom she had subsequently begun sending milk on credit, had left to go and live in a refugee camp, taking the proceeds from their business with her. After this, Saida decided to move to

Eastleigh where she could better oversee the business, feeling she could no longer risk entrusting milk on credit from afar.

In Eastleigh, there is also mistrust and suspicion surrounding plot dispute cases, which are ubiquitous in Kenya, between different groups of Somalis. One informant was defrauded of a deposit he put down for an apartment in a residential block in the estate that was never built, and he turned to the Kenyan legal system to try to resolve his case. Diaspora investors are seen as particularly naïve and vulnerable to deceit, especially if, as mentioned above, they have become used to formal systems of business elsewhere in Europe and North America and are less attuned to spotting the risks of trusting.

The consequences of such naïveté are well exemplified in the story of Abdul, a US-based Somali who had saved up money working as a taxi driver in Chicago. He had managed to purchase a highly sought-after taxi 'medallion' required to operate a taxi business in the United States for 50,000 USD, which he later sold for 250,000 USD. It was this money that he decided to invest in Nairobi, joining a cousin who lived there in his business trading sugar. This is a commodity that has become a mainstay of Somali trade: cheap supplies from Brazil enter Kenya illegally via Kismayu in Somalia and are then traded in northern Kenyan markets (see Rasmussen 2017). But Abdul ended up being swindled: the cousin gave him a fake cheque after a business deal and ran off to South Africa with much of Abdul's savings. Again, trust, including within the extended family, may be spoken of so much in Eastleigh precisely because the repercussions in cases of deceit are so well known (cf. Shipton 2007).

Conclusion

This chapter has examined the possibilities and limitations of the concept of 'trust' in explaining the dynamics of Somali trade, in doing so refining our conceptual understanding of 'trust' in the context of Somali business. Following the above discussion of the risks of trusting, trust in its emic usage also has limits. The narrative that 'we Somalis trust each other'—along with the claim that 'we kin/fellow clan/lineage members trust each other' and 'we Muslims trust each other'—is an idealised one, and buying into it uncritically would make running a successful business virtually impossible. Furthermore, scholars of informal economies have warned that explaining transactions through the notion of trust may mask asymmetrical relations; as Sayer puts it, 'what appears to indicate trust may be largely a consequence of domination, or simple mutual dependency' (2001: 699). In Eastleigh and the broader transnational Somali economic networks in which it is located, people have little choice but to trust, especially when they trade with those with whom they share clan or lineage. Despite all the talk that 'we Somalis trust each other', some are better placed to be trusted than others. Trust networks are not always accessible to less powerful clans, a point made by a representative of the Somali Bantu population in Eastleigh at a workshop in Nairobi in 2014 where we presented a paper on 'trust'.

More than a reflection of actual trusting relationships, trust is a normative discourse that creates a moral code which (ideally, at least) promotes mutuality in trade. Every time trust is emphasised, it further spreads the message that being trustworthy is the correct way to behave, and that one should be prepared to entrust goods and capital to someone else—especially if they are Somali. The same applies to proper Islamic behaviour in trade. These discourses lubricate the flow of capital and goods, reassuring budding traders that plenty of people have trusted before and rich rewards can be reaped by doing so. For those worried about lack of legal recourse, the claim that 'we Somalis don't use contracts' might well be reassuring. Requesting a contract might be deemed evidence of distrust, thus souring relations between potential business partners. This is in a context where, as mentioned, 'trust' creates openings in trading opportunities and renders business more inclusive.

A reluctance to trust might be deemed selfish, especially in relation to the provision of credit, which ensures the circulation of money and the possibility for aspiring traders to participate in Eastleigh's economy. Many, then, find themselves compelled to trust, not only to pursue success in Eastleigh's vibrant economy but also to be considered someone who is acting appropriately within it. In this respect, 'trust' is not merely discursive, but also produces real-world effects, including trust itself, which underpins the circulation of goods and finance in the greater Somali economy, including important business hubs outside of the Somali territories. Multiple obstacles and frictions exist in Somali interregional trading, ranging from the absence of insurance in nonrecognised, fragile or non-existent states; to lack of formal registration or licences for importing, transporting or selling goods; and a lack of formal identification documents. Acts of trusting enable the circumvention of these patchy and often exclusive pockets of formality.

Finally, talk of trust is also designed for an external audience. At the time of our research—when there was a great deal of state and popular suspicion surrounding Somali economic success as reflected concretely in the form of Eastleigh's development— many Somali traders wanted to debunk claims that this success was attributable to dodgy dealings. They were also keen to distance themselves from the clannishness or tribalism that many associate with state collapse, violent conflict and subsequent exile in Kenya. In this way, the narrative of trust serves a wider purpose beyond business in building a unifying vision of what Somali society should be: a counter-narrative to common depictions of Somalia as a conflict-ridden, untrustworthy place, one that emphasises instead *Somalinimo* (Somali unity) and Islamic morality. While scholars, ourselves included, use trust as a concept to elucidate the workings of informal economies, Somalis have seized upon 'trust' to account for the dynamics of their own social and economic lives.

3

WAR, PEACE AND THE CIRCULATION
OF MOBILE MONEY ACROSS
THE SOMALI TERRITORIES

Gianluca Iazzolino and *Nicole Stremlau*

Introduction

On 27 February 2021, the Central Bank of Somalia granted the Mogadishu-based Hormuud Telecom Somalia Inc. the country's first mobile money licence. As the bank governor Abdirahman Mohamed Abdullahi explained in a press conference, 'in formalising our existing digital payments infrastructure, we are accelerating the integration of Somalia's financial system into the global economy'.[1] By issuing a licence to Hormuud, Somali regulators attempted to extend their oversight to the telecom's mobile money platform, EVC Plus, taking stock of a sector that has been thriving for the past decade in the absence of state regulation. During this period, despite the lack of a formal legal framework—or, as we suggest in this chapter, thanks to it—access to mobile networks and mobile money have become a celebrated example of what works across the Somali territories.

The International Telecommunication Union (2018) estimates that, in 2017, just 2% of Somalis had access to the internet but 48.3% of Somalis have mobile phone subscriptions. However, based on anecdotal evidence, this official data seems to be far lower than actual access rates. Business organisations like the GSMA, the telecom industry association,[2] have focused on Somaliland and, to a lesser extent, Somalia to highlight how the popularity of mobile money in the region could be replicated across other low- and middle-income countries. At the same time, the past decade has seen a growing number of media reports drawing attention to the strides made by digital finance across the Somali territories.[3] These reports often contrast a sophisticated digital infrastructure for storing value within the region and transferring it elsewhere with a peculiar, and often violent, dynamic of state formation in the Horn of Africa.

This chapter discusses how the social, legal, political and technological arrangements necessary to develop reliable financial infrastructure emerged in the Somali context, and it asks what the case of mobile money in the Somali territories tells us about the role of business in state making and the hypothesised politics of circulation more broadly (see Chapter 1). Mobile money represents the financial counterpart to the circulation of goods. As Taussig (1997: 132) pointed out, money is itself 'quintessentially' 'circular'. But in the case of post-war Somalia, the financial infrastructure—the very institutions that undergird the circulation of money within and across borders—had collapsed, which had implications for the circulation of commodities. This chapter describes how the vacuum left by state collapse was initially filled by *hawala* companies and, more recently, has seen the rise of mobile money operators. We explore how the collapse of the Somali state in 1991 spurred the emergence of a Somali financial-telecommunication complex characterised by interwoven historical, managerial and operational ties between the Somali financial and telecommunication sectors. These telecoms smooth the circulation of goods across Somali East Africa and, as they forge strategic partnerships with remittance companies, between the region and the rest of the world. We also show how mobile money operators have carved out a new space of value extraction for officials and militias, thus playing a crucial role in reshaping the political economy of taxation in the area.

We combine a political economy and a social-legal perspective to argue that the popularity of mobile money in Somali East Africa builds, on the one hand, on facilitated access to a digital currency pegged to the US dollar in import-dependent economies and with scarce and volatile local currencies and, on the other, on the adaptation of ownership structures and dispute resolution mechanisms to local governance arrangements. However, contrary to most developmental narratives of mobile money across the Somali territories (Pénicaud and McGrath 2013; Hesse 2010), we suggest that the benefits of digital finance are unevenly distributed among populations.

Mobile money services in the Somali territories enable customers to convert local money into US dollars and store them in e-wallets. These services have met a specific demand for hard currency resulting from the absence of a functioning national currency due to the country's economic history and political economy. During Somalia's extended period of limited statehood, which predates the 1991 collapse of the central state, the void of state governance has been filled by a variety of social-legal structures, embedded in kin and business networks and straddling between international norms, practices, compliance requirements on the one hand, and messy, fragmented, dynamic and informal local realities on the other. These fuzzy governance structures, poised 'between the handshake and the contract', as further explored in Chapter 4, have shaped the financial-telecommunication conglomerates that have built the infrastructures through which value and information circulate inside and outside of the Somali territories.

In so doing, these conglomerates have not only met the needs of an import-export economy against a very volatile backdrop but have emerged as key actors in the politics of circulation in Somali East Africa. While the lack of formal state banking systems and regulations has enabled new innovative products to emerge, the popularity of mobile money across the region ought to be linked to a specific experience of state formation and a unique configuration of political, legal and business actors. Apart from Eritrea, where the telecom sector is entirely state-run, Somalia is the only country in Africa where international telecom companies such as MTN or Bharti do not operate; it is solely Somali private telecom companies that provide services. While recipes to transplant the Somali digital finance ecosystem to other contexts may be of limited use, the case of mobile money in the Somali territories offers insights into the socio-legal embeddedness of local institutions and authorities when it comes to conflict and fragile settings.

Our arguments are based on interviews the authors have collected over the past decade of research into this area. Together, and with research teams, we have interviewed hundreds of members of leading telecoms, mobile money providers, political elites and users of mobile money. Moreover, through our interviews, we collected a small corpus of what could be considered oral case law of disputes involving telecommunications companies and mobile money users. We collected oral testimonies of conflict parties, as well as those who assisted in dispute resolution and helped determine appropriate compensation. All of our findings allowed us a better understanding of the role of various authorities in enabling the development of the mobile money ecosystem.

The chapter is structured as follows. In the first section, we chart the development of the Somali financial and telecom systems: from the rapid expansion of the money transfer industry in the 1970s, to its consolidation in the aftermath of the civil war in the 1990s, up until 2001, when the beginning of the War on Terror—following the 9/11 terror attacks in the United States—disrupted the remittance business. Then, we discuss the emergence and transformations of the Somali digital financial sector, focusing in particular on Hormuud (including Golis and Telesom) and Dahabshiil companies (and Somtel). In the third section, we delve into the political economy of mobile money across the Somali territories, highlighting how an import-driven commercial class and a volatile national currency have created the demand for a US dollar-pegged mobile wallet. Finally, in the fourth section, we discuss its socio-legal dimensions, in particular the role of informal governance structures for regulation and taxation.

60

Somali remittances: The birth and infancy of mobile money

Somalia's mobile money infrastructure builds upon a remittance system shaped over more than 40 years by historical circumstances and trust relationships partly based on clanship. Remittances have been a lifeline for Somalis both in the Somali territories and in humanitarian spaces in East Africa (Hammond 2014; Horst 2006; Lindley 2007). According to a conservative estimate, more than 1.4 billion USD per year is sent each year to the Somali territories (Somalia, Puntland and Somaliland) (Majid et al. 2018). This is higher than the amount of Overseas Development Assistance (ODA) to Somalia, which was £1.9 billion in 2019.[4] Most remittances flow to the region through a set of money transfer practices known in Somalia as *xawaalad*, a variation on the Arabic *hawala*, based on the trading of credits and debts among agents (or *hawaladar*), a practice that emerged in the 8th century and has historically been popular across the Muslim world. However, no precise figures on the overall volume or value of *hawala* transactions are available, since many money transfer firms operate outside the scrutiny of national and international regulators.

Somali *hawala* firms, in the large business forms that we see today, first emerged during the 1970s. This was a period of increased transnational mobility—as a growing number of Somalis migrated to the Gulf States to work in the local oil industry—as well as institutional decay in Somalia, particularly during the 1980s, when state-managed financial institutions proved increasingly inefficient (Jamal 1988; Lewis 1994; Marchal et al. 2000). Former British Somaliland was the gateway of the remittance flows to Somalia, thanks to its geographical proximity to the Arabian Peninsula and a long history of trading routes linking the Horn of Africa to the Arab world (Pankhurst 1974). Besides meeting the growing demand for money transfer services from the Arabian Peninsula, traders saw the opportunity to collect hard currency—especially US dollars—to hedge against Somalia's very volatile national currency. Based on networks of agents, often hailing from the same clan, this system was considered more trustworthy and efficient than the state-run banking system managed by the Somali Commercial and Saving Bank, tarnished by its lack of efficiency and high fees.

In 1976, the Somali government formalised these connections to 'stop underground trading activities and to cover the importation of certain local needs with the remittances' (Qassim 2004: 186). It only allowed traders with an import licence into what became known as the *franco valuta* system. Through their agents in the Gulf, these businesspeople were able to collect remittances in US dollars from workers and either deliver the money directly to migrants' families or, more often, use it to purchase goods to be sold in Somalia. In this latter case, the corresponding amount in Somali shillings—or payment in kind—was handed to the recipients, according to a previously agreed exchange rate (Lewis 1994; Qassim 2004). Interestingly, the pursuit of hard currency is a feature which has been playing a central role in Somali traders' decision-making for a long time, as has already been observed by Burton (1943 [1856]: 289) and Lewis (1994: 129) and which, as we discuss below, would significantly contribute to the popularity of mobile money across the Somali territories decades later. Remittances in foreign currency continued outside the scrutiny of regulators, as only a small amount was funnelled through the official banking system and converted into local currency.

In 1982, the *franco valuta* system was phased out by the regime, but the *hawala* system survived and expanded. During the 1980s, the Somali central state buckled under the strain of corruption, economic crisis, political violence and Somaliland's secessionist struggle. Clan-based money transfer firms enabled local businesspeople to move financial assets out of the country and local households to receive much-needed cash from relatives abroad. It was during this period that Dahabshiil, the most popular Somali *hawala* company, consolidated its business model. Dahabshiil was first established in Burao, the capital city of the Togdheer region, in 1970 as an import company by Mohamed Saeed Duale, a remittance broker from the Isaaq clan, which is mostly concentrated in Somaliland (Samatar 2021).

When repression in northern Somalia escalated into civil war in the late 1980s, Dahabshiil moved to Ethiopia, funnelling the remittances of the Isaaq diaspora to displaced populations (Bradbury 2008) and supporting the Somali National Movement (SNM), the main guerrilla group opposing the Siad Barre regime. Crucially, Dahabshiil channelled contributions through clan elders, thus laying the foundation of its political network (Meester et al. 2019). After the central government collapsed in 1991, the crumbling national financial institutions followed suit, wiping out the savings—as well as faith in state banks—of hundreds of thousands of Somali citizens. Somalia, and Somaliland (the former Somalia Italiana and British Somaliland) parted ways. As a result, financial institutions that developed post-1991 in the now separate entities followed different trajectories, shaping local political economies in diverging ways.

In the aftermath of the proclamation of independence of the Republic of Somaliland, Dahabshiil reorganised its commercial structure to meet the growing demands of refugees who were fleeing Somalia en masse. It shifted its headquarters from Burao to Hargeisa and Dubai and opened branches in the countries where Somalis had found shelter and resettlement, both in Africa and in the West. Mohamed Saeed Duale and later his son Abdirashid contributed actively to the state-building process in Somaliland, building on the relationships established with local authorities during the war of independence, contributing to the construction of national infrastructures and becoming a privileged partner of the Somaliland state as well as an influential political player. By 2020, Dahabshiil claimed to 'invest 5% of its profits into community regeneration projects involving the development of schools, hospitals, agriculture and sanitation'. This is higher than the 2.5% *zakat* (a form of religious obligation or tax) that Islam requires its adherents donate to the poor. Dahabshiil employs 5,000 agents in 144 countries and works in partnership with large NGOs and the UN system (FAO, UNDP, UNICEF) to funnel funds to international development projects across the Somali territories.[5]

In Somaliland, Dahabshiil benefited from, and contributed to, the stability of political institutions, propping up the value of the state-minted Somaliland Shilling (SomSh) against the USD. In Somalia and Puntland, businesspeople who were leading or connected to private militias had Somali shillings (SoSH) printed abroad, shipped to Somali ports and injected into the local economy. As Peter Little (2021) calculated, 'With the costs of printing and shipping estimated to be around USD 0.022 to USD 0.028 per 1,000 SoSh note, profits could be earned as long as the SoSh did not devalue to more than around SoSh 22,000 to 28,000 per USD.' While reaping estimated profits of over 1.5 million USD, these businesspeople replaced the state in laying the financial infrastructure for the Somali economy and stabilising the value of the Somali currency against the US dollar in the late 1990s and early 2000s (Luther 2012). The flare-up of violence after the Ethiopian armed intervention in 2006, backed by the United States, and the emergence of the Islamist militia al-Shabaab in 2008 further disrupted the Somali economy. During this period, the circulation of privately minted SoSh was entwined with the flow of US dollars sent to Somali households through local *hawala* firms (Mubarak 1997).

Money transfer and communication industries have thus evolved in parallel. The historical integration of Somali remittance and telecommunication businesses is rooted in both business and socio-cultural factors. In the absence of a stock market, *hawala* companies have played a critical role in raising capital for the telecommunication industry. Most telecoms are public companies—in Somali, *shirkaad* (plur. *shirkooyin*)—started by entrepreneurs who typically set up an account into an *hawala*. Then, selected buyers—usually from the same clan of the founder and main shareholder, or local and religious authorities—would be allowed to acquire a stake in a *shirkaad*. This has enabled the consolidation of strategic partnerships, not only at the business but also at the political level.

However, while *shirkooyin* usually have a fluid and fragmented shareholding structure, one or only a few interrelated shareholders remain at the helm of the company. Therefore, although shareholding bases can include members from different clans, *shirkooyin* are perceived as having a well-defined clan identity: that of the main shareholder(s). It is particularly notable that only Somali telecommunications companies operate in the Somali territories. This contrasts significantly with the rest of the continent, where multinational companies vie for customers. The security and legal environment in Somali East Africa is seen as largely impenetrable for investors who lack the trust of deep-rooted clan and business networks.

Communicating and receiving remittances from relatives are both sides of the social obligations which enable the cultivation of ties within the diaspora as well as between the diaspora and the homeland (Lindley 2007). Long before state collapse, communications companies provided ancillary services to *hawala*, facilitating the coordination between remittance senders and recipients while *hawala* agents offered their customers cheap and fast technologies for exchanging information with relatives abroad and soliciting remittances. Even in Kenyan refugee camps, where displaced Somalis sought shelter from political violence, money transfer services were often located in the sites where people queued to use *taar*, a two-way radio system (Horst 2006) which was the only channel of communication with family members who were resettled or still in Somalia. The entanglement of remittances and communication infrastructures enabled the constant conversion of social capital into financial capital and vice versa, underpinning both social reproduction and the possibility of improving one's living conditions.

It was against this backdrop that the Barakaat Group of Companies (BGC), a business conglomerate that has had a long-lasting influence on the entire Somali telecom sector, emerged in the early 1990s. BGC was established by Ali Ahmed Nur Jim'ale, a businessman from the Hawyie Habr Gedr clan based in Mogadishu. It included the *hawala* company Barakaat Money Transfer, the telecoms Barakaat Telecommunications, Red Sea Telecommunications, Globe Tel Telecommunications, Barakaat Bank of Somalia and Somali Refreshment Company. At its peak in 2001, Barakaat Telecommunications was Somalia's leading company and largest employer. Ali Ahmed Nur Jim'ale remained its majority shareholder. The rest of its shares were divided among more than 600 shareholders. During the 1990s, this conglomerate thrived in a volatile context characterised by the absence of formal financial institutions in Somalia as well as limited access to financial channels for refugees in humanitarian crises. This was dramatically highlighted in the wake of the 9/11 terror attacks when Barakaat

Money Transfer, at the time the largest Somali *hawala*, was included in a list of 62 organisations and individuals suspected by the White House of having connections with Al-Qaeda, resulting in the freezing of all the company's assets (Roth et al. 2004). Thousands of account holders of BGC financial services no longer had access to their savings. Shortly after, Concert Communication, a joint venture between AT&T and British Telecom based in Atlanta, interrupted the international gateway of Al Barakaat's international phone service. The demise of Barakaat Money Transfer had disastrous repercussions on the livelihoods of many families (Cockayne and Shetret 2012), but it cleared the way for the expansion of Dahabshiil[6] and, as we explain in the next section, led to an overhaul of the entire Somali telecom sector.

The emergence of the Somali digital financial ecosystem

In 2002, following the demise of BGC, three new companies rose from its ashes, building upon the conglomerate's assets: Hormuud, established in Mogadishu and operating across south-central Somalia; Golis, based in Bosaso, the commercial capital of the autonomous federal member state of Puntland; and Telesom, established in Somaliland's capital, Hargeisa. We shall focus on Somalia's Hormuud and Somaliland's Telesom in particular.

Since its establishment, Hormuud was a Hawyie-dominated *shirkaad* providing landlines, mobile communication, internet access and, since 2008, mobile banking services. With 3.6 million subscribers in 2020, it was the leading mobile network operator (MNO) in south-central Somalia at the time of writing, with an estimated annual turnover of 40 million USD.[7] When the company was established, its chief executive was Ahmed Mohammed Yusuf, a businessman from Mogadishu who reportedly acquired the premises and the equipment of Al Barakaat. At the time, the company spokesperson denied any link to BGC, but it later emerged that the majority shareholder was once again Ali Ahmed Nur Jim'ale, who since 2001 had been residing in Dubai and Djibouti and who owned the *hawala* Tawakal. The main offices of the company were in Mogadishu and Dubai, where many Somali businesspeople had relocated since the late 1990s.

Drawing on the experience of Safaricom M-Pesa in Kenya, Hormuud launched E-Voucher in 2009. This was the first Somali mobile money service to transfer and store value, relying on a network of agents and allowing transactions of up to 2,000 USD. Shortly after, al-Shabaab, which controlled large swathes of territory, banned the service, ostensibly because it was 'un-Islamic'. The actual rationale for the ban was likely related to the militants' difficulties in monitoring the flows of mobile money. However, because of the unpopularity of the prohibition, they eased the ban shortly after, and the transaction limit was set at 200 USD. In 2011, the platform changed its name to EVC Plus and the maximum amount for a transaction was raised to 300 USD, offering both private and business accounts. On top of that, it enabled transactions to Golis' mobile money platform, Sahal, in Puntland and Telesom customers in Somaliland, thus eroding the internal market share of *hawala*, at least for the transfer of small amounts.

In Somaliland, Telesom soon emerged as the leading MNO, quickly outperforming the existing competitors Sitco (the first Somaliland mobile company), STC, Somtel and Sotelco. While Ali Ahmed Nur Jim'ale retained control of 49% of the conglomerate's shares, the remaining 51% was divided among over 1,400 shareholders. In 2009, Telesom launched the mobile money platform Zaad, which enabled money transfers free of charge. Two years later, it established Salaam Financial Services bank to facilitate the interoperability of mobile and banking services. Through their handsets, Zaad customers were able to move digital funds between their mobile wallets and bank accounts. They also received access to a broad range of services, including *shari'a*-compliant micro-loans, school fees, grants and utility bills payments.

The rapid diffusion of mobile money forced competitors in the telecommunication and money-transfer sectors to adapt. While many small local money-transfer operators (MTO) saw a dramatic drop in the turnover of business, large *hawala* companies had to expand or partner with the sector's leaders to survive. Already by 2008, Dahabshiil, the largest *hawala* operator, had become a major shareholder of Somtel, a telecoms company established in 1997 in Burao. In 2015, it launched the mobile money platform eDahab, which relied on Dahabshiil's agent network and allowed users to transfer or withdraw funds from their Dahabshiil account. Despite large investments in infrastructure in Somalia to provide faster data services and expand its network coverage to underserved areas— such as Middle Juba, Gedo and Bakool—Somtel eDahab struggled to catch up with Hormuud, Golis and Telesom's platforms. Besides enjoying first mover's advantage, these sister companies were successful in building a loyal customer base by creating network effect while meeting a widespread demand for hard currency. Moreover, they managed to embed mobile money into local socio-legal structures through a diffused ownership structure and the reliance on informal traditional governance institutions, as we discuss in the remainder of the article.

Other major *hawala* companies Taaj, Tawakal and Kaah partnered with Hormuud/Telesom/Golis through Salaam Somali Bank based in Mogadishu, Dara Salaam Bank (former Salaam Financial Services) based in Hargeisa, Salaam Bank based in Bosaso and Salaam African Bank headquartered in Djibouti. In 2015, Hormuud/Telesom/Golis started partnering with the online remittance company HomeSend, based in Belgium, to allow online money transfers through a company based in the UK, WorldRemit, and another based in Sweden, Transfer Galaxy. These websites enabled remittances to be sent directly to mobile wallets across Somalia.

The political economy of mobile money

The first set of factors that explains the popularity of mobile money relates to local economies' dependence on imports and a history of monetary instability during which, as previously mentioned, Somali traders have long juggled multiple currencies and financial institutions (Little 2021). In designing their mobile platforms, Hormuud, Telesom and Golis took into account the widespread need in the region for hard currency. The reliance on imports, particularly from Gulf states, has remained a constant throughout the worst years of the civil war and the subsequent decrease in political violence. At the time of writing, the prices of goods for sale across the Somali territories are still often displayed only in US dollars. Mobile money agents initially targeted merchants and traders in strategic economic sectors, such as livestock trade, to help them open mobile money accounts to manage their companies' payrolls. Firms that were already using US dollars to pay their employees' salaries were won over by the fact that mobile money allowed them to bypass the rush on hard currency that took place at the beginning of each month. Entrepreneurs could store US dollars in their accounts and transfer the due to each employee's mobile wallet. As recipients of digitally transferred salaries started drawing on their mobile wallets to purchase items in shops, person-to-business transactions gained momentum. Moreover, the diffusion of mobile money solved what many shop owners call the 'fraction problem', meaning the issue of paying dollar fractions, which was a particular challenge for shops selling imported items (Iazzolino 2015).

Boosting person-to-business payments proved a critical factor in the popularity of EVC Plus and Zaad, as it minimised the need to cash out before each payment. As salaries started being paid directly into employees' accounts, and customers saw the benefits of paying with mobile money, a mobile money ecosystem started taking shape and cash became increasingly redundant (at least in urban areas). In Somaliland, the system was initially met with widespread reluctance by several businesspeople, particularly those loyal to Dahabshiil and accustomed to engaging *hawala* services even for sending small amounts across the country. But as the number of active Zaad users continued to rise, a critical mass of digital wallet holders emerged, reaching 700,000 active users and an estimated 78% of the population by 2019 (Khan and Casswell 2019).

Hormuud's EVC Plus, Golis' Saad and Telesom's Zaad were designed from the onset to address a strong demand for US dollars which, as previously mentioned, has been widespread across the Somali territories since the 1970s. Even in Somaliland, where the state-minted national currency is actively supported by the Central Bank, initially Telesom enabled Zaad to transfer and store only a digital currency pegged to the US dollar. As explained by a Telesom executive, besides meeting the demand for hard currency, this decision was also based on the awareness that Somaliland shillings were not homogeneously accepted across the country, particularly in the Eastern Sool and Sanaag regions on the border with Puntland, where the sovereignty of the Hargeisa government is contested (Hoehne 2015a). Moreover, transferring amounts in Somaliland shillings could be burdensome due to the currency's chronically high inflation.[8]

Despite its popularity, mobile money has neither entirely replaced cash, as observers predicted it would in the early 2010s (Pénicaud and McGrath 2013), nor has it led to the complete replacement of national currencies with US dollars. In fact, since the primary sources of hard currency are remittance companies, international trade and livestock operators, international organisations and NGOs, USD-based mobile money platforms initially built their customer base among urban users. Only recently have they started penetrating rural areas, where the economy is based on subsistence farming and networks and agent coverage are more limited. Mobile money in Somalia has thus further complicated the interaction 'between two intersecting spheres of currency: (i) a dollarized circuit in cities and (ii) a SoSh sphere in rural and poor urban areas' (Little 2021). In rural Somaliland, for instance, Zaad acts as an interface with the urban economy and appears more popular among rural dwellers who mostly use Somaliland Shilling (Sd Sh) in their daily lives but have frequent exchanges with urban traders as in the case of livestock keepers. Up until the time of writing, mobile money platforms have reflected and amplified the gap between urban and rural dwellers and, in general, between those with access to USD (such as large businessmen, NGOs and international organisation workers) and farmers and pastoralists (but also civil servants in Somaliland) who mostly use the national currency. This gap exists not only because of discontinuous access to the dollarised economy but also because the SoSh is utilised 'as a trusted and familiar unit of calculation and payment' (Little 2021).

State and non-state regulation

As we have described above, the mobile money sector in the Somali territories has thrived in a regulatory environment shaped by clan-based dispute-resolution mechanisms (*xeer* law), *shari'a* law and efforts by companies to directly address grievances, often on a transnational scale (Stremlau and Osman 2015). However, since mid-2010, donors have focused on the need to improve the state's fiscal capacity (World Bank 2017) and, more broadly, strengthen oversight of local regulators in a strategically sensitive sector for the economic and political stability of the region (IOM 2016). As shall be argued in Chapter 8—also in the case of mobile money— political and financial institutions, both in Somalia and Somaliland, have increasingly viewed the adoption of a state-based regulatory framework, complying with global standards with regards to preventing money laundering and financing of terrorists, as a way to appease international donors (or, as in the specific case of Somaliland, to advance statehood claims). For instance, in March 2022, Hormuud received Somalia's first GSMA Mobile Money certification, by which the world telecom industry association recognised that the firm met 350 different criteria, including Know Your Customer (KYC) requirements. Hormuud successfully argued that, despite the lack of a national ID, its agents were able to comply with customer identification rules through the verification of records provided by local authorities (Collins 2022).

The Federal Government of Somalia signalled the will to push a regulatory process already under development in order to address issues of consumer security, fiduciary concerns and the conformity of current sector players to better meet international standards. As explained at the beginning of this chapter, this commitment was demonstrated in February 2021, when the Central Bank of Somalia granted Hormuud a mobile money licence to operate.[9] This policy built on the momentum of the National Communications Act that was finally passed in 2017, after years of debate.[10] The powerful technology companies have been ambivalent in their support for further regulation, at times encouraging government legislation and at other times undermining efforts to formalise the sector. Corruption allegations within the telecom sector abound, based on claims that public officials have financial interests within the companies (Rahman 2017), and it would seem that formalising the telecoms and mobile banking sector is actually not in the interests of the companies, which have struggled to reach agreements with the government over tax issues. The informal ways of doing business have become entrenched and—arguably for many stakeholders, including companies and customers—effective, suggesting that these companies have little incentive for government intervention.

While there has been significant movement towards formalising the mobile money, telecommunications and remittance sectors, the reality is that in much of south-central Somalia the federal government has little reach, leaving many disputes to be resolved outside of the state legal system. Indeed, many of these companies in these sectors argue that their operations are already being subjected to extensive taxes. The services and infrastructure one might normally expect to be provided by the state have typically been built by the companies themselves. Examples of this type of collateral taxation include building roads around remittance offices, paying *zakat* to charity and building and providing security for technical infrastructure. Furthermore, while the details are often opaque, it is clear that the companies pay substantial amounts to local authorities, such as al-Shabaab, to be allowed to operate within regions where there is no government control.

The lack of formal regulation means that agreements between entrepreneurs and local authorities, including politicians, are crucial for guaranteeing access to and protection of company assets within different areas across the Somali territories. Somali customary law (*xeer*) and *shari'a* law are central to resolving disputes and safeguarding telecommunication agents and infrastructures. Typical legal issues that repeatedly arise involve infrastructure, including damage—whether accidental, such as crashing into a telecoms tower, or intentional sabotage—and fraud or mistaken transfers with mobile money (Stremlau 2018).

Without centralised planning or investment, telecommunications infrastructure has developed in a relatively ad hoc way, largely financed by the companies themselves. This often leads to substantial duplication of infrastructure, with each business investing in its own lines, tunnels or whatever might be required for a particular service. Cables for telecommunications often use the same pipes or lines as water pipes and electric cables, without guidance or regulation as to how each should be laid. Unsurprisingly, this 'shared' infrastructure has led to conflicts between companies, particularly when there has been inadvertent damage to property.

There is precedent within *xeer* for addressing property issues—including private property, such as livestock—and this has been relevant to telecommunications infrastructure and continues to retain influence (Little 2003). In the context of telecoms infrastructure, companies are often careful to employ people based on clan affiliation to ensure that their property and interests will be protected and that there will be sufficient access to recourse in the case of disputes. Employing individuals from dominant local clans ensures that any property disputes will be resolved because clan relatives will be obligated to address them and find a settlement.

The resolution of disputes involving mobile money depends on the parties involved. Telecommunication companies are regularly confronted with at least three types of disputes: fraud or theft, including password thefts resulting in unauthorised access to accounts and unapproved transfers; mistaken transfers in which one party accidentally or unintentionally transfers funds to another account and seeks to recover those funds; and disagreements on payments between parties. The first place for recourse is the company itself. In the case of Telesom Zaad, for instance, the management has the unchallenged authority to freeze money in a customer's account, block accounts and return money to original senders without the recipient's consent. Zaad management also has access to a variety of information, including the account owner's identity, call history (provided by the parent company, Telesom) and contacts. This information enables Zaad management to investigate disputes and locate individuals who are accused of committing fraud or theft with more efficiency than the government's law enforcement agencies.

However, mobile money companies have no direct role in dispensing justice or enforcing legislation. Their role in resolving disputes is limited to investigation and the gathering of evidence, as well as intermediate steps such as blocking accounts and freezing money. Cases that the companies cannot resolve are then forwarded to the police or local elders, depending on the area and respective strength of state and customary governance institutions. In Somaliland cases are more likely to be referred to state organisations than they are in the South, where the government remains weaker. Disputes within the mobile money sector often involve individuals, and consequently their resolution depends on which clans are involved. The role played by clan elders is often highly politicised, and their intervention varies depending on the social status of the individuals in question; for example, they will engage more vigorously on behalf of those who are wealthier or more powerful (Schlee 2013). Elders are also less likely to be willing to mediate disputes involving individuals who have damaged the reputation of the clan or who are repeat offenders.

Finally, it is important to note the complexities of regulation involving taxation, particularly in south-central Somalia. Because of the Mogadishu government's limited reach, territorial sovereignty is fragmented and played out in different forms at the local level. Anecdotal evidence suggests that local strongmen often extort payments from entrepreneurs and companies, for which they are allowed to operate in a given area. For instance, on 16 April 2011, Ahlu Sunna Waljama (ASWJ), a moderate Sufi group, banned Hormuud from the territory under its control in Galguduud, Central Somalia, because the company failed to pay 2,000 USD per month. Access to the region was granted back after a few weeks. It is well known that the telecom providers, like all other actors operating in south-central Somalia, have to make deals or engage with al-Shabaab to some degree in order to operate within the areas held by the group. Without al-Shabaab's support, the companies' infrastructure would not be protected. As RBC radio, a Somali media outlet, reported, 'in Somalia, the militants frequently demand the private business companies to pay a large amount of money which they describe as taxes or sometimes as "money for jihad"' (Sabahi 2014). Extorting money from private business companies and aid agencies operating in Somalia is seen as the biggest source of investment for al-Shabaab's war with the government (Meester et al. 2019).[11] According to these reports, the amount of the 'taxes' vary according to different factors, including clan relations, business partnerships and external pressure. Research and policy reports also support the arguments that informal taxation by militant groups is a widespread practice across south-central Somalia (UNSC 2020).

Conclusion

This chapter highlighted the critical role of mobile money operators in the politics of circulation within Somali East Africa. Mobile money serves as the financial-technological infrastructure underpinning transnational commodity flows. In doing so, mobile money companies perform 'functional sovereignty' (Pasquale 2017), de facto taking over state functions both in self-regulating as well as addressing the disputes that arise on their platforms. The popularity of mobile money services across the Somali territories emerged within the region's unique trajectory of state decay, internationalised economic informality, civil war and leadership of private enterprises in reconstruction. Political economy factors, such as overreliance on imports and a largely dollarised economy as a means of coping with the chronic volatility of local currencies, contributed to the prominence of mobile money in the Somali territories. Idiosyncratic socio-legal regulations cast in sharp relief the influence wielded by non-state armed actors (mainly in south-central Somalia) and traditional authorities (particularly in Somaliland) in the governance of telecommunication and financial infrastructures across the region.

When analysing the Somali mobile money sector, it is important to move beyond clear-cut dichotomies such as formal versus informal or taxation versus extortion;[12] and, as this book argues, this also applies to the analysis of other state-formation dynamics. Because of fluid conflict and alliance arrangements, telecom entrepreneurs had to develop the ability to adapt to frequent redistributions of power among conflicting factions. Nevertheless, MNOs have leveraged the strategic value of the telecom sector—the fact that no party in a conflict could do without mobile telephones—to continue operating. This is the case for both non-state authorities and state-led bureaucratic administrations. At the same time, the unique capacity of local MNOs to navigate such a volatile political landscape has so far staved off the penetration of foreign competitors, and they have avoided pressures to liberalise the telecommunication and financial sectors. Mobile money has thus remained a Somali success story, not only facilitating the circulation of goods and values across polities with conflicting interests but also creating ties across political divides and a shared pride. In some ways, they have acted out a role akin to that of other media in fragmented contexts, such as when the printed press contributed to modern nationalism in the Americas and, later on, Europe (Anderson 1983).

The diffusion of mobile money has reshaped the Somali financial landscape, leading firms in strategic sectors such as telecommunications and money transfer not only to protect their market niche but also to occupy new ones, as the case of Dahabshiil and its foray into the mobile money business illustrates. While the Somali experience may not directly translate to other countries in sub-Saharan Africa or elsewhere, it does hold significant lessons for understanding state building—including law-making—and the roles of various actors therein, particularly in the private sector (see Musa and Horst 2019). Understanding how mobile money infrastructures emerged and developed in the Somali context produces unique insights into tensions between attempts to comply with international institutions in exchange for recognition—and business—and the reality that ignoring local forms of authority and power structures is not an option. The private provision of a digital currency, as the case of Somali telecoms illustrates, is not so much a return to a pre-fiat currency era—as state-minted currencies are a somewhat recent innovation—but a glimpse into alternative visions of statehood.

4

THE REVIVAL AND RE-EMBEDDING
OF SOMALI PORTS

Finn Stepputat, Warsame M. Ahmed, Omer Qualonbi,
Simon Wallisch and *Mahad Wasuge*

Introduction

Many of the trade-related hubs and flows examined in this book rely on Somali ports that channel and facilitate flows of commodities across and beyond the Somali territories of East Africa. Ports mediate between sea- and land-based modalities of transport and are obvious sites for extracting revenue, as they form chokepoints of commodity flows. As such, they are of key importance in the politics of circulation, which are played out at local, national and international scales and involve military, political and economic actors. The control of port infrastructure and port-related institutions is a highly desired prize, and the access they provide to revenue, political clout and influence on wider patterns of circulation (see Chapter 1) can make or break political entities.

77

With the right location and under the right conditions, ports forge a nexus between—in Tillian terms—war-making, tax-making and state making, as we discuss in Chapter 8. Cooper (2002) too, with his concept of 'gatekeeper states', points to the link between state making and the struggle for control over ports and other 'gates' that mediate flows between a state-territory and the world outside, where the authorities in control can harvest a 'sovereignty rent.' Obviously, the concept of sovereignty is blurred in the Somali case. The central state holds de jure sovereignty, but over time sub-states, warlords, militias, local authorities and al-Shabaab have exercised de facto sovereignty (Hansen and Stepputat 2005) over ports.

While post-colonial, pre-collapse Somalia could be characterised as a gatekeeper state, this chapter explores what has happened to the major Somali ports—Mogadishu, Kismayo, Bosaso and Berbera—since the collapse of the central Somali state, and how state making and gatekeeping have evolved around the ports. We look at the struggles for control over the ports, and at the process of revival that characterised them in the 2010s. We then focus on Berbera Port in Somaliland, exemplifying the most advanced case of port revival, and the specific practices of gate-making and gate-keeping (Hönke 2018) that we have observed since Dubai-based DP World took over port operations in 2017. We make the point that, while outsourcing and foreign investment has increased international control over Berbera Port, changing practices of gatekeeping also strengthen the hold over the port by the government of Somaliland vis-à-vis local authorities in Berbera as well as the Federal Government of Somalia (FGS). In Cooper's terms, the emerging Somaliland state now effectively 'keeps' the gate and harvests the 'sovereignty' rent that can strengthen its state-project as well as its claim for international recognition.

By international standards, Somali ports are small and poorly integrated into global logistical networks and technologies (Humphreys et al. 2019), and the political entities that control the ports lack the necessary human and financial resources to provide upgrades. Their international advisors therefore suggested that they attract foreign investors and operators (AfDB 2016) and pursue the private-public 'landlord model'. This model means that the public authority retains ownership but outsources port operation and development to private investors, which is the current model of choice for port development in Africa and beyond (Trujillo et al. 2013). The hope is to increase government revenues (and spur further development) by increasing throughput, ease access to global commercial networks and lower the transaction costs of trade. In the Somali case, investors are private but also connected to foreign national interests. Even though the ports have mostly served domestic import and export, geopolitical dynamics have been decisive for their development, including those of the Cold War when both the United States and Soviet Union invested in Somali ports. While being of little international interest after the Somali state collapse, Somali ports have attracted the interest of new geopolitical actors in the 2010s, including Turkey, the UAE, Saudi Arabia and Qatar, as well as Ethiopia.

The extensive Somali coast has hosted hubs for intercontinental trading for at least a thousand years (Gonzáles-Ruibal et al. 2017). Over the centuries, the fortunes of a string of seasonal and all-year ports—Zeila, Bullaxar, Berbera, Bosaso, Alula, Eyl, Hobyo, El Maan, Mogadishu, Merca, Barawe, Kismayo and many more—have shifted with changing trade patterns, occupiers, alliances and technologies.[1] Indian, Arab, Ottoman, Egyptian, Yemenite, European and Somali merchants have traded in the ports, while caravan and later truck routes have connected them to hinterlands in what are today Ethiopia and Kenya, as well as further afield.

Given the ports' crucial importance for Somali culture, identity, livelihoods and politics, Dua (2017) has offered a 'port-centric' understanding of Somali East Africa as an alternative to the traditional population- and territory-focused one. He suggests that ports develop through trajectories of regulatory and sometimes violent (re-)embedding within circuits of trade and redistribution. He also notes the different geographical scales that these processes encompass, from local beach ports like Bandarbeyla in Puntland, to ports with a regional scope in terms of hinterlands and the level of political power involved, such as the upgraded Berbera Port.

79

We follow Dua in analysing post-collapse port trajectories as processes of dis- and re-embedding the ports, while understanding the dis- and re-embedding as means of gate- and state making at different scales. Polanyi's (2001 [1944]) term of embeddedness signals that commodities, trade and circulation are embedded in social institutions, such as *abbaan*, a protection and broker institution that for centuries regulated trade and circulation across Somali areas (Abir 1965; Cassanelli 1982; Dua 2019). Further, it signals that the process of marketisation—or in this case port privatisation—leads to the dis-embedding from pre-existing institutions. However, Polanyi's term is analytically vague and does not reflect issues of scale, time, space and agency (Hann and Hart 2009), and dis-embedding can come with the re-embedding in different institutions, such as those of international logistics standards, rather than just a free market. Therefore, we use embeddedness as an observable empirical fact and a methodological principle that directs the attention towards the social processes that structure and shape the political economy of the ports.[2]

In the first part of the chapter, we look at the recent history of the four Somali ports, based on available documents and literature. In the second part, we give a more detailed analysis of Berbera Port in the current process of transition and upgrading. This is based on thirty interviews with officials and stakeholders in Berbera and Hargeisa, carried out between 2015 and 2019, both before and after DP World began operating the port in 2017. We focus on how new practices of gatekeeping and the associated dis- and re-embedding of the port in terms of access, labour recruitment, clearing procedures, logistics and landholding change relations between the port, the town of Berbera, the government of Somaliland and private investors. In the final section, we return to the overall question of how gatekeeping and state making are related in the case of Somali ports.

Somali ports in armed conflict

At the time when the civil war escalated in the late 1980s, Somalia had four larger but mainly domestic ports: Mogadishu, Berbera,

Kismayo and Bosaso. They were all under the Somalia Port Authority, which was established in 1962, shortly after independence.[3] Mogadishu Port, mentioned in the literature as early as in 1228 (Reese 1996), was built in its modern form by the Italians in the late 1920s. It is the largest Somali port and was the most significant one for imports and exports before the civil war. In the late 1980s, supported by the World Bank, the port was upgraded to better service container ships (World Bank 1995).

In the mid-nineteenth century, Berbera—in today's Somaliland—was 'the most important market on Africa's East Coast'(Abir 1965). The port is located across from Aden where from 1839 onwards the British garrison drove Berbera's development as an outlet for Somali livestock. British Somaliland was then established mostly to secure stable meat supplies for the garrison. After independence, the port was extended—first in 1968 by the Soviet Union and then in 1984 by the United States—for civil and military purposes. Berbera was independent Somalia's key livestock export port, accounting for an estimated 80% of the country's export earnings (Brons 2001).

Kismayo in the south of the country was founded in the late nineteenth century (Cassanelli 1982). Its port was modernised with US assistance in 1964 to facilitate the export of bananas and other agricultural products as well as the import of agricultural machinery for the Jubba regions, since the road connection to Mogadishu was not viable year-round.[4] When the military took power in 1969, Kismayo Port became a base for both Soviet and Somali navy forces. Later, in the 1980s, Kismayo Port underwent modernisation with international support.[5]

Finally, in 1984, the Somali government invested in developing Bosaso Port in Puntland, in north-east Somalia, mainly for the purpose of (re-)channelling livestock export. Unlike the other three ports, Bosaso is not a deep-sea port, and is mainly used by dhows and smaller ships. The decision to build this port may well have been influenced by the onset of military actions by the Somali National Movement (SMN) in 1983, thus forming part of what northerners saw as discriminatory economic policies aimed at undercutting trade through Berbera Port (Bradbury 2008), which was dominated by the Isaaq clan. With the construction of the Garowe-Bosaso road in the late 1980s, Bosaso came to provide an alternative outlet for livestock from the Haud, the important pastoral area spreading across the Somali-Ethiopian borders (Dua 2020).

Violence and shifting control of ports

Due to the violence in the north, Berbera Port closed in 1988, while the collapse of the central Somali state in 1991 led to the closure of the other main ports and the discontinuation of the World Bank's port modernisation project.[6] In August 1992, UNOSOM was deployed to protect relief operations,[7] but it was only when the US-led Unified Task Force (UNITAF) arrived in December the same year that Mogadishu and Kismayo Ports came under international control.

In Mogadishu, after UNOSOM II took over from UNITAF in May 1993, the World Food Programme managed the port for some time, setting tariffs, arranging for towage and so on (World Bank 1995). Despite attempts to set up a revenue-sharing arrangement around the port when UNOSOM II left in March 1995, the port closed definitively in October, as the reigning warlords could not agree over the exports through the port (Marchal 2002).[8] Instead, the dilapidated beach port of Merca to the south of the city was reactivated for importing and exporting bananas to businessmen in southern Mogadishu (under General Mohamed Farah Aideed); those in northern Mogadishu (under Ali Mahdi) used the beach port of El Maan. In both places, there were conflicts between former employees of Mogadishu Port and local labour cooperatives. After a storm in 1997 destroyed the road from Merca towards Mogadishu, a cross-clan group of businessmen set up the Benadir Maritime Port Operations to run and secure El Maan, where up to 5,000 people were employed (ibid.).[9]

To the south, Kismayu Port was looted when UNOSOM left it in late 1994. Constant infighting between different clan-militias kept the port out of operation until 1999, when Haber Gidir and Marehaan militias managed to open the port for charcoal export

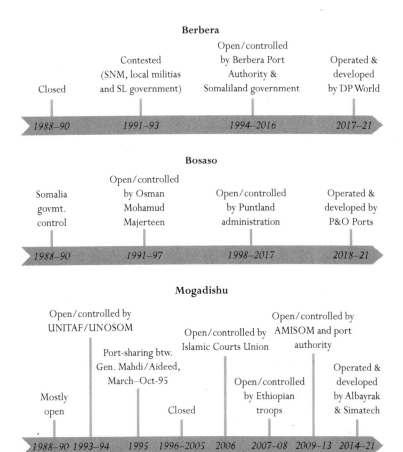

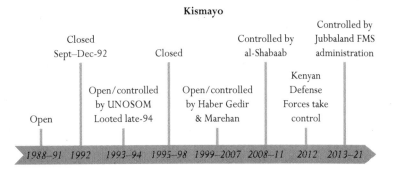

Figure 4.1: Timeline of Somali ports, 1988–2018

and import of food, vehicles and construction materials (ibid.); for security reasons, however, humanitarian aid for southern Somalia was rerouted through El Maan and Merca.[10] In 2008, al-Shabaab seized Kismayo Port, which became an important asset for the organisation due to its taxation of charcoal exports, various imports and the business community.

Reopening the ports

The ports in the north had a different trajectory, closely related to the relative stabilisation of Somaliland and Puntland. In January 1991, SNM took Berbera, and in February—after the fall of the Somali government—Berbera hosted the first peace negotiations in Somaliland. Here, various northern militias agreed that the port was a national asset, which should not be captured by any one clan (Bradbury 2008). In May 1991, the 'Grand Conference of the Northern Peoples' in Burao declared the independence of the Republic of Somaliland. However, even though several ships made it into the port, humanitarian aid was looted and numerous competing checkpoints along Berbera corridor frustrated attempts to reactivate the livestock export. Following this, the 'sheep wars' between different Isaaq sub-clans closed the port again for a year (ibid.).

Unlike Somaliland's first president, who never managed to control the port, the second one—President Egal, who himself hailed from Berbera—was able to demobilise clan militias in Berbera in exchange for jobs at the port and decisive influence in the Berbera Port Authority (BPA), which he established in 1993 (Musa and Horst 2019). Furthermore, with port revenue and economic support from returning Isaaq businesspeople, he managed to demobilise other clan militias, develop a national army, free up circulation along the corridor and set up a minimal administration (Balthasar 2013). Nevertheless, the majority clan in Berbera maintained control over a good part of the revenue through the port manager, who headed Berbera Port Authority almost uninterrupted from 1993 to 2016 (Steppuppat and Hagmann 2019).

Something similar took place in Puntland, where Majeerteen and other Harti traders fled the violence in Mogadishu to seek safe havens and outlets in their clan homelands, including Bosaso (Hoehne 2016). From 1991, the Osman Mohamud Majeerteen sub-clan controlled the port, which benefited both from Berbera's problems in 1991–92 and from being the only outlet for the Majeerteen-based Somali Salvation Democratic Front (Mukhtar 2003). From 1995, UNCTAD assisted rehabilitation and training of a port administration in Bosaso (UNCTAD 2000: 16). When Puntland was formed in 1998 after consultation among Harti clans, port management fell under the authority of the Puntland administration, with revenue from the port serving as the administration's lifeline. Due to overseas connections and the road to Galkayo and Mogadishu—which made it possible for Bosaso Port to compete with Mogadishu Port—Bosaso grew twenty-fold from a sleepy port town of 15,000–25,000 inhabitants in 1991 to almost half a million inhabitants in 2009 (World Bank 2020: 65).

In Mogadishu, businesspeople also had a decisive role in reopening the port. They were a driving force behind the Unity of Islamic Courts (UIC) that defeated the competing warlords and took control of Mogadishu in June 2006 (Ahmed 2014). In August 2006, the port reopened under a re-established port authority, while a WFP food-for-work programme helped clean up the facilities.[11] But the UIC rule was short-lived. In late 2006, Ethiopian troops invaded Somalia, and in 2007 they took control of the entirety of Mogadishu, including the port. The African Union Mission in Somalia (AMISOM) has been securing Mogadishu Port since 2009, while the Port Authority has been appointed by the federal government.

In 2012, the Kenyan Defence Forces (KDF) invaded southern Somalia as part of the AMISOM and pushed al-Shabaab out of Kismayo. Since then, the KDF has managed the security of Kismayo Port, allegedly also profiting from the (illicit) import of sugar to Kenya (Rasmussen 2017). When Jubbaland Federal Member State was established in 2013, control of the port fell under the Jubbaland administration, which is responsible for the collection and management of revenue from the port. According to the UN Somalia and Eritrea Monitoring Group, this revenue includes taxes from illicit charcoal export to countries like Oman, Iran and the UAE (UNSC 2018).

A revival of Somali ports?

In the 2010s, the major Somali ports were subject to various projects of revival and upgrading. Armed conflict and insecurity on land as well as piracy at sea limited the use of these ports for commercial purposes in the first half of the decade, and while major shipping companies like MSC, Maersk and CMA-CGM did call at Somali ports,[12] the limited container facilities, inefficient management, high insurance rates and a degraded road network in the hinterlands resulted in an estimated berth occupancy rate of only 20%.[13] Nevertheless, ports constituted the primary sources of revenue for states as well as non-state actors like al-Shabaab; in 2016, estimated revenues from Berbera Port were 150 million USD, Mogadishu Port 80 million USD, Bosaso Port 23 million USD and Kismayo Port 4.5 million USD (Majid et al. 2021: 26). More importantly, the proximity of landlocked and logistically challenged Ethiopia with over 100 million inhabitants provides prospects for the future of Somali ports. It is no coincidence that Ethiopian prime minister, Abiy Ahmed, visited Mogadishu shortly after his appointment in 2018, with Somali ports being one of the core items he discussed with Somalia's president. As their joint communiqué emphasised, they 'agreed on the joint investment in four key seaports between the two countries, and the construction of the main road networks and arteries that would link Somalia to mainland Ethiopia'.[14]

Due to limited financial and human resources, the upgrading of Somali ports depends on foreign investments. As recommended by the international development banks, such investments have been ensured by the ports of Mogadishu, Bosaso and Berbera outsourcing port management to private companies; only Kismayo Port has yet to undergo such a transition. After decades of neglect, 80% of the port facilities were out of use when Jubbaland took over the administration in 2013 (AfDB 2016), and a large part of Kismayo's hinterlands are controlled by al-Shabaab. Furthermore, a WFP project to renovate the port failed because three shipwrecks that limit the access to the port proved harder to remove than expected (WFP 2018).

In 2013, Somalia's federal government agreed on a 20-year contract with the Turkish company Albayrak for the management and development of Mogadishu Port. The Dubai-based shipping company Simatech was then awarded a contract to develop and manage a container terminal in the port. Turkey was interested in expanding its political influence beyond the Middle East and had provided humanitarian assistance to Somalia since the 2011 famine, but it was also motivated by financial interests (Wasuge 2016). When Albayrak took over port operations in September 2014, the agreed port revenue sharing was 55% for Somalia and 45% for Albayrak.[15] Since then, the revenue has increased considerably, but Somalia's Financial Governance Committee has criticised the government for not following a transparent tender process, as well as for failing to negotiate a fair agreement on revenue sharing and the required level of investment.[16]

Mogadishu Port is the largest domestic revenue source for the Federal Government of Somalia, but it is the only port that contributes to the federal state's revenue. Other ports are under the control of Federal Member State administrations or Somaliland, who in practice set, charge and keep custom duties. Somalia has adopted a federal system of governance, but fiscal relations and Mogadishu's status in a federal Somalia have not yet been settled. In Bosaso and Kismayo Ports, charges have reportedly been lowered to attract business, to the detriment of Mogadishu Port and businesspeople who allegedly pay higher custom duties (van den Boogaard and Isak forthcoming). In Mogadishu there is furthermore discontent over the FGS' management of port and airport revenue, as only 15% of the port revenue goes to the city's administration, Benadir Regional Administration (ibid.). An agreement of fiscal federalism and the status of Mogadishu will have a significant impact on the current arrangement.

In the north, the ports of Berbera and Bosaso have followed a similar path of upgrading as the governments of Somaliland in 2016 and Puntland in 2017 gave 30-year port management concessions to the two (related) Dubai-based companies, P&O Ports (Bosaso) and DP World (Berbera).[17] The latter started operating Berbera Port in 2017, having promised to invest 442 million USD in upgrading the port in terms of berths, cranes, yards and operating systems, as well as constructing a Free Trade Zone. Unsurprisingly, the FGS disapproved of the port deal.

Since 2020, the Somaliland government has received 5 million USD plus 10% of the handling fees. For the purpose, a joint venture was formed, of which DP World owns 51%, Somaliland 30% and Ethiopia, as the greatest customer, 19%. Ethiopia was included in the venture following a memorandum of understanding (MoU) from 2016, in which Somaliland and Ethiopia agreed on signing a transit agreement and re-routing up to 30% of Ethiopia's imports through Berbera to relieve its dependency on Djibouti. In practice, Ethiopia has not taken any action in this regard, and as of 2022 the UK government's British International Investment has acquired a 6% share, investing 700 million USD.[18]

The DP World deal was landed as part of a larger agreement of cooperation between Somaliland and UAE, which, somewhat controversially, gave the latter access to extend and use Berbera Airport for military purposes and build a naval base close to Berbera. The background was partly commercial, as DP World had been kicked out of Djibouti's Doraleh Port in 2016, and partly military due to the UAE's engagement in the civil war in Yemen at the time. The agreement also included investment by the Abu Dhabi Fund in upgrading of the road from Berbera to Ethiopia, also supported by the EU, Germany and the UK.

The port of Bosaso, apart from being a seasonally busy outlet for livestock to the Middle East, is called by small ships—in particular dhows—with flexible itineraries and standards that provide cheap alternatives of trade in the 'underbelly of a variety of political and commercial systems' (Dua 2017: 18). The 2017 agreement between the Puntland president and P&O Ports was, like the DP World concession in Berbera, never published, but according to the company they will invest 336 million USD in a multi-purpose facility including a Terminal Operating System, mobile harbour cranes and container handling equipment.[19] The FGS did not consent to this agreement either, but the Puntland parliament approved the deal.[20] However, on 4 February 2019, a gunman killed the CEO of P&O Ports in Bosaso in the fish market while going to the port. Al-Shabaab claimed responsibility.[21] In 2022 Puntland renegotiated the contract, now with DP World as the port operator.[22]

The question is how the current revival of Somali ports will impact the relations in which the ports were embedded before their upgrading and partial privatisation. To gain an idea, we take a more detailed look at the ongoing changes in and around the port of Berbera, partly because the port and corridor project is the most comprehensive one in Somali territories, and partly because of accessibility.

'The port is closed now': The dis- and re-embedding of Berbera Port

Our interviews in Berbera town and port suggest that the arrival of DP World in early 2017 was met with a mixture of high expectations and deep fears of how the changing arrangements around the port would affect Berbera. During the first year, DP World introduced changes in employment, salaries and organisation of those working in the port; gave extensive training in upgraded security and safety procedures; discontinued previous paternalistic practices by the (head of the) port authority whereby different groups in the town received support for various purposes; and changed procedures for clearing goods from the port. Security, which was not bad before, was tightened and linked to online systems with ID cards and fingerprints, so that 'everybody is known now' and government and port personnel can be distinguished by the colour of their uniforms.[23] The technical and infrastructural changes however—the 400 metre extension of the berth, the extended area for container storage and handling, the new cranes and the construction of Berbera Free Trade Zone—were much slower in coming, which caused much frustration and impatience in Berbera.

As part of the rearrangement of the port regime, the government of Somaliland started transforming Berbera Port Authority, turning it into 'Somaliland Port Authority' where the influence of the local majority clan, Issa Muse, was reduced to give advantage to the central government, and with representation of other

Somaliland regions (Awdal and Sool) on the board. Alongside these changes, the double taxation of imports, whereby both the customs authority and the port authority claimed separate import taxes, was discontinued. This practice, together with high insurance costs and the slow handling of cargo, had contributed to the excessive costs of importing goods through Berbera.[24]

Almost two years after DP World's takeover of port operations, an elder from Berbera's majority clan and former SNM fighter summarised the effects it had for Berbera's community in a way that illustrates the process of dis-embedding. Now, he says, except for the salaried workers, people from Berbera 'have nothing to do with the port .... The port is closed now':

> Let me tell you, Berbera port was a government-run entity in the past. Even if I don't work, I can get something. For example, as *Aqil* you could get fuel from there ['fuel' here means money]. Then, if there was a conflict, we were told to settle it. But now there is nothing ... Before, the people of this city were getting lots of benefits from the port. For example, if you have a job at the port as a porter, you can get a hand from someone in the city when there is extra work. People used to profit from one another. All that trading and profit between people have just become a salary, the rest goes to DP World.[25]

The *Aqil* is a 'father of peace', as he describes it, with a role in conflict mediation. He describes well the economy of favours that existed in the port/town assemblage, which was now being disrupted by the new port regime. Below we analyse how the new practices around the port have dis- and re-embedded the port as changes have unfolded in (at least) five different but overlapping domains: labour; communal benefits; clearing procedures; land; and the logistics sector.

Port labour

When DP World took over operations, it also took over most of the staff of 800, raising their wages considerably.[26] The company then began to discipline and train the workforce, in particular in new safety rules and procedures. DP World fined employees who came late to work, and after a trial period of four months they eliminated ghost-workers, i.e., people who are included on the payroll but never show up to work. As an employee describes it himself, instead of choosing either not to go to work, to sleep at work or to go downtown during work hours, as they did before when they received very low and unstable government salaries, employees are now 'motivated' and 'working hard', resulting in productivity going up.[27] The 'documentations department', for example, used to employ 50 people; now there are only 15, with the rest being relocated to other tasks.[28] The increased presence and productivity have not gone unnoticed by port customers, who now find the employees actually working in their offices: 'The irony is that it's the same people' as before, one businessman remarked.[29]

Recruitment procedures have also changed. Before, young men would usually apply for jobs in the port through their clan elders; as elsewhere in government offices, the Berbera Port Authority (BPA) would hire employees based on a set distribution between the different sub-clans in Berbera (Bradbury 2008). After the changes, as several interviewees confirmed, recruitment is based more on what you can do than on who you are: 'The first question they'll ask is "what are you good at?" Before people used to get jobs for all other reasons.'[30] As an elder noted, 'It's the contract and the law that is between the port workers and DP World.'[31]

Two groups of workers, the stevedores and the porters, were not given DP World contracts right away. They used to be organised in 'unions' on which the BPA had relied. Characterised in a World Bank report as 'private' entities (Humphrey et al. 2019), the unions saw themselves as self-organising business-like entities rather than (just) a union of workers. They were organised in work crews or 'sections' and were hired and paid directly by the ships or the clearing companies. Section secretaries kept records of the goods unloaded, and members pooled together to help if someone in the section was injured. The unions drew on a pool of temporary workers who they called in during peak times, which expanded the included workforce far beyond the permanent employees and the unions. While DP World discontinued this practice and left out occasional workers,[32] in 2018 the company finally offered contracts, with their 'scales and grades',[33] to stevedores and porters. As a clan elder explained, 'DP World is taking over all activities; the last they did was [to include] the Stevedores and I hear they are taking the porters too.'[34]

The chairman of the stevedores' union told us, 'Previously we were independent and managed our own work, now they [DP World] have taken over.'[35] Thus, the workers just receive their salary, while DP World manages the unions' operations. The unions see themselves as having served the government as a group since 1995, when they agreed to 'join the [port] administration' in exchange for promises of holiday, gratuity and indemnity for injuries. By their own account, the stevedores built 'Wajale', the container storage and clearing space from where goods go to Togwajale at the Ethiopian border.[36] The unions therefore see the government as being indebted to them, and they expected the government to protect them when negotiating their contracts with DP World. However, their hopes were in vain: after President Bihi came to power in 2018, the government informed the unions that '"if you don't join DP World, we will bring competitors with equipment and everything and you will be thrown out." Our effort was taken away by the government and we have saved nothing'.[37]

As the chairman expressed it, the workers were not happy to become salaried employees instead of working through the unions; and one detects a certain disdain for wage labour, similar to so many other places around the world that have experienced the spread of capitalism and proletarianisation:[38]

> I am going to become a salaried person … The poorest person in the world is the salaried person. You will be told that you are 'just a worker'. But Allah said [speaking in Arabic]: 'I have raised some of them above others in degrees [of rank] that they may make use of one another for service.'[39] You are no longer independent, you will do what you are told to do. That is what I expect.[40]

Other employees however, described to us how their lives had improved once they were receiving salaries that they and their families could live from. This has created expectations about the future, and, as several leaders asserted in 2019, employees were now building on their houses and considering buying cars, while sons supported their elders who used to receive handouts from the port manager.

Communal benefits and land

Before DP World's takeover, the (head of the) port authority literally handed out funds to people and institutions in Berbera that were in distress or otherwise needed support. Through such benefits, BPA provided support towards children's school fees, war veterans and old community leaders, disabled individuals, mosques, football clubs and schools. But after DP World's arrival and with the new Somaliland Port Authority in place, towns-people cannot make tacit claims for a share of 'the little revenue from the port that circulated among people in the community'.[41] DP World has of course launched various corporate social respon-sibility projects, such as the distribution of humanitarian aid dur-ing droughts, provision of support for the hospital, drilling of new wells in Berbera, construction of a training facility for local logis-tical firm employees and so on. 'They're not stingy,' as one of the counsellors said, but their contributions have been less visible than what people in Berbera had expected from the deal with the Emirates.[42] But, no doubt, the municipality will seek benefits from its new patron, as was the case in late 2019 when the mayor sought financing from DP World for the tarmacking of the last half-kilometre of the street leading to the port.[43]

The process surrounding the arrival of DP World to Berbera has contributed to 'freeing' (dis-embedding) municipal land and land claimed through the lineage system for sale and productive occupa-tion, thus feeding into an accelerating land market. Since he entered the municipal office, the mayor explains, he has been giv-ing away municipal land to persons or organisations that had pro-ductive investment plans, including DP World and 'non-residents', that is, investors from other clans.[44] This has helped increase the tax basis of the municipality. But in the period when 'the winds of DP World were blowing'[45]—that is, from the signing of the accord in 2016 until early 2018, when disappointment with the lack of construction and visible progress set in—land has been sold for more speculative purposes. In this period, prices went up four times. As a broker stated, 'We sold Berbera to the diaspora, local people, Djiboutians, Arabs and everyone.'[46]

Clearing procedures

Another way in which Berbera Port was socially embedded was through a system of redistribution involving informal payments to clear goods from the port. This used to complicate the process of clearing, which was a business that employed many operators and government employees in the town. Before, as described by the clearance agent of an import company,[47] the customers had to pay multiple fees and taxes both in the port and in the customs. In the port you would have to go through seven or eight offices that, rather than 'being legal', were there to 'squeeze people and as a show of power', which made it a 'backbreaking job' to get things out of the port. Now 'the system is legal', and you only pay a pre-set handling fee for the container plus the customs; payments go through the bank (Dahabshiil or Darasalam) rather than through the BPA and government offices.[48] Customers save a lot of time this way. Before it could take three to four days to wait, to find the persons in charge, negotiate and so on. In 2019, it took 30 minutes and two office visits, several customers confirmed. As a port employee asserted, 'now life is easy for the customer', and in the future 'the customer will not have to meet any official; everything will be done online'.[49]

In the case of the clearing of goods, the dis-embedding from the previous system of *bacadjoog*[50]—the informal payments—was accompanied by a process of re-embedding, partly through online procedures going through registered (bank) institutions and partly through the licensing of clearance agents. After DP World's arrival, only licensed agents could operate in the port, so they had to register with the state and accept being taxed by both local and central government. The agents have also organised in a Union of Clearance Companies in Berbera, with some 120 members as of 2022, to facilitate negotiations and exchanges between the agents and the port operator.

THE REVIVAL AND RE-EMBEDDING OF SOMALI PORTS

Logistics between the handshake and the contract

At the time of writing, the logistics sector has not yet been deeply affected by the privatisation and upgrading of port operations, but some changes have predated the arrival of DP World. Transport between Berbera, Hargeisa, Burao, Puntland and south-central Somalia is dominated by individually owned small and medium-sized trucks that are registered, licensed and taxed in Somaliland, while larger Ethiopian trucks dominate transport to Ethiopia.[51] Individual truck-owners are usually organised in unions. They operate as cooperatives that distribute tasks among themselves. Large importers have their own in-house truck services, which is seen as highly unethical by the local truckers' union.[52] As well as this, since 2012–13 several increasingly professional logistics companies have emerged in Berbera. The main driver of this development is the presence in Berbera of the regional office of the World Food Programme (WFP) and the network of humanitarian NGOs working with them, but logistics companies have also emerged in anticipation of the announced port development (Wallisch 2018).

Like most of the business sector in Somaliland, truck owners and logistics companies operate on informal credits and pooling of resources by family and friends, not least through remittances from the diaspora. Until recently, insurance companies did not exist in Somaliland, where lineage-based mechanisms—'the language of clan', as one businessman put it[53]—serve the purpose of insurance. From 2019, the government started legislating, regulating and nurturing commercial insurance, as traffic accidents in particular represent serious problems for the existing practice. Previously, truck owners' unions used to pool together assistance for repairs and for bringing back vehicles when accidents occurred. However, while clan- and union-based insurance provides some basic protection for truck owners and drivers, there are limits to the system, both geographically and in terms of compensation for damaged goods.[54] For example, contracting NGOs must consider that some traders and transporters cannot deliver humanitarian aid in some clan territories, since receiving clans insist on having their own people bring the aid.[55]

For logistics companies and large importers, the clan-based system of insurance is of less importance, but they still rely on individual truck owners and drivers for whom it is fundamental. Deals with truck owners are closed with a handshake, whereas the logistics companies themselves sign contracts when taking orders from international companies, agencies and NGOs.[56] For these, it is difficult and administratively burdensome to operate directly with the truck owners who are embedded in local practical norms and relations, even when interactions are mediated by their union. Hence, the international companies and organisations— that are embedded in the norms and standards of global logistics and business—increasingly turn to the more expensive logistics companies for the mediation of transport assignments with the truckers. Logistics companies then function as brokers, allowing for operational relations across differently embedded businesses. As discussed in the introduction to this volume, this broker function is an example of one of the mechanisms by which 'supply chain capitalism' currently incorporates difference and heterogeneity (Tsing 2015).

In this way, the upgrading of ports has not produced a sudden dis- and re-embedding of the logistics sector. Rather, in the 2010s a slow process took place in which local logistics companies and clearing-and-forwarding agents served as translators between global logistical networks and local ones. As one of the logistics firms in Berbera explained in 2017, 'In the last five years we have seen an improvement in people's understanding of how the outside world is working and connecting—so businesses professionalize.'[57] In fact, in the new Union of Clearance Companies in Berbera, this kind of professionalisation is seen as necessary to protect Berbera and Somaliland business from competition from foreign companies that is expected to arrive in the future.[58]

Gatekeeping and state making on the Somali coast

In this final section, we look across the recent trajectories of the four ports and take the insights from Berbera on board to discuss the ports' relations to state making.

The Somali case indeed illustrates how ports and airports have been at the centre of political-military struggles, but they have also, like Berbera, been 'at the heart of peace'.[59] In at least three of the four ports described here, businesspeople have been instrumental in local and regional peace processes, as they have pushed for and supported arrangements that would allow the ports to reopen for business.[60]

The collapse of Somalia's central state interrupted the upgrading in the 1980s that sought to integrate the ports better into the progressively containerised global logistics networks. The revival of Somali ports in the 2010s renewed these efforts, but it was based on a neoliberal development model with outsourcing at its heart. In the 1980s, the World Bank and donors were important drivers of modernisation. These actors are still involved, but rather than giving loans to the state(s), they provide strategic and technical assistance, with the aim of outsourcing port operations and setting the ports up for competition over domestic markets and (mainly) Ethiopian transit trade. Such competition is already taking place between the ports in Kismayo, Mogadishu and to an extent Bosaso, where Jubbaland and Puntland FMSs are lowering taxes to attract trade (in sugar and other goods), causing a great deal of discontent among Mogadishu-based businesspeople (Raballand and Knebelmann 2021).

In the future, Somali ports will indeed compete with other gateways for goods going to Ethiopia and Kenya, such as Lamu Port in Kenya, Djibouti's ports, possibly also the Port of Sudan and, depending on political developments, the Eritrean ports of Assab and Massawa. In the Somali territories, development actors, investors and authorities increasingly regard the location between the sea and Ethiopia as the most valuable Somali resource. In October 2022, a deep-sea port in Gara'ad was inaugurated in Puntland close to the border with Galmudug, partly financed by private investors in Galkayo (Abdirahman 2021),[61] but other port and corridor projects abound. Within the same 350 kilometre coastline where Gara'ad is located, it is rumoured that the Chinese have been developing a port project in Eyl in Puntland,[62] while contracts have supposedly been signed—first by Qatar's port authority and more recently by a British-Turkish-Somali consortium—for the construction of a port in Hobyo in Galmudug FMS.[63] According to DP World, however, there will be trade enough for twelve ports the size of Djibouti's Doraleh terminal in the Horn of Africa, depending, of course, on political and military developments in the area.[64]

Except for Kismayo, and the new port in Gara'ad, the larger Somali ports are being upgraded by foreign companies that bring capital, know-how and logistical networks to the ports, and which share rents with authorities that can claim more or less effective sovereignty over the ports (the governments of Somaliland in Berbera, Puntland in Bosaso and Gara'ad, Galmudug in Hobyo and FGS in Mogadishu). However, negotiations over concessions have been accused of being untransparent and shrouded in secrecy, as has been the case in Mogadishu and Berbera.

The current modality of port upgrading via outsourcing gives the investor a lot of control over the port, while wider logistical networks and international standards and technologies delimit and reconfigure access to port facilities and revenues. Nevertheless, an interesting point is that this modality has also increased control over the port by the authorities that give the concession. In this way the development confirms Béatrice Hibou's (2004: 18–28) point that privatisation can be understood in terms of the Weberian notion of 'delegation' or 'discharge', which, she claims, never meant a loss of power but rather an increase of the points where the state can intervene. Furthermore, the 'privatisation of the state' is 'in part the fruit of globalisation, but it is just as much the product of local history' (ibid.: 25).

As we saw in Berbera's case, the new practices of gatekeeping—by concessions and public-private partnerships—opened up the introduction of state-of-the-art port management practices that have the effect of dis-embedding the port from its local moorings and re-embedding it in relations that are at once more centralised and more international. New online procedures for payment, new clearing and recruitment procedures, security and safety standards and a new terminal operation system have increased productivity and rents while reducing handling time. More importantly however, the new practices, in combination with the 'nationalisation' of port authority, have led to a reduction of local brokerage and the frictions resulting from corruption, multiple taxation and slow handling.

In sum, the outsourcing and investments tend to reorient parochial, port-centred political economies away from locally dominant clans around the port and towards more centralised authorities that can cash in on a sovereignty rent, even without enjoying de jure sovereignty. Only in the case of Mogadishu Port, it was the holder of international recognition who gave the concession. But whereas the changing practices of gatekeeping have increased the central Somaliland authority over Berbera Port, laws for regulating ports, maritime affairs and public-private partnerships have been identified as key shortcomings in the development of the port (Humphreys et al. 2019). State institutions are not strong, and they are still permeated by practices of negotiation and rule-bending, as is shown by the ability of large telecom companies to avoid taxation. This leaves a great deal of ambiguity and room for negotiation at and between various levels and agents of governance. As an official in the Ministry of Commerce once suggested to us, 'the problem is that we have a collaborative and not a regulating government'.[65]

Turning to the perspective of the townspeople in Berbera, the local majority clan lineage clearly stands to lose out on access, influence, privileges and claims to revenue. Our interlocutors talked about how proletarianisation, merit-based recruitment, work discipline, written contracts, the law, professionalisation and other tropes of modernisation were gaining influence at the cost of clan-centred norms, practices, authorities and negotiations. Yet, while clan elders in Berbera counted their losses, there also seemed to be an acceptance of a government that is capable of arm-twisting and bullying, but also of bringing investors and hopes for development to Somaliland:

> When you see the role of government is getting stronger and stronger, the role of tribes is diminishing. Now, workers at the port earn five times more than before, so you see this is development and the result of strong government … We were subjugated [in the process]: All other regions in the country told us that we

[Issa Muse] are anti-development. Then we abandoned our resolve. Now when they ask us what happened, we tell them, the development you wanted so much is going on. Now we don't see it as a problem anymore.[66]

As the first phase of the port upgrading was finalised in early 2022, the visible signs of change have given reason for optimism in Berbera as 'a place that waters the Horn of Africa', and which could potentially come to resemble the cities of the Emirates,[67] a popular image in Somaliland and beyond. But, as is the case for other Somali ports and port projects, the revival also brings risk of conflict and disappointed hopes. Several ports on the Somali coast—such as Lamu Port in Kenya, the Port of Sudan, Djibouti's ports, and maybe even the ports of Eritrea—will be competing for the traffic between Ethiopia and the sea. Furthermore, exceptional economic growth in Ethiopia is slowing down due to the country's continued political turmoil, and foreign investors are motivated by a mixture of economic and (geo-)political interests that threaten to disturb the already fragile balances of power and contestations over sovereignty and rents in Somali territories.

5

GOVERNING MARKETPLACES

SELF-REGULATION, STATENESS AND MATERIALITIES

Fana Gebresenbet, Kirstine Strøh Varming
and *Philemon Ong'ao Ng'asike*

Introduction

Marketplaces are key sites of circulation, where commodities change hands between producers, smaller and larger traders, wholesalers, retailers and consumers. While these transactions are instrumental in conveying commodities along supply chains, the marketplace is also the site where the value of commodities accumulates and becomes visible, where profits materialise and where friction from transactions and congestion slows down circulation. However, the convergence of commodity flows in marketplaces, the 'slowing down' of these flows and the visibility and accumulation of commodities provide an opportunity for public authorities to regulate trade and extract revenue from commodity flows. In fact, as we suggest, marketplaces are sites for the production of

101

authority, be it state, state-like or non-state authority (see also Chapters 1 and 7).

This chapter highlights factors that have shaped Somali market-places and their governance in the context of shifting political and security dynamics across Somali East Africa since the early 1990s.[1] We draw on our studies in Ethiopia (Jigjiga), Kenya (Garissa and Eastleigh) and Puntland (Garowe), in addition to Ahmed Musa's (2019) study from Somaliland (Burao and Hargeisa), Abukar Mursal's (2018) study of the Bakara Market in Mogadishu and others. Rather than a systematic review of Somali markets, this chapter synthesises key insights from select marketplaces, identifying their characteristics and pointing to a variety of market dynamics. These dynamics depend on the commodity and the supply chain in question—whether livestock, staple foods, vegetables, fuel, textiles, electronics or *khat*—as well as their materiality. Other factors include the geographic location of the market, population movements, the existing infrastructure and logistical networks and the availability of services, such as banking, water or veterinary control. Marketplaces are further influenced by the availability of protection of goods as well as mechanisms for conflict mediation and the enforcement of (predominantly unwritten) contracts. Services are not always provided by local or central governments, nor do authorities necessarily provide much in return for traders' tax payments (see also Chapter 7). Producers and traders thus have an ambiguous relationship with (state) authorities: on the one hand, they rely on the provision of security to move and trade goods, but on the other hand, they often seek to evade authorities who tax and regulate trade.

Such dynamics are examples of how politics of circulation are formed through the interaction of authorities, security providers and various kinds of trade operators in and around Somali market-places, as pointed out in Chapter 1. While large traders may be able to influence policies of state and other authorities—in terms of infrastructure, taxation and transport regulations, for example—smaller traders claim their stakes in the politics of circulation through their everyday operations and, as we show in this chapter, various forms of organisation that have been key for the continued operation of marketplaces under shifting conditions since the early 1990s.

Finally, we consider how marketplace interactions shape state formation. These interactions are not only practical—involving various forms of taxation and coercion—but also performative and symbolic as competing public authorities project stateness in marketplaces. Marketplaces are thus, in the words of Muñoz (2018: 199), 'quintessential spaces of *encadrement* and provide a frame for commercial transactions'. Marketplaces (and ports) are the locales where commodity flows and trade operators are governed and taxed most intensively, and where the balance between facilitation of circulation and the 'frictions' of regulation, taxation and congestion become apparent.

The remainder of this chapter has five parts. The first provides a summary overview of political developments in the Somali territories after 1991, whereby insecurity and displacement refashioned marketplaces in often unexpected ways. The subsequent section identifies key drivers of dissimilar Somali marketplaces pertaining to their variegated economic significance, geography, infrastructure, social hierarchies and temporalities. The third section focuses on diverse forms of marketplace regulation, drawing particular attention to how the materiality of commodities produces different interactions between traders and public authorities who seek to govern marketplaces. The fourth section delves into non-state or private governance of marketplaces, highlighting the importance of market associations in the daily management of urban markets. The last part examines interactions between state and non-state authorities in governing marketplaces as well as dynamics of contestation, interdependence and boundary-making between them.

Politics and marketplaces

Marketplaces in Somali East Africa have been shaped by post-1991 political developments in the region. 1991 was a watershed year for Somalia and Ethiopia: Siad Barre's dictatorship crumbled after 22 years of rule; Somaliland, the north-western part of the country, declared independence; and in Ethiopia the TPLF/EPRDF (Tigray People's Liberation Front/Ethiopian People's Revolutionary Democratic Front)[2] toppled the *Derg* and decentralised the country after 17 years of guerrilla warfare.[3] By instituting a federal political system structured along ethno-linguistic lines, Ethiopia's new rulers brought monumental changes to politics in the country's peripheries, including in what became the Somali Regional State. This transformation created an opportunity structure for local Somali elites in regional political and economic affairs, notwithstanding interference by the federal government. Despite recurrent political violence and instability in Ethiopia's Somali Regional State (Hagmann and Korf 2012), economic vibrancy characterised the following three decades, particularly in the regional capital Jigjiga with its long history of 'contraband' trade (Thompson 2021) (see also Chapter 6). But, as elsewhere in Ethiopia, economic and political empowerment of the regional majority—Somalis in the case of the Somali region—came at the expense of the economic and political privileges that the non-Somali population, locally referred to as *habesha*, used to enjoy (Tibebe Eshete 2014).

In Somalia, marketplaces and transport routes were heavily affected by armed conflict, chronic insecurity and lawlessness in the absence of functioning state authorities. Irrespective of state failure, marketplaces continued to function or re-emerged in many parts of Somalia, while some commodities—in particular livestock exports to neighbouring Kenya—experienced a veritable boom (Little 2003; 2005). New and old market centres experienced different, often unpredictable trajectories over the past three decades. Insecurity, displacement and transnational trade linkages benefited some marketplaces while they undermined others. Bakara Market in the capital Mogadishu and Eastleigh in Nairobi, to name the two more prominent examples, have continued to grow throughout the post-1991 period. Other marketplaces—like Hartasheikh in Ethiopia and Yirowe near Burao in Somaliland, which were linked to the booming refugee economy of the early 1990s—eroded after a few years of flourishing (van Brabant 1994; see also Chapter 1). Likewise, when people fled Mogadishu during the Ethiopian invasion in 2006–7, the market of Elasha Biyaha flourished for a while until the displaced returned to the capital. Over the years, competing armed groups, often clan militias, have contested major markets in Beledweyne, Baidoa, Galkayo, Kismayo, Lasanod and Mogadishu, as well as important towns on the Somali-Kenyan border, such as Balad Hawa, El Waq and Dhoobley.[4]

The collapse of the Somali state spurred the transnationalisation of Somali commodity trading, which drew on pre-war labour migration and later diaspora networks. Somalia's 'border economies … became globalized, with links throughout the Horn and beyond' (Little 2014: 169). Dubai and Eastleigh grew as key market hubs outside of Somalia, as did Garissa in the Kenyan borderlands and Jigjiga in Ethiopia's Somali Regional State. Conflict, drought and economic opportunity increased Somali social and economic capital in Kenya and Ethiopia and extended social and kinship ties across the border with the possibility of influencing business relations based on clan-lineages. For example, the incoming Somali entrepreneurs in Garissa— which became one of the largest livestock markets in East and Central Africa—benefited the local economy by bringing financial capital as well as business acumen. By the mid-2010s, Eastleigh estate, with more than forty shopping malls and accompanying multi-story apartment blocks and hotels, was attracting interest from other parts of the world, primarily Dubai, China, Europe, and the United States (Carrier 2017).

While some marketplaces quickly went from 'boom' to 'bust' (Little 2014), reflecting the opportunistic nature of commodity trading under uncertain political and economic conditions, urbanisation across the Somali territories made important strides. Cities in the more stable parts of Somalia—Somaliland and Puntland in particular, but also conflict-stricken Mogadishu and hubs along important trade routes—grew in size due to population inflows from south-central Somalia and neighbouring countries. For example, Puntland's administrative capital Garowe grew from a small town of approximately 14,000 inhabitants in 1991 to a population of 70,000–120,000 in 2011. The population of Bosaso, commercially a far more important urban centre, increased from around

30,000 in the late 1980s to some 300,000 in 2007, and between 600,000 and 800,000 in 2015 (Varming 2017).

Conflict-related displacement and the expansion of Somali trading networks throughout the 1990s coincided with economic policy reforms in neighbouring countries. Ethiopia's economy sluggishly transitioned from a tight command economy towards a more open economy. Private actors inserted themselves in trade and other sectors that the government did not consider of strategic importance for industrialisation (Fantu Cheru et al. 2019; Little 2003). This gave way to a bustling cross-border trade, in particular livestock exports and commodity imports, using Somali Regional State as a linchpin (Tegegne Teka and Alemayehu Azeze 2002; Eid 2014).

In Kenya, the economy was further liberalised and law enforcement by state authorities was limited. This benefited Somali cross-border trading and investments in Kenya (Little et al. 2015). After constitutional changes in 2010, Kenya devolved its polity and strengthened county governments, including in the management of trade and markets. Local Somali-Kenyan politicians have been heavily involved in trade and transport, and Somali entrepreneurs have dominated trade in Garissa and other Somali-inhabited parts of northern Kenya. Until recently, non-Somali entrepreneurs have shown little interest in investing in these areas, which has contributed to the dominant position of Somali trade entrepreneurs. In Ethiopia's Somali Regional State, Somalis have also dominated trade, partly because local authorities have actively favoured Somali traders vis-à-vis other Ethiopian traders (Emmenegger 2013; Fana Gebresenbet 2018).

Dynamics and features of Somali markets

Providing an overview of Somali marketplaces is impossible given the lack of reliable comparative data on their size and economic significance, for example, the volumes of particular commodities traded.[5] In spite of this lacuna, differences in terms of geography, infrastructure, social hierarchies, gender and temporality can be identified. Marketplaces in rural areas are usually smaller in terms of volume and diversity of commodities traded, as well as the number and range of trade operators involved. They are also more difficult for state authorities to protect, regulate and tax. For example, in the case of livestock markets in Ethiopia's Somali Regional State, 'bush markets', from which brokers and traders source animals for export to Somaliland and further afield, are typically located far away from main towns and political centres (Eid 2014). Rural markets are often marked by ethnic and clan homogeneity and operate under trees or stands made of simple bushes. As they are 'closer to home', these markets give producers the advantage of access, while traders benefit from lower prices and low or no tax requirements.

Large urban markets like Bakara, Garissa or Burao boast more significant and diversified trade volumes and are more open to traders from different ethnic and clan groups. Due to their economic importance and as sites of exchange interlinking production areas, smaller markets and seaports, they attract state and municipal authorities who seek to tax and govern transactions. Within large urban settlements, main markets host both wholesalers and retailers and co-exist with smaller marketplaces in other parts of town.[6]

The physical appearance and infrastructure of marketplaces differ considerably. Nairobi's Eastleigh estate has seen a proliferation of malls and other multi-story buildings. But livestock markets continue to operate with minimal physical infrastructure and services, apart from loading ramps for livestock in secondary or terminal markets as well as basic veterinary services. Similarly, Jigjiga's central vegetable market, locally known as *Kudra Terra*, consists of mud houses built over four decades ago as storage and selling spaces. In addition to shops and warehouses, most marketplaces host street vendors who sell goods on the sides of streets, whether second-hand clothes in Hargeisa, vegetables in *Kudra Terra* or textiles in Eastleigh.

Somali marketplaces are strongly gendered, as female traders and vendors typically market less profitable goods, while wholesalers and large-scale traders are predominantly men. With the notable exception of *khat* trading (Hedemann 2011), the more expensive the commodity—and the higher the profits garnered in trading in it—the higher the proportion of male traders. Gender differences also apply to particular commodities. The marketing of *khat* and vegetables—but also sheep, goat and camel milk in small quantities—is dominated by female traders, while large livestock and electronics are in the hands of male traders (Koshin 2021; Nori 2009). The gendered nature of markets is most evident in Somali livestock markets. The very 'language of bargaining' livestock sales—i.e., special hidden 'finger-speak' in the case of Somaliland's livestock markets—excludes female traders and brokers (Musa and Schwere 2019), with female traders relegated to side negotiations, particularly of goats and sheep for local consumption, as touching the hand of a random man would be considered inappropriate. Of the three livestock-marketing value chains identified by Ng'asike in Garissa, only the local value chain is in the hands of female traders, while the transnational and export livestock value chains are controlled by men. The profit margin of the local value chain is small and thus left to poorer female traders. Upward mobility is possible for enterprising female traders in livestock, however, and possibly more so in vegetable and *khat* trading (Hedemann 2011; Koshin 2021).

In addition to gender, Somali marketplaces are stratified according to traders' social belonging, including their genealogical and ethno-linguistic identification. Relations between identity-based economic networks and locally dominant authorities—whether state or non-state—determine opportunities and hierarchies in markets. Jigjiga's *Kudra Terra* vegetable market perfectly illustrates this point. In this marketplace, traders are ethnically mixed, consisting of Somali as well as non-Somali—or *habesha* (here Oromo, Amhara, and Gurage)—traders. In the context of Ethiopia's ethno-federal arrangement, Somali traders benefit from their smooth relations with the Somali-led municipality and regional government, as well as their economic entitlements as 'sons of the soil'. These have allowed Somali traders to dominate the ownership of stores from where wholesalers operate. Non-Somali trade operators—who deploy most of the physical labour and capital in Jigjiga's vegetable market—find themselves in the position of second-class citizens, while Somalis have come to occupy the highest rungs of the accumulation ladder in the market. The non-Somali truck drivers who bring vegetables from the highlands to Jigjiga dread encounters with regional police officers in the Somali Regional State, and consequently hire Somali replacement drivers (*shefagn*) for this part of their trip. In other parts of the Somali territories, similar market hierarchies exist between 'majority' and 'minority' Somali clan lineages. While the former typically belong to descendants of 'noble' pastoralist clan families, the latter often belong to occupational minorities, mixed groups or clan lineages with lesser prestige (Hoehne 2015b).

Similarly, trekkers who help in sourcing Somali livestock for the market in Garissa join together according to the different clan territories they pass through on the Somali side, including areas where al-Shabaab and clan militias are in control. Trekkers report being subjected to higher taxes and more aggressive behaviour when these groups consider them to be 'outsiders'. On the Kenyan side, due to widespread discrimination and distrust of Somalis, trekkers and truckers have smoother encounters with Kenyan security personnel if they have a Kenyan ID and speak Swahili. Displaying a 'Kenyan identity' affords Somali market operators better protection.

As trust is vested in genealogical relations (see Chapter 2), the perceived 'trustability' among market operators varies with social stratification of (sub-)clans and ethnic groups. Traders from larger and wealthier lineages have better access to credit and dispute settlement mechanisms; they are more easily trusted, as it is easier to 'enforce trust' bestowed on such individuals, and they are more likely to be part of self-governing bodies such as market associations.

Marketplaces not only differ in terms of their economic significance, geography, infrastructure and social hierarchies, they also have different temporalities. While large-scale urban markets such as Eastleigh or Bakara operate throughout the day, livestock markets across the region or Jigjiga's *Kudra Terra* would see peak activity occurring very early in the morning and would be nearly deserted by mid-day. Thanks to the absence of permanent structures, and the fact that livestock trade occurs only in the mornings,

Somaliland's livestock markets turn into football fields in the afternoon (Musa and Schwere 2019). In Ethiopia's Eastern Hararghe—a main *khat* production site—Awaday's *khat* markets are busy in the evenings as local workers put the produce into bundles destined to reach their destinations early the next morning, including across the border in Somaliland. Similarly, the cattle market in Garissa is active every Wednesday to Friday and dries up towards the weekend. Markets also undergo seasonal changes, reflecting dry and wet seasons as well as major livestock exports to Arab Gulf states during Ramadan (Mustafe M. Abdi 2021). Finally, markets see more unpredictable shifts when macro changes occur in demand—for example, when Saudi Arabia imposes bans on Somali livestock imports (Halderman 2004)—or in supply, caused for example by the frequent droughts.

Varieties of marketplace regulation

Ever since the early writings on the informal sector in Africa (Hart 1973; ILO 1972), African markets have been associated with a lack of state regulation. The 'informal sector' has been viewed as devoid of 'footprints' from the state, as an aberrant economic activity existing outside the regulatory tentacles of post-colonial administrations. In this line of thinking, the state can only realise its full potential once it is able to 'formalise' the 'informal' economy (Banks et al. 2019). This one-sided view of informality has long failed to capture the diversity of economic activities and their institutional effects. More than 60% of the global labour force is estimated to be employed informally, while most businesses in developing countries are estimated to be unregistered with revenue authorities (ILO 2018, cited by Gallien and van den Boogaard 2021). The dominant policy view on economic informality as something to be dealt with through state-led formalisation has got in the way of more empirical investigations into how economies and state authorities interact and mutually shape each other in real life (ibid.).

Somali marketplaces and cross-border trading have often been understood from an 'informality' vantage point (Hagmann 2021).

The resilience of commodity trade, despite state failure and political instability, has led observers to assume that Somali markets are essentially 'stateless' and thus 'informal', drawing on kinship relations and driven by opportunistic motives. While this interpretation cannot be entirely dismissed, it glosses over the fact that markets are indeed regulated by a complex mix of state and non-state actors, rules and routinised practices.

Conceptually speaking, the governance of Somali marketplaces oscillates between 'self-regulation', in which state officials play no or very minimal roles, and hybrid forms of 'co-regulation', in which private and state actors manage marketplaces, at times in a complementary manner and at others in competition with each other. Generally, smaller markets in peripheral localities are left more to self-regulation. Conversely, larger central markets have a higher degree of regulation and taxation by local and national state officials as well as non-state actors that assume public authority in marketplaces, including market associations, *shari'a* courts and insurgent movements like al-Shabaab.

Importantly, in spite of their dissimilarities, all marketplaces discussed in this chapter encounter some form of state regulation. Overall, state institutions are much stronger in Kenya and Ethiopia than in south-central Somalia. Yet even the Somali-inhabited areas of Kenya and Ethiopia have long been known for a limited state presence, predatory national policies and insufficient public services (see Chapter 8). Although devolution and decentralisation have partly transformed relations between local communities and state officials, these challenges persist. But variegated state capacity is not the only variable accounting for the way in which market commodities are governed and taxed. In addition to state capacity, the intensity and quality of state regulation in Somali marketplaces vary according to, first, the different types of trade corridors, and second, the materiality of goods traded.

In his classification of trade corridors in sub-Saharan Africa, Dobler (2016) distinguishes between three types of circuits: first, 'green' circuits, traversing bush routes and bush markets, with no or highly episodic control and regulation by the state; second, 'grey' circuits, along roads where state and state-like institutions

111

control hubs and chokepoints,[7] including the marketplaces in major towns where the exchange and transshipment of commodities slow down flows and where values concentrate; and third, 'blue' circuits, the international air and sea routes that (in principle, at least) allow for more intense regulation by national and international state bodies in sea- and airports. Reflecting three different levels of circulation, Dobler's three circuits or trade corridors correlate with various levels of state authority involved in regulating and taxing the circulation of goods in Somali East Africa. While national and regional state authorities, and the international companies they subcontract, manage and tax sea- and airports, local authorities— whether municipal or county governments—regulate trading in urban marketplaces.[8] Meanwhile, rural markets and trade routes are left to self-regulation to a larger extent, as the potential for tax gains are low.

In addition to differences in infrastructure between various trade and transport routes, the materiality of commodities also has a bearing on the intensity of government regulation. Focusing on the taxation of agricultural commodities in the Somali Regional State, Fana Gebresenbet (2018) has suggested that the value per volume and the degree of perishability influence relations between traders and state authorities. Agricultural commodities that are both valuable and perishable and thus have low storage life are amenable to greater state taxation, partly because trade operators do not want to risk a loss of value by trying to evade authorities' roadblocks. Moreover, given the scope for profits, the likelihood of an oligopolistic trade is high.[9] The risk of loss of value is lower with high-value agricultural commodities that are more durable and mobile, like trekked livestock, making state capture of revenue along cross-border trade routes more difficult.

For example, khat markets are characterised by haste to respond to the high perishability of the leaves, whereas a window of marketability is not an inbuilt characteristic in electronics, shoes or textiles, whether new or used. Moreover, while khat and livestock marketplaces operate predominantly in the mornings and afternoons, clothes and shoe markets operate the whole day. Similarly, the former do not need permanent physical structures (with the exception of high-end shops selling *khat* in Jigjiga that operate from rented spaces), while the latter commodities are more likely to be sold from permanent shops.

In the case of livestock trading, which forms the backbone of the rural Somali economy, livestock markets or sale yards provide officials the best opportunity for taxation. This has been the case in the borderlands. Here, attempts by government agents to control livestock trade and—in the case of Ethiopia—to wage 'war on contraband' have been largely unsuccessful (Devereux 2006: 49; Little et al. 2015) (see also Chapter 6). In the case of low-value agricultural commodities such as vegetables, the drive for state regulation is lower. In his study on the everyday governance of small cross-border trade routes in the Gaashamo corridor in the Ethiopian-Somaliland borderlands, Mustafe M. Abdi (2021) has identified various degrees of 'state capture' of traded goods in accordance with their materiality. Hence, camels trekked from Ethiopia's Somali Regional State to Somaliland along (Dobler's) 'green' circuits evade taxation. Sheep and goats transported on main roads—meaning 'grey' circuits—are taxed in bulk by district revenue agents or the *Liyu* police. The latter have a particular interest in inspecting high-value imported goods, namely electronics, entering Ethiopia from Somaliland, as they allow the extraction of fees from transporters (Mustafe M. Abdi 2021).

Private or non-state governance

To a large degree, Somali marketplaces have survived and prospered because societal actors have governed them, stepping into the void created by state failure (see Menkhaus 2006). As has been the case with other public services and goods—whether education, health, mobility, water or electricity provision—the daily governance of marketplaces has often occurred with minimal state involvement (Hagmann et al. 2022). This situation corresponds to what Grossman, in her study of Lagos Market associations, describes as 'private governance', meaning the ability of 'private group leaders … to provide services that support contractual trade' (2021: 111). Key among these 'services' is the provision of basic security in the marketplace, the enforcement of contracts—

essentially business agreements pertaining to sales, credits and debts—and dispute resolution.

Market associations and local committees of varying permanence and significance have been an enduring feature of the 'private' or non-state governance of marketplaces in Somali East Africa. In many instances, traders have formed more or less institutionalised market committees to fill the gaps left by state collapse or weak administrations. In the words of one of the founders of such a market committee in Mogadishu, quoted by Abukar Mursal (2018: 20):

> As long as there was a state, well, there was a state between us. The municipality was standing between us with witnesses and all. If there was a problem, they [the municipality] dealt with it. When the state removed itself from between us, we had to create committees. The circumstances forced us to create committees.

In the context of limited state presence, for long periods of time in Mogadishu markets, shop-owners and market committees have had to deal with insecurity, crime and disputes in the market, effectively taking the place of the municipality.

In other marketplaces, associations have formed in response to, rather than in the absence of, state authority. This has been the case in several Kenyan markets. In Garissa's livestock market, a Somali council of elders that had represented traders vis-à-vis the local government in the 1990s was formalised as a Livestock Market Association (LMA) in 1998. With devolution in 2013, associations like the LMA have been formally mandated to 'co-manage' markets together with county authorities (Njiru et al. 2017). In 1994, when large numbers of Somalis were settling in and starting small businesses in Eastleigh, they formed the Eastleigh Business District Association (EBDA). As a former leading member of the EBDA explained to one of the co-authors:[10]

> The business association was formed by indigenous Kenyan Somalis to approach the government and to improve the situation for them [Somalis arriving from Somalia]. So the government started giving 'alien cards' to them, rather than refugee [status]. That meant they got the rights to do business, banking, owning property, everything. The only thing they could not do was vote, but every other right, they got it.

In 2015–16, the Micro and Small Enterprises Leaders' Summit (MSEL)—an umbrella organisation with 60,000 members across the 17 constituencies of Nairobi City County—advocated on behalf of street hawkers in Eastleigh when registered traders and City County authorities sought to remove them from the streets of Eastleigh. The MSEL also contributed to the formation of the Eastleigh Hawkers' Association to represent Eastleigh hawkers in negotiations with traders and authorities (Indimuli 2022).

With increased state building occurring in Somalia, along with devolution and decentralisation in Kenya and Ethiopia, the overall influence of local, regional and national governments in regulating and governing markets has grown. This has led to a change in the roles and functions of market associations. In Mogadishu, the members of market committees, whose primary function in the 1990s was to ensure protection, have become more like 'elders', responsible for traders in the market 'as parents are for their children' (Abukar Mursal 2018, 13). This role has involved resolving disputes, providing information and assuring good relations among traders as well as between traders and state authorities. In some committees, members have been selected on a logic of clan lineage representation. In others, they have been chosen by a particular sub-section of the market specialising in the marketing of a particular commodity, such as clothes or charcoal (ibid.).

Genealogical descent is important in terms of social capital, allowing an individual trader to become a figure of authority in a marketplace. In the case of Mogadishu's shops, booths and open markets in the 1990s, traders belonging to one of the dominant clan lineages in otherwise mixed markets became authorities because they could mobilise and finance armed fighters among their clan constituency. They effectively functioned as protectors or *abbaan*, engaging in the age-old practice of protecting travelling traders and their caravans that re-emerged after the Somali state collapse (Cassanelli 1982).

Abukar Mursal (2018) illustrates how market committee members mobilise personal skills and qualities that are often ascribed to Somali elders. These skills are needed because of the challenge of enforcing sanctions on market operators in a context of weak or absent judicial frameworks, as explained by a member of a Mogadishu market committee (ibid.: 21–2):

> We don't arrest people. We also don't fine anyone. It is with the Somali language, and brotherhood that we solve things, as well as with 'it used to be like this, or like that'. That is the way. More than that, the state deals with it. It will imprison the one that is wrong, and the others carry on with their work. That's it.

Like the council of elders, the Mogadishu market committees rely on tradition (*dhaqan*), customary law (*xeer*) and 'Somali language'. The latter refers to a form of communication that allows them 'to find compromises through speaking an intelligible language to all, through entering into dialogue as opposed to using force' (ibid., 14). Settling disputes in the marketplace is among their most important tasks, particularly when conflicts over the predominantly trust-based credit systems arise, as most trading in the Somali territories is based on credits without written contracts (see Chapter 2). In cases of breach, state authorities have no basis to intervene, while non-state authorities such as market associations are better suited, as they can enforce principles of trustworthiness and utilise lineage as a collective insurance mechanism.

Apart from market associations, other actors—especially brokers and wholesalers—play a role in the organisation of markets. Over 40 years ago, Clifford Geertz (1978: 30) identified the search for information as 'the central experience of life in the bazaar', suggesting that competitive 'clientship relations' allowed market operators to reduce this search to manageable proportions and transform 'a diffuse mob into a stable collection of familiar antagonists'. In Jigjiga's *Kudra Terra* vegetable market, for instance, wholesalers with over a decade of trading experience assume considerable responsibility for the working of the market. They have an incentive to do so, as they bear most of the risks involved in the trade, as their working relationships with agents in production areas and retailers are based on trust. There are no formal sanctions or enforcement mechanisms in place, except that these wholesalers will not work with agents and retailers who prove themselves untrustworthy, thus pushing them out of business. Consequently, trust and trustworthiness are important norms that produce tangible compliance and ensure the effective running of the market.

Brokerage is another integral part of the private governance of Somali marketplaces. It serves as an effective governance mechanism in livestock trade, which makes the sale, transport and certification of animals possible. Connecting buyers and sellers, sometimes in different locations, brokers play crucial roles in transactions of livestock. Brokers are 'connective agents', linking actors with differing interests and logics across space and the formal-informal divide (Koster and van Leynseele 2018). As Garissa-based livestock trading highlights, brokers are the effective buyers and sellers in the market. They often have authoritative market information and potential solutions to market challenges (Ng'asike et al. 2020). On top of this, they also possess the required social capital within their lineage as well as across clan and ethnic boundaries, enabling trust-based transactions. Brokers embody and ensure the largely credit-based long-distance flow and circulation of livestock across international and social boundaries.

Livestock producers and small-scale traders value clan and kinship relations when it comes to seeking out brokers to work with. In Garissa and other livestock markets, brokers of particular lineages congregate around the gates that their (distant) relatives use. Nevertheless, family ties have their limitations when it comes to governing marketplaces. When the volume of commodities traded by a broker or a trader increases, his or her relations with other lineages and ethnic groups also increase over time. In Jigjiga's *Kudra Terra*, wholesalers embolden their position in the vegetable trade through the size of their capital and the number of retailers they work with, rather than by mobilising lineage or ethnicity. In sum, the personal attributes of traders, brokers and wholesalers matter as much as their family ties when it comes to governing transactions in Somali marketplaces, and the two are interlinked.

(Un)making the state in the marketplace

Multiple state-, state-like and private entities govern Somali marketplaces, which are sites of contested state making and unmaking, as well as revenue generation (see Chapter 7). Even though marketplaces across the Somali territories are taxed by state officials, traders often obtain few tangible benefits in return. This creates a constant reminder of the disconnect between governments' ambitions of governing economic life and the persistence of non-state actors in doing so. For example, in Mogadishu markets, traders observed that 'when the state collapsed, that's when [taxation] stopped. Since the government is back [in 2012], taxes are back in town'.[11] Taxation typically comprises indirect taxes in the form of payments for annual or biannual licences, in addition to daily taxes (*ardiya*) when business—in stalls, shops or on the street—is open. In livestock markets, traders and brokers pay taxes per animal traded. In the case of shops in Hargeisa, taxes are based on visual assessments (as opposed to, e.g., value-based or *ad valorem* assessments) of the level and value of business (Campos 2016). In livestock markets, traders pay veterinary authorities for various permits and certificates proving that animals are free of disease, a service which is not always entirely trustworthy (see Musa 2019).

Providing security and taxing profits stand out as the most prominent tasks performed by agents of local and national governments—as well as other entities vying for public authority—in marketplaces. Chronic insecurity in many parts of south-central Somalia in the 1990s and onward brought to the fore the challenge faced by traders in securing their goods and profits in a context where property rights were not guaranteed and political instability prevailed. Without municipal police or soldiers, traders had to arm themselves or pay for protection from clan militias to avoid having their wares looted. In Mogadishu, businessmen funded the *shari'a* courts in 2006, since their police force was considered more reliable and predictable than clan militias and warlords (Ahmed 2014; Hansen 2007). Since the 2010s, the protection of markets in south-central Somalia has been shouldered by local and regional governments, including the capital's huge Bakara Market, which spreads across several of the capital's districts. Bakara Market has been devastated by bombs and fires in the past and is heavily contested between the government and al-Shabaab. The latter co-governs this marketplace at a distance through taxation, dispute resolution and intimidation (Abukar Mursal 2018).

If the taxation of marketplaces provides state authorities across the Somali territories with substantial revenue,[12] market traders often question the level of public services they receive in return for their fiscal contributions. Substandard market infrastructure, lack of sanitation and other subpar services serve as motivations to resist state taxation in the marketplace. Varming's following exchange with a young fuel trader in Puntland's capital Garowe captures traders' scepticism towards state taxation:

> 'We don't have a problem with them collecting the money, or with the price. But we have a problem, and we always talk about what it is that we get in return. The municipality is always collecting, but there is always rubbish lying around here.' He points out the door, towards the main street. I ask him what the money was spent on, and he replies: 'I think that question is for the government. I really don't know.' He sends me a knowing smile: 'But if you ask them, they will say that they spend it on security' (Varming 2017: 13).

Interactions between market associations, who assure the daily functioning of marketplaces, and local government are equally insightful examples of the contested processes of state making and unmaking. For example, brokers in Garissa (Kenya), Burao, Hargeisa and Tog'wajaale (Somaliland) collaborate with local officials by helping to register, tax and formalise livestock transactions (Musa and Schwere 2019). In Garissa, brokers serve as intermediaries between buyers and officials, facilitating the documentation and taxation of animals sold. In practice, they thus function as auxiliaries to local authorities, helping to reduce the scope for tax evasion.

Market associations have entertained shifting relationships with the state. While market committees in Mogadishu emerged in the state's absence, by the end of the 2010s municipal authorities had themselves created market committees and registered some (but not all) committees, to facilitate the work of civil servants. This has generated discussions and resistance on the part of some market committee members who fear being co-opted by local government, a process that might undermine their authority in the marketplace. But even when market committees resist state co-option, they still contribute to the production of state-like ideas and practices, both by distinguishing themselves from the state as well as signalling boundaries between state and society. As Abukar Mursal (2018: 25) has pointed out in her analysis of Mogadishu market committees, 'Unlike state officials, [market committees] do not claim taxes, issue fines, or receive a salary; they are not armed; and they do not want to be registered as committee members, since this would make them part of state law as they see it.'

Aside from a potential loss of recognition, close association with the government puts committee members at risk of harassment and attacks by al-Shabaab. Abukar Mursal (2018: 17) provides the following vignette that describes the delicate balances that traders and market committees must strike as they navigate the overlapping claims of local government and armed groups:

> On the 1st of July 2015 [Somali National Day], after the ceremony in which the Somali flag was raised had been televised the night before, shops on main streets hung flags. Two rows of shops on both sides of the street had Somali flags of varying sizes ... [But] the streets were [empty] and most shops were closed, although it was a Wednesday, a regular working day. ... The order [to fly the Somali flag] had actually been associated with a fine of US$100 ... but traders were also afraid of being accused of being supporters of HMS [Harakada Mujahidinta al-Shabaab] or militants themselves. At the same time, shop-owners were worried that if they flew flags, HMS's militants would attack them, destroy their shops, or identify them as supporters of the government ... To display the flags while keeping their shops closed was the strategy shop owners came up with. So, the flags were hung, hence avoiding the fine, while the shops remained closed and were guarded from a safe distance in order to assure their safety.

In Kenya's Eastleigh and Garissa, circumstances are different from those in south-central Somalia, and markets and market associations are registered by and operate in the context of Kenyan legal frameworks (Njiru 2017). However, everyday operations in these marketplaces are often far removed from official rules. The relationship between market associations and local state actors can still be fraught with tension and contestation. In Eastleigh, the Eastleigh Business District Association (EBDA) filed several court petitions against the Nairobi City County (NCC) between 2010 and 2016 to force them to provide services to the business community. They complained of depleted infrastructure, insufficient sanitation, and the spread of street hawkers in the area.

When court petitions did not provide the desired result, the EBDA entered into a hybrid arrangement with the NCC. The association collected funds from the traders in Eastleigh's malls and used the money to pay for police reserves to remove the hawkers and patrol the streets. Until this point, the NCC had been collecting unofficial taxes from street hawkers, thus giving the latter de facto permission to operate. Following the re-negotiated tax agreement between the EBDA and NCC, clashes between street hawkers and traders—who by now possessed a higher degree of state recognition—ensued, eventually leading to the forceful removal of hawkers from Eastleigh's streets. This example illustrates how, in cases where government institutions are (made) effective, market operators have an interest in being recognised and even taxed by them.

Relations between state and non-state authorities across Somali marketplaces thus vary from stark opposition, in the case of al-Shabaab and the local government in Mogadishu; to collaboration and partial incorporation, in the case of the EBDA and NCC in Eastleigh; and to marketplaces that are essentially self-regulated by private actors with minimal state involvement. These hybrid or shared forms of market governance reduce economic insecurity, increase protection and build trust. As argued by Grossman (2021), market associations have an interest in liaising and collaborating with state institutions precisely because they seek to avoid government interference and regulation of 'their' markets.

Local traders and private actors are often sceptical of what the government does with the collected tax revenue (Abukar Mursal 2018; Varming 2017, 2019). In some instances, like in the case of Eastleigh, traders feel more confident that their needs will be met by paying extra fees to the business association, rather than paying contributions to the NCC. While the long-term effects of such hybrid governance arrangements have not been assessed (see Meagher 2014), we suggest, based on observations in Somali East

Africa, that state institutions have often benefited from hybrid and informal arrangements of taxation (see also van den Boogaard and Santoro 2022b).

In the governing of marketplaces in the Somali-inhabited areas, as in other places around the world, state authority is under continuous negotiation and its limits are constituted in an iterative process of representing, inferring, problematising and disclaiming the state (see Chalfin 2001b). In this process, the very idea of the state (Migdal and Schlichte 2005) is produced by traders, brokers and market committees, not only by civil servants who represent the state, such as the official who explained to Abukar Mursal (2018: 18) that '[t]he market is a public good. Everywhere there is a market, it belongs to the state'. When criticising state (in-) action, traders and other market operators contribute to cementing imaginations of the state. Similarly, interactions, collaborations and negotiations between state and non-state authorities make the state present and relevant in the marketplace, even when state authority seems to be negated, circumvented or replaced.

Conclusion

Contrasting empirical insights from different study sites, this chapter has drawn attention to the evolving role of marketplaces in the politics of circulation and state (un)making in Somali East Africa over the first three decades after Somali state collapse. Rather than stateless or ungoverned spaces, markets have been critical sites for producing authority and (re)forming states, even though local government typically plays a limited role in their daily workings. Whether 'self-regulated' by market committees, contested between competing interest groups or managed collaboratively between traders and state agents, marketplaces across the Somali territories have continued to operate. Despite insecurity, political instability and economic uncertainty, small- and large-scale traders have generally been able to protect their goods, resolve disputes and enforce contracts.

The regulation of marketplaces in the Somali-inhabited parts of East Africa has evolved in tandem with post-1991 developments related to the state collapse, the dramatic diasporisation of Somali society, the attempts to rebuild or reform Somali state institutions, as well as devolution and decentralisation in Kenya and Ethiopia. Trade operators have had to cope with and take advantage of these changes. Self-regulated or private market governance shouldered by traders initially emerged as a way of managing marketplaces in the vacuum left by receding or persistently weak public administrations. The presence and actions of these depend to some degree on the materiality of the goods traded. The gradual strengthening of state institutions in the 2010s created the interdependence and need for cooperation between market operators and government officials. In this interaction, the state is invoked and imagined as an entity separate from society, which is empowered to sanction, tax and (in ideal cases) secure accumulation, exchange and the flow of value.

Marketplaces have been critical sites for both the projection of stateness—even with limited and contested presence of local and central governments—and for the continued circulation of commodities. Looking at the supply chains of livestock and imported commodities, we may distinguish between two different arenas in which market operators partake in the politics of circulation. On the one hand are oligopolistic livestock exporters and import/(re-) export companies whose agents mostly operate in the blue and grey circuits and market hubs, in Dobler's (2016) terminology. These 'blue operators', as we may call them, are big enough to have political connections and influence on decisions relating to infrastructure projects (ports, roads); incentives for trade (taxes, customs and services such as quarantine stations); and regulation of the transport sector (licensing, standards).

On the other hand, a range of operators who animate the marketplaces of the grey and green circuits exist: the wholesalers, retailers, brokers, agents, hawkers, transporters, trekkers and the people providing associated services of banking, catering and so on. These actors mainly play into the politics of circulation by voting with their feet—or, rather, with their trucks—by choosing by which routes and to which marketplaces they take their trade. However, as this chapter shows, these predominantly 'grey opera-

TRADE MAKES STATES

tors' are also organised into market or business associations and market committees. Having mostly local governments—or other local public authorities—as counterparts, these organisations have a stake in politics of circulation that relate to marketplace conditions. These conditions in turn can either facilitate or hinder the circulation and exchange of commodities, including market infrastructure, access, public services, security, taxation, licensing and dispute resolution.

Finally, this chapter has shown how markets are also places of accentuating and entrenching inequality and social hierarchies. Insecurity and political dynamics in circuits and marketplaces favour certain clan and ethnic communities over others. In many cases, cultural and religious norms keep women from high-profit enterprises. Market actors and authorities interact in various ways to dismiss the lower rung of traders, such as hawkers, as nuisances and push them out of the marketplace. As such, like elsewhere, trade and state making dynamics primarily favour better-off traders, whose wealth indirectly is hinged on clan and other social markers.

6

GOVERNING COMMODITY FLOWS
IN THE SOMALI BORDERLANDS

Asnake Kefale and *Jacob Rasmussen*

Introduction

This chapter centres on the governance of commodity flows across
national borders in the Somali territories of the Horn of Africa. It
highlights mutually reinforcing causal relations between state-
formation processes and the circulation of goods. On the one hand,
state policies and practices impact on the direction of cross-border
flows of goods in variegated ways. On the other hand, struggles
over the circulation of goods have been—as argued in Chapter
1—an important element in the process of (re-)building state and
state-like authorities across the Somali territories. However, the
governance of commodity trading is far from a state monopoly,
with a multiplicity of differently positioned actors involved that
compete to insert themselves at key junctions of the trade. While
governments implement policies that seek to limit or at least control the circulation of commodities, cross-border trading in the

125

Somali borderlands plays a central role in providing livelihoods for local traders, and in making goods accessible to local communities. As a result, borderland communities often resist policies introduced by national governments, as well as other attempts at disciplining cross-border flows (Dereje Feyissa and Hoehne 2010; Bruzzone 2019). These types of transgressions are locally legitimised by reference to historical state marginalisation; through generational, clan and family relations across borders; and through narratives of irregular state practices (see van Schendel and Abraham 2005).

Our chapter draws on empirical examples of two trade and transport corridors that traverse these borderlands: the Berbera corridor connecting the Port of Berbera in Somaliland with landlocked Ethiopia, as well as the Kismayo corridor linking the Port of Kismayo in southern Somalia with northern and central Kenya (Hagmann and Stepputat 2016).[1] The two corridors present contrasting insights into how the politics of circulation of goods play out. The chapter offers a de-centred view of the governance of commodity flows in the Somali borderlands. We give prevalence to local traders and their practices, to cross-border relations and to local and regional politics. Rather than emphasising the logics of the central state, in this chapter we consider how state institutions are related to and embedded in local practices. It is important to note the presence of a myriad of state and state-like actors, often with divergent—if not conflicting—approaches to the governance of commodity flows in the borderlands. Recent reforms in regional and local government structures in Kenya and Ethiopia have created local administrations whose interests regarding cross-border trading do not necessarily converge with the policies and priorities of their national governments.

Despite the local importance of cross-border trade, national governments in Ethiopia, Kenya and Djibouti—the countries bordering Somalia and Somaliland—have until recently shown little interest in developing cross-border trade and economic relations. Governance in the border regions has mainly focused on security related issues, and governments have rarely taken the borders seriously as logistical frontiers (Murunga 2005; Hagmann

2014). State regulation, governance and revenue collection in the borderlands have often taken an ambiguous form, meaning state policies and practices are either insufficient—as in lacking capacity—or deliberately selective (Carrier 2017; Asnake Kefale 2019). In addition, governance reforms in Kenya and Ethiopia have given more opportunities to local political elites who gained influence in decentralised institutionalised domains, enhancing the so-called 'Somalisation' of local politics (Thompson 2021). Despite the ambiguous institutional presence of the central state, these changing policies and regulations have affected the politics of circulation in the two corridors considered here (Stepputat and Hagmann 2019: 797).

This chapter comprises the following sections. The first section addresses shifts in trading patterns along the Berbera and Kismayo corridors. The second section discusses shifting governance interventions and formalisation drives by Somalia's neighbouring states and how these impact the circulation of goods. While this section contributes to arguments about relational governance and trust, it also reveals how cross-border relations are politicised and intertwined with security dynamics and the 'Somalisation' of local government. The third section focuses on goods and the trading practices in the border regions, especially efforts put into maintaining the flow of goods along trade corridors. The attention to traded goods highlights the importance of arbitrage and testifies how differentiated value and durability of commodities inform their gatekeeping and the authority to control their circulation (see also Chapter 5). The fourth section provides insights into the myriad of actors involved in governing cross-border trade. On the one hand, the multiplication of authorities and state-like entities competing and negotiating over the control of cross-border trade reveals the fragility of regulatory frameworks in the Somali borderlands. On the other hand, it points to how cross-border commodity trading informs state-building processes. Finally, we provide a few concluding remarks, emphasising the intertwining of cross-border commodity flows with political influence and state-formation dynamics.

Border communities and business elites along the Berbera
and Kismayo corridors

The borders shared by Somalia and its neighbouring countries are porous and arbitrarily divide communities that share identical ethno-linguistic features. These trans-border ethnic and linguistic ties provide a strong social basis for cross-border trading (see also Chapter 2). The Somali borderlands largely remain marginalised in terms of receiving services from the central parts of both Kenya and Ethiopia. For example, border communities in the Berbera and Kismayo corridors obtain most of their vital supplies such as food and clothing from Somali traders crossing the borders. Hence, local authorities in both countries largely tolerate small-scale trading between the border regions.

Peter Little has shown how the transformations of the Somali economy after the collapse of the state in 1991 informed the growth of a 'second economy' based on cross-border trade, informal money transactions and a global network of remittances (Little 2003; Little et al. 2015). He highlighted how pastoralist mobility combined with kinship relations affected the Somali economy as well as political and social institutions. However, state collapse also meant the collapse of public taxes, opening up possibilities for private businesses to act in an almost unregulated manner, and those with capital and political connections benefited enormously (see Ahmad 2014; Hagmann 2016).

Somaliland's de facto independence and the secession of Eritrea from Ethiopia in 1991 brought about new inter-state relations and increased the importance of sea corridors (Bradbury 2008; Reid 2011). Following the 1998–2000 Ethio-Eritrea border war, Ethiopia became completely dependent on Djibouti for maritime imports (Medhane Tadesse 2015). Securing an alternative means of accessing the sea has therefore been one of the key foreign policy objectives for post-1991 Ethiopian governments. This revitalised the importance of the Berbera trade and transport corridor (see Chapter 4). Importers from the Isaaq clan, based in the Middle East or Somaliland, used to operate from Djibouti following Mohammed Siyad Barre's accession to state power in 1969.

They moved back to Somaliland to exploit trade opportunities at the less crowded Berbera port and to access a larger market and the relatively open economy in neighbouring Ethiopia (Ciabarri 2017). Wholesalers, mainly from the Isaaq clan, became dominant commodity traders in trading hubs along the Berbera corridor, for example, the border town Tog'wajaale. As these wholesalers operate within Somaliland and follow local business requirements, they do not face the risk of having their goods confiscated by state agents.

Similar patterns exist along the Kismayo corridor, where a trust-based transnational economy built on links between clan, politics and trade has developed, in part supported by diaspora connections to the Gulf states. Charcoal exports and sugar imports through the port of Kismayo increased from the mid- to late 1990s. This trade was facilitated by members of the Hawiye clan and their connections to the Arabian peninsula, but the distribution and transport of commodities was shouldered by other clans, in particular members of the Ogaadeen clan family, who straddle the border and are dominant in Garissa County on the Kenyan side (Marchal and Yussuf 2017; Hagmann 2016; UNSC 2018).[2] Multi-clan collaborations at Kismayo Port played a central part in shifting dynamics from being primarily anchored in clan networks to broader business coalitions focused on common economic interests, and this had effects on local politics as well (Hagmann 2005). To protect their goods while en route, these business networks employed their own militias for security, set up checkpoints and demanded taxes (Bakonyi 2013).

However, the emergence of a business elite founded on international and cross-border trade is far from benefiting all Somalis: the majority of pastoralists in the region depend more on livestock and charcoal production than trade (CSSF 2019; RVI 2013). Large-scale livestock trade and the sharing of pastures across the Somali-Kenyan border were already widespread in the 1980s (Ng'asike 2019; Mahmoud 2008), although the direction of the export was re-oriented from Kismayo towards Nairobi after the Somali civil war (Little 2003). While the new business class in southern Somalia forged new alliances and linked up to global networks, partly facilitated by Somali diaspora members, especially in the Gulf, they also benefited from local livestock trade and charcoal production that fed exports through Kismayo (Marchal and Yussuf 2017).

At the Port of Berbera, livestock trade is the most important outbound trade. Animals are bought at small 'bush markets' or secondary markets by mid-level traders and are either trekked or trucked to terminal markets across the border, such as Tog'wajaale and Hargeisa in Somaliland. To evade interception by the police or the militia, livestock trekkers use bush roads. On the Ethiopian side, traders rely on informers to tell them about the movement of local militia and the federal police who aim to intercept livestock crossing the border to Somaliland. Traders then give trekkers the task of driving the animals to the terminal markets. The economic gains from the transaction bind traders and trekkers together, but in the absence of formalised contracts, trust vested in intra- and inter-clan ties as well as Islam plays a central role in allowing the continuation of the business (see Chapter 2).

Livestock traders in the Berbera corridor are connected to large-scale traders who are predominantly based in Somaliland and buy large numbers of animals from terminal markets. These large-scale traders either supply exporters or export the livestock themselves to Arab Gulf countries, predominantly to the Saudi market. Since the lifting of the Saudi ban on the importation of live animals from the Horn of Africa in 2009, the exportation of live animals from Somaliland has increased dramatically (Muhumed 2016). The establishment of three export quarantine stations in Berbera helped formalise the export of sheep and goats, further boosting livestock exports from Somaliland. Similar upgrading of the abattoirs in northern Kenya has helped the establishment of the Garissa livestock market—the largest in the region—feeding most of Nairobi (Mahmoud 2008; Ng'asike 2019). Despite the phenomenal growth of livestock exports from Berbera and southern Somalia, the gains from the trade appear to be concentrated among a few operators who dominate the sector.

Cross-border trading in both corridors has been boosted by the large-scale movement of people triggered by multi-layered conflicts and humanitarian crises that continue to affect the region.

Refugee camps and urban settlements hosting Somali refugee communities have grown into important hubs for cross-border trading in both corridors (Montclos and Kagwanja 2000; Jaspars et al. 2020). Across the Berbera and Kismayo corridors, similarities in the consolidation of business elites around diaspora networks and their ability to import and export goods using the existing logistical infrastructures are evident. These business elites have partly relied on cross-border clan networks to establish their positions and facilitate trade. Furthermore, pastoralist networks and practices of raising cattle with limited consideration for political borders have also positively influenced cross-border relationships and ease of passage. It is, however, important to note that trade in both the Berbera and Kismayo corridors could not have thrived without trust-based relations established through generations and across borders.

Central states, cross-border trade and the 'Somalisation' of local government

In his classic work on commodification and commodity flows, Arjun Appadurai (1986) argued that political elites often have an interest in freezing the flow of commodities in closed circuits of regulation and fixed prices. He highlighted how political elites are challenged by innovative merchants and traders who, driven by the politics of demand, introduce new commodities and new tastes, or cheaper products (Appadurai 1986). Increased cross-border trade (Little 2003) and the emergence of Somali business elites along the Berbera and Kismayo corridors fit with Appadurai's description. The circulation of goods in both corridors can be seen as an outcome of protectionist economic interests and policies by the Kenyan and Ethiopian governments on the one hand, and the exploration of new markets by innovative Somali traders on the other. In recent decades, state reconfiguration in the form of ethnic federalism in Ethiopia and devolution in Kenya has brought autonomy to local communities (Asnake Kefale 2019; D'Arcy and Cornell 2016).

After its ascendance to power in May 1991, the former Ethiopian Peoples' Revolutionary Democratic Front (EPRDF) initiated a process of ethnic decentralisation, which culminated in the formation of an ethno-federal state structure. One of the newly formed regions was the Somali Regional State. From being historically peripheral to Ethiopian politics, the region began to play an increasingly important role in the governance of cross-border commodity flows (Tezera Tazebew and Asnake Kefale 2021). As part of the Ethiopian government's ambition to discipline cross-border trading activities (Stepputat and Hagmann 2019), it allowed regional governments like that of the Somali region to play an important role in the prevention of cross-border trade, which the central state sees as contraband. An immediate consequence was that the Somali Regional State's special or *liyu* police paramilitary forces became involved in cross-border trade management, supporting the federal customs police in inspecting vehicles passing through government checkpoints. In addition to its participation in the governance of cross-border trade, the Somali regional government and its local agents have become major actors in the circulation of goods in the borderlands (Mustafe M. Abdi 2021). Accordingly, the regional government has given licences to petty cross-border traders and manages the lucrative *franco valuta* trade, which the federal government made an exception for in borderland communities (Tezera Tazebew and Asnake Kefale 2021).

While Somaliland showed a remarkable state-building performance—despite not achieving international recognition—internationally supported state-building efforts in south-central Somalia faced serious challenges (Clapham 2017). Since 2004, efforts at reconstituting a Somali state on the basis of federalism have proven highly divisive (Chatham House 2013; see also Chapter 8). For one thing, the military Islamist group al-Shabaab has a strong presence in much of the south-west of the country. Because of insecurity, the Kenyan-Somali border has been officially closed since 2007, but it has remained porous, and the influx of refugees and arms continue to cause political problems for Kenya. As early as 2010, the Kenyan government was lobbying for the establishment of Jubbaland as a semi-autonomous state so it could act as a buffer zone to it (Lind et al. 2017; Anderson and McKnight 2015). While the participation of Ethiopia and Kenya in the fight against al-Shabaab did not defeat the militants, it did alter the security landscape in south-west Somalia. When Mogadishu recognised Jubbaland as a prospective federal member state in 2013, Kenya's hope of a buffer zone in southern Somalia was met.[3] However, the increase of internationalised state-building endeavours within Somalia after the adoption of federalism rarely boosted state capacity, instead creating rents for political entrepreneurs, which further destabilised the country (Hagmann 2016).

In the wake of the 2007/8 post-electoral violence, Kenya underwent a constitutional reform process which culminated in the adoption of a new constitution in 2010 (D'Arcy 2020). The constitution established 47 counties and introduced devolved governance, giving greater autonomy and more leverage in national politics to the historically marginalised north-eastern regions (Carrier and Kochore 2014). Devolution in Kenya enhanced local stakes in politics, business and trade (D'Arcy and Cornell 2016; Cheeseman et al. 2016). In Garissa, Wajir and Mandera, where local politics traditionally had been informed by intimate cross-border relations, devolution enhanced interactions between local politicians and cross-border traders (Chome 2016). Locally elected officials in these counties appear to permit—and some even actively facilitate—cross-border trading, which provides employment, cheap consumables and foodstuffs like sugar, rice, powdered milk and vegetables to their communities. A former MP for Garissa openly stated his involvement in the lucrative cross-border sugar trade on national TV.[4] Other examples are two lower-level bureaucrats who admitted they had been offered money from local businessmen for turning a blind eye to the flow of goods through their jurisdictions.[5] While these examples point to the pecuniary power of commodity trading, the importance of building relations through trade—even for politicians and lower-level bureaucrats— must be taken into account.

Despite the historical marginalisation of Somalis in northern Kenya, over the years central governments have attempted to co-opt them into patronage relations. President Moi refined this type of politics and groomed Somalis, especially from the Ogadeni clan around Garissa, into the Kenyan military, as well as appointed them to key government positions (Lind et al. 2017). Ogadeni from the Garissa area have thus held prominent positions, both in business and in Kenyan politics. Moreover, they maintained cross-border relations to Jubbaland in southern Somalia through trade and politics. In Jubbaland, politicians have relied on taxes levied from cross-border trade to mobilise the support of militias, key clan constituencies and the emergent Somali business class (see also Chapter 7). Cross-border trading along the Kismayo corridor has been instrumental for Jubbaland politicians in drawing together a 'political budget' to win local elections (see de Waal 2015). Part of the bargain with Kenya is to maintain Jubbaland relatively autonomous from central Somalia. Another part is to maintain relations with the political leadership in Garissa County who facilitate cross-border commodity flows as far into Kenya as Eastleigh. Most Somali traders in Eastleigh rely on links to Garissa, Wajir, Mandera and even to Somalia, and they take pride in the entrepreneurial and innovative characteristics of Somali-led trading (Carrier 2017; Hassan 2019). These commercial skills are informed by trust networks that rest on a combination of lineage loyalty and experiences of mobility and displacement, allowing small enclaves of Somali settlers to insert themselves in trade networks throughout Kenya (see Chapter 2).

State reconfiguration along the Berbera and Kismayo corridors reveals that the inclusion of local Somalis in positions of state power had the paradoxical effect of producing more autonomy for the historically marginalised Somali borderland communities while increasing the presence of central states at local level. By becoming involved in policing and revenue collection, in the Ethiopian case, Somalis increasingly became incorporated into state institutions over recent decades, even if their view of the state remains very much informed by local context and continues to reflect existing cross-border trade networks. Similarly, in the Somali-Kenyan borderlands Kenya's military presence alongside al-Shabaab and the Jubbaland authorities has coincided with increased Somali influence in regional decision-making on the Kenyan side of the border. Whether it is former Kenyan President Moi's (1978–2002) attempt at establishing Somali loyalty, or the Kenyan Defence Forces' (KDF) engagement in the charcoal and sugar trade, or the presence of Somalis in the *liyu* police of Ethiopia's Somali Regional State, attempts at involving Somali communities in state governance effectively activated and reconfigured cross-border relations. The gradual 'Somalisation' of governance at the edge of the Ethiopian and Kenyan states thus must be understood not only as an expression of ethnicity or clan belonging, but as the outcome of cross-border relations and trade networks that rely on trust and obligation, and which allow for the maintenance of commodity flows.

Maintaining the flow of goods

An international embargo on the import and export of arms, charcoal and drugs to and from Somalia, adopted by the United Nations Security Council in February 2012, effectively made cross-border trading of these products illegal.[6] But the embargo brought on new dynamics in the politics of circulation underpinning the trading of these commodities. Despite the ban, the charcoal trade has thrived across the Somali-Kenyan border, with al-Shabaab playing an active role in the illegal export from Somalia, and this trade has continued since the KDF took control of the port in Kismayo (JFJ 2015; UNSC 2018; Fanusie and Entz 2017). Even though al-Shabaab, the KDF and the Jubbaland authorities pursue conflicting goals, in practice they have cooperated to allow the flow of contraband sugar into the Kenyan hinterland and the export of charcoal through Kismayo Port, quietly sharing the profits of this lucrative trade. One might conclude that this continued trade, and the KDF's takeover of the charcoal stockpiles, is solely driven by greed and the wish to realise profits based on arbitrage. While economic motives clearly matter, so does the political influence associated with the power to keep goods circulating despite the presence of multivarious actors with vested interests.

In Kenya, the historical oppression of the Somali population and their animosity towards the Kenyan state has shaped the provision of public and private goods and services in its north-eastern counties, which have consequently had to rely on imports from their neighbours Ethiopia and Somalia. Historically, few goods from central Kenya tend to reach the Somali parts of the country, partly due to a lack of interest by the government and partly due to high transport costs (Mboya 2002). In the case of food supplies and sugar, northern Kenya relied on small-scale cross-border imports from Ethiopia and Somalia until the mid-1990s, when innovative Somali traders began bringing in larger quantities of sugar through Somalia (Marchal 1996). The main driver of the booming sugar smuggling in the Kismayo corridor is the huge difference between the prices of imported and domestically produced sugar in Kenya. Because the Kenyan government protects local sugar manufacturers, domestic sugar prices are high. Price variation along with high levels of sugar shortages in the Kenyan market are thus the main incentives for sugar smuggling (Rasmussen 2017).

As a consequence of the historical lack of goods and services distributed from central Kenya to the north-eastern borderlands, local traders and communities have invested additional efforts towards maintaining a steady flow of goods across the border. As we noticed during fieldwork in Eastleigh in 2015—and repeatedly thereafter—commodity traders and businesspeople pay constant attention to 'their' goods, and even when they are far away they receive updates on their progression and potential disruptions on the way. When a truckload arrives, repackaging and onward distribution must be immediately organised. But that is the easy part; payments for passing roadblocks, informal fees and taxes are all part of the calculation and organisation of the trade. Awareness of roadblocks, weighbridges and toll stops, as well as obstacles such as poor roads and bad weather, are likewise fundamental parts of the business. Moreover, there is always the risk of unplanned interruptions, expensive delays or even capture, which means loss of goods, additional cost and difficult negotiations.

In these cases, the goods need to be 'released', as the local phrase goes. This work of putting goods back into circulation can take place from anywhere, but it requires a network of trusted contacts who are based in different locations along the corridor and who have access to different layers of society, and an ability to activate this network instantly. While money is a key factor for releasing the goods, trust and social relations are far more important, as explained by a Nairobi businessman: 'It is not a question of what I can do, it is a question of who I know.'[7] Bribes and payments are integral to release captured or delayed goods. These include governmental import taxes, but most traders do not make a moral distinction between these and other under-the-table payments, because their main concern is to provide passage for their goods. In the Kenyan-Somali borderlands, official tax receipts might provide traders documentation to pass, but that is only half the battle: actual passage requires intimate knowledge of trade routes as well as a strong network with officials stationed along the way.

We find similar dynamics in the borderlands of the Berbera corridor. Ethiopian(-Somali) traders organise the smuggling of merchandise—in particular new and used clothes, shoes, electronics and foodstuffs—across the border from Somaliland to Ethiopia's Somali Regional State. They face the risk of having their goods intercepted by customs and security checkpoints along the main asphalt roads connecting Somaliland with Ethiopia. Ethiopian traders travel to Tog'wajaale, the border town, to buy large amounts of goods, or else they order from a wholesaler. The task of crossing the border is given to the drivers who use Isuzu lorries or specially reinforced Toyota minibuses to transport the merchandise to secondary distribution hubs inside Ethiopia, like Jigjiga or Harar. A single lorry often carries goods for several merchants, with merchants writing their names or putting a special mark on their bundles.[8] Traders and drivers use a variety of ways to circumvent control by customs officers. One is arranging the passage of the lorry by bribing the authorities. In Jigjiga, this method is euphemistically referred to as 'purchasing airtime', where during the agreed-upon time drivers will be allowed to pass through inspection points. The other, and riskier, way of bringing in commodities is to use one of the bush roads.

Small-scale traders who travel to Tog'wajaale to buy small amounts of goods usually travel by bus from Jigjiga and back again, purchasing foodstuffs and clothing in the border town. They run a lesser risk of capture by authorities, and if caught they have to either pretend to have bought the goods for personal consumption;

otherwise, they contribute a small amount of money for the driver to pay off the police manning checkpoints (Tezera Tazebew and Asnake Kefale 2021). Once commodities arrive at secondary distribution markets like Jigjiga or Harar, marketing strategies and tactics of state avoidance become more diversified. Sometimes traders distribute their merchandise among ordinary passengers whom they do not know, so as to avoid having it confiscated by the federal police. Once the bus has passed the main inspection checkpoints, traders collect their merchandise from their fellow passengers. Solidarity among passengers is maybe best understood as a form of everyday resistance against the state (Scott 1985). More importantly, it is also worth noting that cross-border trade in the Berbera corridor—although officially resisted by Ethiopian state authorities—cannot happen without state officials colluding with traders. As was made public in 2018, the import of goods through the Berbera corridor all the way to the country's central highlands has occurred with the close cooperation of traders and government officials in regional and federal security forces, as well as customs officials (Tezera Tazebew and Asnake Kefale 2021).

While livestock dominates Ethiopia's outgoing trade and is the main export commodity from the Port of Berbera, incoming trade is largely made up of manufactured goods such as new and used clothes, footwear, food items, electronic goods and others. Since the 2000s, there has been a substantial increase in small but high-value electronic devices imported to Ethiopia through the Berbera corridor, with mobile phones progressively making up the lion's share of informal imports. Indeed, electronics figure only second after used and new clothes in Ethiopia's Revenue and Customs Authority's (ERCA) data on the confiscated 'illegally' imported goods. But the statistics of seized electronics goods by ERCA do not tell the full truth about the smuggling of mobile phones. By 2016, over 60% of mobile apparatuses in Ethiopia were likely to have been smuggled through Berbera and other Somali-dominated trade corridors. The main reasons for the flourishing import of mobile phones are high government tariffs and the fact that mobile phones are small in size but high in value, making them easy to transport and difficult for authorities to intercept (see Chapter 5).

This said, the importation of mobile phones is dominated by only a few traders, as it requires large amounts of capital and good networks to evade seizure by customs authorities.

The arbitrage gained from moving goods in the Berbera and Kismayo corridors across state borders—from one market into another—is a combined effect of both state and non-state barriers. Profits depend on the cost of passage and the risk of capture, but also on the materiality of the goods. Electronics, livestock and food supplies not only have different mobility patterns, but they are also subject to different risks of state capture. The examples from the Somali borderlands reveal that the history of circulation and past access to goods inform the current day flow of goods, not only in terms of old back routes and long-established trading relations, but also in terms of the habitual perceptions of border regimes and their role in either facilitating or preventing access to goods over time.

Multiple authorities and state contours in the borderlands

The borderland literature offers important insights into everyday life, politics and economics in border regions. It fundamentally challenges our tendency to think of borderlands as marginal to the state. If border regions are physically distanced from the centre of the nation, they are neither economically nor politically marginal. On the contrary, border regions exist in synergetic relation to the state they are part of and politically separated from (Bøås 2014; Scheele 2012). State making processes and the enactments of state authority manifest themselves in visible ways in border regions.

After state collapse in Somalia in 1991, most Somali borderlands experienced an abundance of competing actors trying to assert power or institute some form of control, often simultaneously. On the one hand, violent conflict, humanitarian crisis and the absence of stable institutions to accommodate Somali border populations have strengthened existing clan and family networks across the borders. On the other hand, external security forces and international humanitarian actors extended their presence into the border regions. For traders, governance in the Somali borderlands became a question of securing the protection of their goods while either minimising taxation or evading it entirely. For authorities, whether state or non-state, regulating cross-border commodity flows has primarily been an exercise in balancing loyalties to local, regional and national power holders. As shall be argued below, cross-border trade produced distinct economic and political dynamics in conversation with logics of state schemes of 'formalisation' but, nevertheless, constantly resisted these schemes.

Jubbaland in southern Somalia represents a good example of how authority, trade and political legitimacy intertwine. Over the years, the Port of Kismayo has been a hotly contested economic and political hub claimed by various armed factions and interest groups in the region. The Somali Federal Government, al-Shabaab, the KDF and the Jubbaland government have all controlled Kismayo Port at different times, enabling them to insert themselves in the Kismayo trade corridor in different ways (see Chapter 4). Despite these shifting and at times overlapping authorities, al-Shabaab's control of overland trade is widely perceived as fairer and more transparent than taxation by the KDF or the Jubbaland authorities (Hiraal Institute 2018; Fanusie and Entz 2017).[9] Receipts that truck drivers in the Kismayo corridor receive from al-Shabaab in exchange for payment of taxes provide passage through checkpoints along the entire stretch from Kismayo to the Kenyan border. The receipts include information on the vehicle, the owner, the driver, the points of departure and the destination, as well as the name of the al-Shabaab officer who issued the receipt.[10] Such evidence suggests that the insurgent group needs to balance their use of coercion with garnering local acceptance (see Chapter 7).

In the Ethiopian-Somaliland borderlands, the Ethiopian government has used a variety of policies and strategies to govern Somali populations and cross-border trading, the modalities of which have 'mutated' from formal to informal (Tezera Tazebew and Asnake Kefale 2021). From 2015 onwards, the role of the Somali Regional State's *liyu* or special police in the management of cross-border trading and border control was enhanced as the federal government had to re-deploy many of its federal police forces to the protests that hit regions of Oromia and Amhara (Mustafe M. Abdi 2021). Furthermore, the government's decision to give licenses to a limited amount of petty cross-border traders was used as a cover by local authorities and traders to engage in large-scale cross-border trading.

Likewise, traders and local officials used the Ethiopian government's *franco valuta* policy—which allows for importing vital goods such as food and basic clothing to borderland communities—to import a wider range of goods, which were then transported onward to the central parts of the country, including Addis Ababa, where they found a lucrative market. In addition to state authorities, (inter-)clan networks and traditional authorities all partake in managing commodity flows through the Berbera corridor by enforcing credit and sales agreements between traders, brokers and buyers based on social sanctions (Tezera Tazebew and Asnake Kefale 2021). The governance of commodity flows across the Ethiopian-Somaliland borderlands is thus marked by a broad range of actors and normative complexity.

The politics of trading across the Kenyan-Somali borderlands is not that different from the Ethiopia-Somaliland borderlands. To reach Garissa, smuggled goods from Kismayo need to bypass the Kenya Revenue Authority (KRA), which involves the cooperation of officers from the KRA and KDF posted on the Somali side of the border.[11] Before reaching the border, sugar shipments have to pass through al-Shabaab-controlled roadblocks as well as territory controlled by the Jubbaland authorities. The border crossing of trucks through the Dadaab refugee camps on the Kenyan side is a meticulously organised undertaking, involving a network of carefully organised passages and several branches of the Kenyan police and the KRA. For Kenyan police officers and county officials, appointments in the north-eastern counties are infamous for being lucrative (JFJ 2015).[12] In 2015, Kenyan authorities implemented a multi-agency collaboration, involving various branches of the police and several Kenyan authorities (e.g., anti-counterfeit authorities, the Kenya Bureau of Standards, etc.), to combat economic crime. Since then, the orchestration of government collusion has become more complex, and smuggling networks have begun influencing and controlling the placement of officials in public office (Rasmussen 2020). Not only has the Kenyan state increased the number of its agencies in the borderlands, but long-established Somali trade networks have also refined and systematised their collusion with the authorities. The implications of these complex relations extends well beyond the border regions. Trade arrangements between the otherwise warring al-Shabaab and KDF might provide temporary predictability for traders in the region, but they undermine Kenya's security objectives in Somalia. Hence, the governance of trade and security on the Somali side of the border has implications for the regulation of trade and security on the Kenyan side because of the economic interests of Kenyan-Somali political and business elites and their clan loyalties across the border.

Similarly, on the Ethiopian side of the Berbera corridor, the number of authorities who partake in the governance of commodity flows has increased over time and so has the complexity of their relations. Agents of both the federal and Somali regional governments—including customs, federal police and army, the region's *liyu* police and militia—participate in border control and interception of incoming and outgoing 'contraband' goods (Mustafe M. Abdi 2021). To give coherence to the activities of all these state agencies, in 2017 the federal government established anti-contraband task forces at federal and regional levels, the latter of which was led by the then president of Somali Regional State. But the proliferation of state officials, including those involved in the formation of these task forces, did not lead to a significant reduction of cross-border trade, as traders found ways to either circumvent the restrictions or collude with the authorities.

While political authority is partly acquired through the control and facilitation of trade, the spike in numbers of authorities in the Somali borderlands has increased contestations and competition between them (Musa et al. 2020). The frictions produced by competition over influence and shares in cross-border trading has direct implications for the flow of goods and the routes taken by traders and commodities. The collusion of state actors in commodity trading along main trade and transport corridors in the Somali territories highlights the 'politics of smuggling' (Gallien and Weigand 2021: 27) between authorities and cross-border traders. On the one hand, state involvement in cross-border trade increases risks of violence, as its agents rely on secrecy and physical sanctions. On the other hand, collusion stabilises trading relations, as it gives government actors privileged knowledge about commodity flows in the border regions. Complicated relations between state officials, traders and local communities over cross-border trade and its governance in the Berbera and Kismayo corridors draw attention to the ambiguous ways in which trade produces stateness in the Somali borderlands.

Conclusion

This chapter has examined the governance of commodity flows in the Berbera and Kismayo corridors, highlighting relations between state-formation processes and borderland trading. The post-1990 period reconfigured both international and intra-state borders through the establishment of new states—de jure (Eritrea) and de facto (Somaliland)—as well as a localisation of public administrations due to state collapse (Somalia), ethnic federalism (Ethiopia) and devolution (Kenya). An increasing number of actors and interests in the Somali borderlands thus added to the complexity of governing the circulation of goods across borders. While national governments seek to manage, limit or control cross-border trading, local and regional government officials in the border areas of the Berbera and Kismayo corridors partake in facilitating cross-border flows, complicating the role of the state in the borderlands.

Our historical review of cross-border trading in the two corridors highlights how the circulation of goods and state-formation processes are mutually embedded. Trade and transport corridors are continuously negotiated and reaffirmed through the contested facilitation, regulation and reappropriation of commodity flows, what this book frames as 'politics of circulation'. Newly established local and regional authorities in Ethiopia's Somali Regional State and in north-eastern Kenya have been more supportive of cross-border trading. The ability to facilitate the cross-border circulation of goods is important for acquiring political influence at different levels. But the positions of central governments both in Kenya and Ethiopia continue to be ambiguous. On the one hand, they work to limit the flow of commodities. On the other hand, their officers in different agencies collude with traders, smugglers and armed groups in facilitating the circulation of goods.

While the boundaries between different state authorities are blurred, loyalties and interests of local communities are often historically informed. They hinge on lineage, clan and trust relations established through trade as much as—if not more than—citizenship and attachment to the nation-state. However, the economic rationality of cross-border trading is what sustains commodity flows in both corridors—producing lucrative profits for traders, rents for state agents and affordable commodities for borderland communities. These motives account not only for the resilience of Somali-dominated trading of commodities since the 1990s, but also for its expansion into the Kenyan and Ethiopian hinterlands. Somali traders and a host of other actors have specialised in maintaining the flow of commodities, releasing them when they (inevitably) encounter friction, to put them back into circulation.

7

RAISING FISCAL REVENUES

THE POLITICAL ECONOMY OF
SOMALI TRADE TAXATION

Ahmed M. Musa, Kirstine Strøh Varming and *Finn Stepputat*

Introduction

Collecting taxes is at the heart of any state-formation process (Tilly 1975; Herbst 2000). To create a viable administration, funds are needed to pay salaries, provide services and invest in infrastructure. However, taxation also has a performative dimension, and, as scholars of the New Fiscal Sociology insist, taxation is part of the non-material aspects of state formation, such as the 'social contract' between taxpayers and taxing authorities (see Moore 2004; Bräutigam 2008; Martin et al. 2009). Basing their conclusion mostly on studies of tax systems where 'direct taxes'—generalised taxes on income and property—is the norm, Martin et al. (2009: 1) have suggested that taxation '*is* the social contract', as it defines the boundaries and obligations of a political community and

145

generates collective bargaining. But what about countries where taxes on trade, a form of 'indirect taxation', provide the bulk of tax revenues? This was the case for post-colonial states in sub-Saharan Africa well into the 1990s (Moore 2021). By then, internationally promoted tax reforms reduced custom tariffs in order to remove barriers to international trade. In exchange, Value-Added Tax and other reforms were introduced to broaden the tax base (ibid.). Because of instability and conflict, such reforms only reached the Somali territories by the mid-2010s, when the World Bank began implementing a series of projects to increase the capacity of the Federal Government of Somalia (FGS) and the Federal Member States (FMS) for tax mobilisation and financial administration. Taxation is considered central to state building in post-conflict contexts (van den Boogaard et al. 2018), and, indeed, the World Bank has qualified these projects as its 'primary instrument for supporting Somalia's state-building'.[1]

Nevertheless, as of 2021, trade taxes—mainly from ports and other customs points—still provided the bulk of tax revenue for Somali administrations, and will most likely continue to do so for the foreseeable future (Raballand and Knebelmann 2021; Hagmann 2021). Given the importance of trade taxes during the first three decades after state collapse, this chapter examines the forms, actors and implications of trade taxation in various parts of Somali East Africa, suggesting that a fine-grained analysis of taxation is needed to better understand the political economy of taxation, the (un) making of public authorities and the dynamic relations between authorities and political subjectivity. We thereby contribute to an emerging but still limited literature on taxation in the Somali territories, which, refuting former conceptions among policymakers and aid agencies that the Somali economy was unregulated and untaxed, shows that a range of public authorities engage in taxation (see Campos 2016; Abshir et al. 2020; Raballand and Knebelmann 2021; Hagmann 2021; Musa et al. 2021; van den Boogaard and Santoro 2022b; Varming 2017, 2019, 2021). If Somalia was once described as 'the largest duty-free shop in the world' (Menkhaus 2004b: 51), this is far from the reality today.

Taxation of trade is directly related to politics of circulation as authorities capture revenue from goods that are moved through gateways, hubs and corridors of the 'greater Somali economy'. While a range of state, sub-national and state-like authorities rely on trade taxes, and as such seek to manage and capture flows of circulating goods, taxpayers are often mobile and change their routes to avoid payments. Hence, relations between taxpayers and taxing authorities are not straightforward. First, trade operators move across several territories without necessarily belonging to the political community of the taxing authorities, which has implications for any 'social contract'. Second, jurisdictions—de facto and de jure—are sometimes blurred and overlapping, with multiple authorities claiming the right to tax the same goods and transactions. As our chapter shows, al-Shabaab engages in taxation alongside FGS and the FMSs outside its areas of control, but fiscal relations between FGS and its member states also remain unsettled (Raballand and Knebelmann 2021; Isak and Wasuge 2021). Furthermore, ongoing disputes over territory between Puntland and Somaliland have resulted in overlapping taxation regimes (Musa 2021), while the taxation practices of local administrations are often legally ambiguous.

Looking at the practical and symbolic aspects of trade taxation, we ask the questions: which authorities are taxing Somali trade, where and how? What effects does trade taxation have on processes of state formation? And how does the creation of fiscal revenue from traded commodities relate to the politics of circulation? Empirically, this chapter draws on the authors' published work and insights from fieldwork in Puntland, Somaliland and Nairobi, but because of the transboundary reality of taxation—including competition between authorities, comparison of taxation practices by trade operators and shifting trade routes—we also consider other analyses of taxation and state formation in Somali East Africa.[2]

The chapter is divided into four sections: in the first, we examine different forms of trade taxation in the Somali territories, focusing on the actors who claim the right to tax. We highlight the plurality of taxing authorities, pointing out that legality, regularity and legitimacy do not follow any simple state/non-state distinctions. The second section explores the question of social contracts and what we refer to as 'tax games'. These include negotiation, bargaining, avoidance, exemption, extortion and other fiscal practices marked by different degrees of agency by taxpayers. In using the term 'tax games', we hope to move beyond the understanding of taxpayers as either compliant or non-compliant, and instead show how social contracts can take different forms, including ones that do not involve improved services, governance or representation for the taxpayers. The third section analyses the relationship between taxation and political subjectivity, considering how insider/outsider identifications are central to understanding taxpayer motivations and strategies. The fourth section focuses on the (un)making of authority through trade taxation, illustrating the argument that some types of non-state taxation can strengthen state-society relations, while taxation by competing actors, such as al-Shabaab, tends to weaken state authority. As evidence from the Somali territories suggests, the relationship between taxation and state building is complex and non-linear (Raballand and Knebelmann 2021; Musa 2021).

The chapter concludes by arguing that a state-centred approach to taxation in Somali East Africa is inadequate; that fiscal social contracts, in the context of administrations that depend on trade taxation, are piecemeal and rudimentary with limited forms of reciprocity; and that revenue from trade taxation is the prize for public administrations that take part in the politics of circulation. Nevertheless, since trade operators through their choice of routes also become actors in these politics, administrations must balance the revenue harvested with the friction induced by their fiscal practices.

Trade taxation in Somali territories

Developing a typology of taxation in Somali territories since the collapse of the Somali state is difficult given the shifting and ambiguous status of state, state-like and other forms of public authorities engaged in taxation, as well as the ambiguous or undefined legal status of different types of taxes. In this section, we will organise the overview according to the taxing authorities: 1) state and sub-state actors, meaning FGS and its member states, Somaliland, Ethiopia and the Somali Regional State, the Kenyan state and county governments; 2) local governments, referring to districts, municipalities and *woredas*, or districts, in Ethiopia; 3) state security forces; and 4) non-state authorities, ranging from al-Shabaab to clan, religious, community and business authorities. Along the way, we make distinctions between types of taxation according to whether they are inscribed in a legal framework or not, whether they reach the coffers of public authorities or not and whether they are bureaucratic—meaning routinised and regular—or more random and ad hoc.

Taxation by states

In this section, we consider taxation by the FGS, the FMSs and the government of Somaliland. State taxation is regulated by public finance laws that are based on modifications of the 1960 Somali Republic legislation, which only in the late 2010s became increasingly subjected to reforms in the case of Somaliland and the FGS.[3] As Raballand and Knebelmann (2021: 5) pointed out, 'tax rates, valuation methods, the definition of taxable goods, lists of taxpayer categories and tax or exempted goods and services, have (for the most part) remained unchanged over the last thirty to fifty years'. The FMSs have tax provisions in their constitutions, but since Somalia's provisional federal constitution has not yet been finalised, questions of authority and resource sharing between the FGS and the FMSs, including fiscal arrangements, remain unanswered (Isak and Wasuge 2021). The FMSs retain the fiscal revenue they collect, including from ports under their control, without coordination and oversight by the central government (Abshir et al. 2020).

With a tax revenue profile dominated by taxes from international trade—making up 60% of tax revenue (Raballand and Knebelmann 2021: 8)—the control over customs in ports, airports and border posts is the biggest source of the glaring inequality in terms of domestically generated revenues in the Somali territories. As Table 7.1 shows, Somaliland (with Berbera Port), the FGS (with Mogadishu Port), Puntland (with Bosaso Port) and to some degree Jubbaland (with Kismayo Port) are in a different league than

Galmudug, Hirshabelle and South West. The latter member states depend on fiscal transfers by the FGS of 1.8 million USD per year (Isak and Wasuge 2021). Unlike Puntland and Jubbaland, they cannot allow themselves to push back against the FGS in negotiations about a decentralised federal system (Abshir et al. 2020).

Table 7.1 also highlights to what extent the different states depend on customs revenue—with Puntland being the most dependent—and the (limited) degree to which they have managed to 'move the revenue further inland'. This is the expression that government representatives in Somaliland used in conversations with the authors when explaining the aim of internationally backed tax reforms aiming to build the state and potentially remove tariff barriers to trade. Nevertheless, in the case of Somalia, tariffs are only at 7%, which is low compared to the East African Common Market and other parts of the world (Raballand and Knebelmann 2021). The FGS is lagging behind Somaliland in terms of developing direct taxation as well as indirect taxes like sales tax, Value-Added Tax (VAT) and excise taxes,[4] but the overall improvement of the FGS's domestic revenue mobilisation and public financial administration was enough to convince the International Monetary Fund (IMF) that Somalia, by 2020, was eligible for debt relief.[5]

Apart from Berbera Port, where upgrading of customs is most advanced, Somali states' custom operations are still largely manual. Officials count the taxed items, which is not only inefficient but also causes delays in the flow of commodities and increases the cost of trade.[6] Moreover, when manually checking commodities, customs officials, sometimes at more than one customs point, will ask for the unloading of cargo for inspection, which can cause damage, affecting the commodity value. In Somaliland, taxes are applied on an *ad valorem* basis at 3% of the value of imports and exports, whereas other Somali customs taxes are specific, based on the weight, number or volume of goods (Raballand and Knebelmann 2021). Neither rates nor rules for tax exemptions are uniform across Somali customs, and officers have discretionary powers, which makes bargaining common. In general, luxury items such as cars and electronics are fully taxed while authorities are more relaxed about other commodities such as basic staple foods.

Table 7.1: Breakdown of tax revenue in Somali territories (in USD millions, 2019)

	Somaliland	FGS	Puntland	Jubbaland	Southwest	Galmudug	Hirshabelle
Total tax	174.6	173.3	43.5	19.3	3.5	2.7	2.7
Tax on income & profits	18.3 (10.5%)	11.7 (6.7%)	0.5 (1.1%)	1.3 (8.0%)	0 –	0 –	0 –
Tax on goods & services	59.1	47.1	6.1	8.3	2.2	2.7	2.7
Tax on international trade	97.2 (55.7%)	109 (62.9%)	36.5 (83.9%)	9.6 (49.7%)	1.3 (37.1%)	0 –	0 –
Other tax	0	5.5	0.4	0.1	0	0	0

Source: Adapted from Raballand and Knebelmann (2021: 9).

Importers of the latter are sometimes eligible for tax reductions (*cashuur dhimid*) or tax exemptions (*cashuur dhaaf*), and the tax rates are often negotiable (Hagmann 2021; Khalif 2021; Musa 2021; Mustafe M. Abdi 2021).

The heterogeneous, incoherent and de facto independent fiscal policies of Somali states lead to competition for revenue between the different polities as well as an overall trend towards lower tariffs and taxes. For example, FGS/Mogadishu Port, Jubbaland/Kismayo Port and partly Puntland/Bosaso Port compete to capture the import of vehicles, electronics and sugar (Raballand and Knebelmann 2021). Similarly, Djibouti, Puntland and Somaliland consider export tax rates as an incentive to make livestock traders choose the respective ports for export to the Middle East (Musa et al. 2020). States with border posts at the borders with Ethiopia and Kenya, official as well as unofficial, are also competing for revenue from customs, a major source of which is imported *khat* from Ethiopia and Kenya.

Since the Somaliland government's official stance is to treat territories outside the former British Protectorate as foreign countries, its border posts impose import tariffs on commodities arriving from these 'foreign territories'.[7] Likewise, although Puntland does not consider other Somali states as foreign countries, in practice it imposes import duties on commodities from these territories, excluding those coming from eastern Sanaag and Sool where both Somaliland and Puntland claim sovereignty. This creates ambiguity. For example, in Lasanod, the capital of Sool Region—which has trade relations with both Bosaso and Berbera Ports—businesspeople pay customs duties for commodities that enter through Bosaso in Puntland for Lasanod (Somaliland). But as an employee in a construction company in Lasanod told us, 'They sometimes receive the wrong order, but when they try to return the commodity to Bosaso, the customs authority in Puntland yet again levies customs duties and other fees on the returned commodities.'[8]

Other than tariff duties, the Ministries of Finance of several state administrations have recently put efforts into developing the capacity for collecting sales and other indirect taxes and fees on goods and services. These indirect taxes make up three to four times the direct taxes in the cases of the FGS and Somaliland (see Table 8.1). In 2018, the FGS imposed a 5% sales tax on goods at the point of import and a 15% tax on telecommunications (Raballand and Knebelmann 2021). Somaliland has introduced VAT and collects sales tax on imported commodities at the point of entry. However, there has been a debate about whether sales tax should be collected at the point of entry—which favours municipalities with customs points, such as Gabiley, Berbera and Zeila, which receive a certain percentage of the sales tax collected by the Somaliland government—or at the destination. Somaliland moreover requires service providers such as hotels, restaurants and electricity companies to charge 5% sales tax. In addition, the state collects sales tax on commodities entering marketplaces. In Puntland, Musa observed that its Ministry of Finance collects between 30 and 50 USD per truck, depending on the commodity, in the destination districts. In Garowe, the administrative capital of Puntland, Varming observed that businesspeople pay monthly sales taxes to the Ministry of Finance.

Taxation by local government

Local governments such as municipalities, regions, districts, counties, zones and *woredas* collect revenues from trade in markets and at checkpoints (and custom points, in the case of Somaliland) in their territories, sometimes alongside tax collection by central state authorities. As we have observed in Somaliland, Puntland and Ethiopia's Somali Regional State, local government taxation is often not legally circumscribed or formally authorised by state institutions. State officials and institutions might be fully aware that local governments are collecting taxes but turn a blind eye to it, and in return local governments will receive limited budget transfers from the state. In south-central Somalia, institutions of the FGS and FMSs continue to be weak, with limited authority or territorial presence to stop this practice. As Moore (2021) notes, this is a very common phenomenon across sub-Saharan Africa due to the limited and often ambiguous institutionalisation of local government.

To give an example, Somaliland's Regions and Districts Self-management Law, No. 23/2019, does not allow local municipalities to collect transit fees from trucks passing through with commodities. Nevertheless, many districts still do it, even though these charges feature under names such as garbage collection fee (*qashin gur*) in Somaliland, or district development tax (*cashuurta horumarinta degamada*) in Puntland, where the same conditions apply. The transit taxes collected at district checkpoints along the Bosaso corridor to Garowe are technically illegal but are widely accepted by administrators and taxpayers alike. The checkpoints are official and manned by police officers from the municipality, and the revenue ends up in the municipal coffers. These charges are, as a Garowe administrator put it, 'socially accepted but not legal'.[9] In Puntland, checkpoints are only supposed to collect an 'offloading tax' from trucks delivering goods at their destinations. Truck drivers interviewed about the checkpoints did not question the legitimacy of the charges but stated that the fees were for 'district development'.[10]

The total amount of transit fees collected by the districts varies, as some districts are more open to fees negotiation than others. Each district in Puntland's Bosaso trade corridor collects 6 USD per truck, while Somaliland districts in the Berbera-Burao corridor collect a total of 10 USD per truck.[11] As a manager of a general trading company in Lasanod, which is part of Somaliland but contested by Puntland, told us:

> The tax collected by districts in Somaliland is called the garbage collection fee, but this money is lower than what is collected by Puntland districts. We pay a total of 100 USD or less per truck to all the districts, compared to 240 USD which we pay as a district development tax to Puntland districts along the Bosaso-Lasanod corridor. The money that districts in Somaliland collect is not rigid; there is flexibility. However, since we are a company, we pay the required money to build a relationship with the district authorities since we constantly use the road, and also for protection.[12]

Below, we will return to such practices that are grounded in the wish to uphold good relations with local authorities and the promise of protection for trade operators. Local governments are not different from state governments in that they depend on trade taxation and attempt to capture revenues from the circulation of goods such as livestock for export or imported fuel, building materials, electronics and foodstuffs. Municipalities that host larger markets for livestock, for example, take advantage of this by charging sales tax. Thus in 2018, the municipalities managing Burao and Hargeisa livestock markets collected 0.20 USD per small ruminant (sheep or goat) sold. In addition to sales tax, municipalities collect revenues such as a 'budget supplement' (*kab*) of 0.064 USD per head of livestock sold in Burao's market. The revenue from this tax goes to the regional branches of public institutions, such as the General Hospital and the Ministry of Education, which receive insufficient fiscal transfers from their headquarters in the capital, Hargeisa.

Taxation by security forces

Our findings from the Somali territories illustrate that security officials commonly collect taxes, a kind of protection fee. These have no legal basis but may well be known to higher levels of state authorities and take place with varying degrees of consent. Police officers in Puntland and Somaliland, stationed at the checkpoints along the important trade corridors, collect small, standardised, yet negotiable fees. Somaliland checkpoints collect a 0.50 USD 'road usage' fee (*wado maris*), while Puntland checkpoints collect a 2 USD 'checkpoint opening fee' (*bir qaad*).[13] In government-controlled areas in south-central Somalia, soldiers stationed at checkpoints collect a fee commonly known as *baad*, meaning 'extortion' or 'informal taxation' (Abshir et al. 2020: 5). Commenting on these fees, a businessman in Mogadishu, quoted by Abshir et al. (2020: 5), said: 'At our stores, 45–50 trucks are lined up and trying to unload. Soldiers show up and you have to pay them. What happens if you don't? They stop the work. You can go to higher-ups to complain but this means we lose time. The truck drivers also complain. It is just easier to pay. ... The government doesn't control these soldiers.'

Moreover, security forces in the fragmented Somali security landscape collect unofficial but institutionalised fees to support official security provision. For example, regional security forces in

Somaliland's Sool region collect an 8 USD protection fee (*amaan*) from every truck with commodities that enter Lasanod city, the administrative capital of the region. The above examples illustrate the spectrum of fees that state security forces charge from circulating commodities. These charges differ in their degree of consent, negotiability and enforcement, as well as the degree to which the payments remain in the pockets of security officials themselves, reach higher echelons or indeed end up in the coffers of official security forces to support their existence as well as the state entities they represent. However, the opponents of the latter also engage in various forms of taxation.

Taxation by al-Shabaab

The revenue that al-Shabaab collects from trade operators in areas under its control, or from networks of circulation that the organisation taps into, is extracted coercively and thus lacks a base in state law or governmental frameworks. Nevertheless, businesspeople who are subjected to various forms of extraction by al-Shabaab generally consider its fiscal practices as 'taxation' (Ahmad et al. 2022), akin to a state practice. Various reports indicate that a substantive part of the extraction is regular and bureaucratised, following certain rules, which makes the costs predictable and calculable from the point of view of trade operators (Ahmad et al. 2022). As the 'rebel governance' literature suggests (Mampilly 2021; Bandula-Irwin et al. 2022), revenue extraction by rebels exists on a continuum between extortion and state-like taxation, between coercion and consent. Furthermore, while extraction is always economically motivated as funds are needed for military campaigns, administration and sometimes services, it can also be a way of performing and producing authority among the population by mimicking taxation as a 'language of stateness' (Hansen and Stepputat 2001).

Al-Shabaab reaps revenue from trade in several ways. Before losing control of the ports in Kismayo and Brava, taxation of imports and exports provided the organisation with a handsome revenue. But even without being physically present around the ports, al-Shabaab manages information from port administration and commercial shipping agents, which allows them to spot imports coming through Mogadishu port and tax the goods at their destinations (UNSC 2018). Also, through a sophisticated system of remote taxation, the organisation extorts revenue from trade operators in the huge Bakara market in Mogadishu and submits businesspeople in Mogadishu and Bosaso to the payment of 'donations for God's grace' (Abshir et al. 2020: 4).[14] Furthermore, a 'service charge' of 10% is levied on commercial operations to fund al-Shabaab's drought relief (ibid.).

Most importantly, the organisation has developed an extended system of checkpoints in remote areas in south-central Somalia where vehicles as well as goods are taxed in cash or in kind, according to standards for different vehicle types and the goods they carry. Livestock is taxed with one per twenty-five camels, and one per forty goats, while trucks, depending on size and goods, are charged between USD 555 and 1150 (Hiraal Institute 2018). According to a conservative estimate for 2017, al-Shabaab collected USD 15 million in cash from checkpoints and 8 million in kind, as livestock *zakat* (ibid.). Based on interviews with former al-Shabaab tax officers, the UN estimated that one key checkpoint alone, between Mogadishu and Baidoa, collected up to USD 70,000 per day and some USD 10m in revenue for the whole year (UNSC 2018). At border crossings between Jubbaland and north-eastern Kenya, al-Shabaab also taxes trade in commodities such as charcoal, livestock, sugar, and other imported food staples (Rasmussen 2017).

Analyses of al-Shabaab taxation conclude that its system outperforms taxation by the FGS and FMSs, both in efficiency, oversight, accountability and enforcement, leading some taxpayers to prefer al-Shabaab taxation, which is more predictable, to the government's (Hiraal Institute 2018; UNSC 2018; Harper 2020; Ahmad et al. 2022). Unlike the latter, al-Shabaab taxation was highly centralised, standardised, predictable and accountable during the 2010s, with tax collectors issuing receipts and the system being responsive to taxpayers' and businesses' complaints about double taxation or fraudulent tax collectors (UNSC 2018). Nevertheless, the high degree of tax compliance with al-Shabaab is owed not only to efficiency and accountability, but to the use and threat of violence. At checkpoints, people have been killed and trucks burned, and in general, al-Shabaab's tactic of 'pay-up or pay the consequences,' combined with its effective intelligence to find and squeeze businesspeople who are trying to avoid taxation has been an important part of its fiscal strategy.[15] As Hiraal Institute concludes (2020: 6), payments have 'little to do with recognising the legitimacy of the group and more to do with the practicality of real life.'

Tax games and social contracts

Schumpeter (1991 [1918]) proposed that 'tax states'—administrations who finance their operations through routinised taxation of the population—more than other types of states will tend towards accountable, representative government as taxpayers will demand some reciprocity in their relationship, thus forging a social contract. In the new fiscal sociology literature this is seen as a causal relationship, meaning that tax bargaining and reciprocal tax relations foster liberal democracy as well as state capacity (Moore 2004; Bräutigam 2008; Martin et al. 2009). But when revenues primarily stem from taxation of international trade, such 'social contracts' remain abstract or piecemeal as they do not include the broader population that only indirectly contributes to the tax revenue by paying higher prices. Looking at microstates in West Africa, Togo and the Gambia in particular, which rely on ports and entrepôt economies for their tax revenue, Nugent (2010: 44) identified a 'permissive' social contract, which he described as a 'halfway house' between purely coercive and more productive social contracts in which the state waives (some of) its sovereign rights 'in return for securing a measure of *de facto* compliance'. Thus, permissive contracts are lenient on taxation in the remainder of the state's territory and leave taxation to local elites, borderland populations or others. While this applies to Somaliland and states with ports, the FGS depends mainly on foreign aid and has not achieved 'de facto compliance' in much of its territory. As Ahmad et al. (2022) have argued, al-Shabaab is the only authority in Somalia which has established something like a civil contract based on extensive and coercive taxation of the rural population.

But what about relations between traders and taxing authorities? Traders who are often itinerant engage in what are maybe best described as 'tax games' with multiple taxing authorities. 'Tax games' cover a spectrum of fiscal relations between coerced and consensual, including negotiation, bargaining, protest, evasion, and avoidance of heavily taxed trade routes and hubs. Drawing on observations from Somaliland, Puntland, Ethiopia and Kenya, this section discusses such examples. Without pretending that these are exhaustive, these examples illustrate trade-tax dynamics and the motives of Somali taxpayers who engage in commodity trading. These are still insufficiently understood and permeated by colonial and post-colonial stereotypes of tax avoidance and resistance, which were reinvigorated during the 1980s when policies by the Siad Barre regime produced a highly unregulated economy (see Chapter 1). As an academic observer from the US wrote in 1981: 'Even in colonial times, most Somalis lived outside the system set up by Italian and British regimes. To beat them in their own game—whether through illegal trade, illegal poaching, smuggling, or tax evasion—was as much a form of economic sport as anything else' (Miller 1981: 7).

Since 1991, multiple attempts to build public administrations through taxation have provoked a range of reactions in the Somali territories. In Somaliland, an embryonic fiscal relationship emerged between livestock exporters and local state authorities in the early 1990s as part of negotiations about the introduction of an 'export duty levy'. This allowed major livestock exporters to continue receiving hard currency outside of the state's financial institutions and regulations while the Somaliland state received its share of hard currency through the relatively high export duties levied on livestock. At the time, the Somaliland administration did not provide services for livestock exporters apart from the relative security that allowed them to bring their livestock to Berbera and further afield.

At a later stage, after years of Saudi bans on Somali livestock had made their impression, in 2009 the Somaliland government started reciprocating its taxation of livestock export with the introduction

159

of veterinary health posts in the markets of Burao, Hargeisa and Tog'wajaale, as well as the port of Berbera. At these posts, officials of the Ministry of Livestock have been undertaking animal health inspections and issued veterinary certificates. Together with Saudi quarantine stations in Berbera, these services have been essential for compliance with international standards and hence for the continued export of livestock out of Somaliland. In terms of politics of circulation, the provision of veterinary services was indispensable for the flow of livestock to Gulf states from which Somaliland authorities could capture hard currency and revenue at the gateway. Security and protection are often stated as main reasons for paying taxes. In south-central Somalia, as mentioned above, businesspeople 'exchange' taxes for protection by al-Shabaab, which provides more effective protection in their territories than state actors (Hiraal Institute 2018). As Musa observed, traders from Lasanod are willing to pay taxes to the district authorities along the Berbera-Lasanod trade corridor as these provide basic security of their goods (Musa 2021).

Reciprocity in the form of service delivery and infrastructure investments in exchange for taxes is difficult to achieve in areas where revenues of public administrations remain low. In most FMS, state budgets are primarily used for security and the salaries of public employees (Haas 2017). But even so, and despite the absence of a social contract deserving this name, some kind of reciprocity may materialise when officials are lax in their application of fiscal regulations and turn a blind eye to illicit trade activities to ensure the cooperation of taxpayers—an accommodation of private interests that Tendler (2002) calls the 'devil's deal'.

Nairobi is an example where public authorities do have resources to provide services, but Somali businesspeople in Eastleigh feel that they, despite paying their taxes, have been marginalised in this regard. To remedy this, they pay fees to the Eastleigh Business District Association (EBDA), partly to support the lobbying for government services and improved infrastructure, such as the pavement of main streets, and partly for the association to organise and provide services itself. As Varming observed in 2016, the EBDA managed to remove unregistered street hawkers, to mobilise more security and to provide private garbage collection. Such trust in and willingness to support local non-state actors in providing services has been confirmed by van den Boogaard and Santoro (2022b) who observed a much higher legitimacy of community committees and clan and religious leaders than local and central government in the Somali context.

In Puntland we find another example of tax games that involves negotiation with public authorities, in this case Garowe Municipality, which in 2014 rolled out a new 'parking tax'. At the time, there were forty-five registered gas stations operating within the city limits.[16] Fuel is a highly valuable commodity, the circulation of which has been key for Puntland authorities to regulate and capture revenues from. Fuel traders in Garowe felt that they were already being taxed heavily, paying a monthly sales tax to the Puntland Ministry of Finance and a biannual tax to Garowe municipality. The parking tax amounted to USD 10 monthly for every shop within the city limits that used the space in front of the shop for purposes other than parking. In practice, only fuel traders were required to pay because of the fuel pumps. Other shop owners simply removed their stalls or minor structures that had been occupying the space in question.

At an individual level, many fuel traders deployed various tactics to avoid paying the tax. Some argued with tax collectors and refused to pay. In reaction, municipal authorities would close their business and take the trader to the office or the police station. As Garowe traders who refused to pay the parking tax saw their business interrupted and their income threatened, 'usually they pay, rather than spend the night [in the police station]' as a municipal administrator explained.[17] Eventually, feeling targeted by the parking tax and other attempts to regulate and control the fuel trade in Garowe, the small scale fuel-traders organised and used their collective bargaining power to have the parking tax and other regulatory initiatives revoked. As one trader said: 'The fuel traders are so many. It will cause a social uprising, if they do this to us.'[18] Another trader explained how some of the wealthier and better-connected fuel traders had used their personal networks to put pressure on the municipal administration to give up the parking tax.[19]

Another kind of tax game involves traders' avoidance of taxation, highlighting how they engage in the politics of circulation as they try to reduce costs, in this case related to the taxation of circulating livestock. Historically, livestock was trekked from producer to market on the hoof, and trekkers were often able to choose remote border crossings, where no taxes were imposed. Nowadays, most livestock is trucked to the markets and must therefore follow roads with checkpoints and border posts. However, it is still possible to choose alternative routes, as in the case of livestock from south-central Somalia that is exported through Berbera or Bosaso ports.[20] Traders that bring livestock from south-central Somalia to the north choose between the two gateways, but also, if they choose Berbera, between two different routes to this port: One route follows the tarmac road through Puntland entering Somaliland via the contested town of Lasanod, while the other route passes through Ethiopia's Somali Regional State. Puntland levies customs duties of USD 3 per head of small ruminant at Burtinle, amounting to between USD 1050 and USD 1200 per twelve-ton truck, depending on the number of animals on board. In comparison, when crossing through Somali Regional State, a truck encounters four to five checkpoints, paying some USD 500 in total.

Due to the stark difference in tax expenditure along the two routes, the Somali Regional State route is preferred by most livestock traders and transporters. However, the route is only available to trucks carrying Ethiopian number plates. This has caused bottlenecks in vehicle registration on the Ethiopian side of the border. The Somali Regional State authorities have been trading number plates of damaged or out-of-service trucks at lower fees and have at times allowed unregistered Somaliland trucks to cross the border. This illustrates how many Somali livestock traders, despite their reluctance to pay taxes to Ethiopian authorities, prefer to pay lower rates to Ethiopian authorities rather than higher rates to Somali authorities in Puntland. Tax games are not limited to small and medium-sized businesses. Larger telecommunication companies and commodity importers, for example, are insufficiently taxed because they do not share their income revenues or

162

sales documents with the taxing authorities, and at times, they lobby for lower taxes or make philanthropic contributions during crisis, which they later use to negotiate taxes (Musa and Horst 2019) (see Chapter 3).

Taxing citizens: Subjectivity, identification, and representation

Implementing and improving tax collection is an important part of the quest to constitute and (re)create the idea of the state as the primary authority within a given territory (Migdal and Schlichte 2005). As the backbone of a powerful narrative of the self-reliant state, taxation constitutes a critical ideological and symbolic battleground of statehood (Varming 2019). When considering taxation in areas of limited statehood such as the Somali territories, it is important to recognise the link between political subjectivity and popular attitudes toward taxation and tax collectors. If the population does not identify with the state project, tax claims by state officials are likely to be unsuccessful or highly coercive (Campos 2016). Yet, it is important to note that taxation always contains an element of coercion. As Martin et al. (2009: 3) note, '[t]axation consists of the obligation to contribute money or goods to the state in exchange for nothing in particular,' an obligation that 'the state imposes on its citizens and, if necessary, enforces.' Unlike this state-centric definition, this chapter highlights how many other public authorities engage in taxation and that taxation—as a practice associated with statehood—can be a way of conveying and constituting authority over subjects in a given domain. However, as we discuss below, a strengthened identification with the taxing authority may lead to greater acceptance of certain levels of coercion.

The effects of taxation on state-society relations cannot be reduced to either a success or failure to implement specific taxation frameworks, nor to the tax revenue collected. Significant impacts of taxation lie in the contestation and negotiation that form multiple and often competing social contracts. The state is constituted through subjects' experiences and imaginations, and interactions related to taxation become 'key sites where social actors come to imagine and instantiate state sovereignty in both its regulatory and its territorial dimensions' (Chalfin 2001b: 202).

Campos (2016: 6), who studied taxation in Somaliland's capital Hargeisa, suggests that when citizens identify with the political project of the tax collecting authority, they come to view taxes as money owed out of genuine adherence and tax collectors as 'agents of the common collective project'. This contrasts with a situation where taxes are viewed as a primordial debt, and tax collectors are seen as 'authority of the sovereign state', collecting their debts by force if necessary. In Puntland, state authorities have long recognised the importance of taxation in the creation of a Puntland political identity among its citizens. In efforts to increase inland taxation revenues, an elaborate campaign in 2014 appealed to national awareness and a sense of responsibility among the population. With slogans such as 'The state is a tree that grows through the taxes of the citizens' and 'The real national is the one, who pays tax,' the Puntland administration demonstrates a vision of imagining taxation as a collective owing, based on a collective political project.

Although taxes in Puntland are often collected by force or the threat of it, fiscal revenues have been part of an emerging national identity, which increasingly manifests itself in everyday economic transactions. As a result, such political subjectivity is becoming relevant to the everyday lives of Puntland citizens. This is reflected in the fact that traders in Garowe often recognise that state and municipal authorities have the right to use coercion to secure tax compliance. However, traders often raise questions about the accountability and reciprocity of state taxation—in other words the type and quality of services they receive in return.

In Somaliland, livestock traders belonging to the main Isaaq clan family have often shown positive attitudes towards official taxation. The Isaaq have dominated the Somaliland's post-1991 state-building process (Bradbury 2008), and the political identification of livestock traders with the state project underpinned their willingness to pay taxes. In contrast, a very contested taxation relationship exists between Somali livestock traders and the Ethiopian (federal) government (Eid 2014; Tezera Tazebew and Asnake

Kefale 2021). This relation has been shaped by a history of predatory taxes imposed on Somali pastoralists by Ethiopian authorities.
In both Kenya and Ethiopia, the looting of Somali livestock was a
commonplace 'taxation' practice in the late nineteenth and early
twentieth centuries. These trajectories of predation and alienation
have shaped interactions between both states and their Somali
minorities, and today Isaaq traders see Ethiopian taxation as lacking
reciprocity, since they don't get anything in return for paying
taxes. A significant reason for the strained relationship between
Somali traders and Ethiopian tax authorities is that the bulk of livestock crossing the Ethiopian-Somaliland border originates from
Ethiopia's Somali Regional State. While Somali livestock producers, traders and officials see it as 'Somali', Ethiopian state officials
consider it 'Ethiopian', and they tax it as such. In return, Somalis
see this Ethiopian taxation as an expression of (post-)imperial
Ethiopian claims to Somali livestock assets.

In Eastleigh, the hub of Somali-dominated trade in Nairobi, the
relationship between the Kenyan state and its Somali minority has
similarly been fraught with historical enmity and predatory behaviour (Carrier 2017). In Eastleigh today, the Somali business community complains of state neglect in the form of depleted infrastructure and a lack of sanitation services. The continuous
complaints and conflict-filled environment of Eastleigh speak to the
fact that historical trajectories of authority and the exclusion or
inclusion of Somali populations into collective definitions of who
belongs to the nation are central to contemporary statehood
dynamics, including taxation.

A myriad of taxes are levied in Eastleigh, including regular state
taxation (as well as irregular non-state taxation) of registered businesses; formalised and routinised taxation of unregistered street
trade; as well as irregular taxation of unregistered traders. Taxation
in Eastleigh has given rise not only to conflicts between Kenyan
authorities and Somali traders but also between registered traders
and street hawkers. On the one hand, Somali shop and mall owners
have argued that the Nairobi City County should stop collecting
taxes from street hawkers, as street hawking is illegal and the
extensive street trade in Eastleigh hampers the business of the

'proper' taxpayers.[21] On the other hand, a representative of the Eastleigh Hawkers Association has stated: 'We are Kenyans, we have our rights. We don't want to sell on the street, but we want to be given a [piece of] land.'[22] Both Somali shop and mall owners and street hawkers of various backgrounds rhetorically used these categories of 'citizens' and 'taxpayers' to appeal to Kenyan authorities for rights and services. Thus, as Juul (2006: 830) pointed out, 'tax payment may serve to signal membership of a certain locality or social group ... just as non-compliance may justify exclusion not only from membership of social or spatial entities, but also from specific political representation'.

From these different claims and counterclaims in Eastleigh, we learn that while the formal-informal distinction in taxation practices is of limited use, there is a constant battle of (il)legitimisation surrounding taxation practices and disputes. In the process of making claims to rights and services, labels of insider/outsider identities—like taxpayer/non-taxpayer and citizen/non-citizen—will often be used to legitimise one group's claims against another's. In this way, taxation contributes to defining the role of the subjects in a state project and creates specific types of subjectivity (Juul 2006; Campos 2016).

Making (and unmaking) authority through taxation

Raising revenues is one of the cornerstones of the making and unmaking of public authority. Political subjectivity as discussed above is created through interactions between the population and figures of authority. Such interactions constitute both political subjectivity and relations of authority; these exist neither prior to nor independently of each other (Lund 2011). Rather, the governance of political subjects and resources produces (state) authority. Likewise, effective rights do not represent pre-existing natural rights, as the latter are political constructs and achievements as argued by Lund (2016). When a state or a state-like entity makes a claim to taxation, it is recognising the individuals included in the claim as within its jurisdiction. Conversely, these individuals recognise—even if only reluctantly—the authority of the state when they pay their taxes.

With the plurality of public authorities that compete for tax revenue from the circulation of goods in the Somali territories, the implications for state-formation dynamics are not causally straight-forward. On the one hand, irregular and non-state taxation are often seen to undermine state institutions and authority, and indeed the 'institutionalised informality' of tax exemptions at street-level and around powerful business elites in Somalia appear to have this effect (van den Boogaard and Isak forthcoming). On the other hand, some evidence suggests that irregular and non-state forms of taxation may, under certain conditions, reinforce state authority and strengthen state governance (Roitman 2005; Titeca and De Herdt 2011; van den Boogaard 2020). Van den Boogaard and Santoro (2022b) argue that the perception and legitimacy of sub-national governments in Somalia benefit from increased service delivery enabled by payments to non-state actors. Varming (2019) observed a similar effect in the case of the hybrid cyclone relief in Puntland, where a collaboration between state and non-state actors enabled fundraising and effective relief aid for victims in cyclone-affected areas. In both cases, non-state tax collection contributes to increased acceptance of—and compliance with—state taxation, as taxpayers associate or attribute the net effects of service provision to state actors.

This somewhat counterintuitive effect is not in play when armed groups compete with state actors for revenue and authority. Hoffmann et al. (2016: 1435) give the example of armed groups in the Democratic Republic of Congo creating authority through taxation. They argue, 'first, that taxation is at the core of armed groups' production of public authority and citizenship and, second, that taxation practices are strongly conditioned by institutionalised registers of authority and practices of order making', what Hansen and Stepputat (2001) call 'languages of stateness'. In Somalia, as discussed above, al-Shabaab collects taxes through highly routinised coercive practices, which include issuing receipts. Livestock traders who pay taxes to al-Shabaab do not necessarily find these taxes predatory in the sense of being exorbitant or unreasonable, and indeed consider them moderate compared to taxes imposed on the livestock trade by state authorities (Musa et al. 2021).

Drawing on state-like registers and bureaucratic procedures allows al-Shabaab to increase its authority, enabling the group to attract and regulate flows of goods through its territory. Furthermore, while the organisation uses the revenue to strengthen its military and administrative capacities, al-Shabaab's taxation also hampers the capacity of FGS and FMSs to extend taxation by pre-empting the will and ability of traders and of businesspeople to pay taxes to them. For example, in 2022, al-Shabaab and ISIS groups imposed parallel taxes on livestock exports through Bosaso, while Puntland also levied duties on livestock exports through that port. This triple taxation burdened livestock traders who shifted their trade to Berbera Port, further limiting Puntland's revenue base as a result of overlapping taxes imposed by competing state-builders. In the south, where both al-Shabaab and ISIS are effective in their taxation, these multiple taxations complicate the internationally supported attempt to build a Somali state.

Conclusion

Despite recent tax reforms, direct taxation remains extremely limited across the Somali territories, where public administrations and security forces continue to depend on foreign aid, revenue derived from taxing international trade or, in the case of Ethiopia and Kenya, fiscal transfers. Focusing on different forms of taxation, their dynamics and implications for state-society relations, this chapter has highlighted the limitations of state-centric approaches to fiscality in the Somali territories: state and sub-state taxation has limited legitimacy and is liable to tax bargaining and exemptions for large traders and businesses in particular; security forces engage in taxation without official authorisation; local governments, which sometimes are not even officially recognised, levy taxes at markets and checkpoints with no legal foundation and varying degrees of legitimacy; and business and non-state actors charge fees and provide public services, which in some cases contribute to the legitimacy of state- or sub-state authorities, contrary to the perception that such 'informal' taxation undermines their position. This is certainly not the case with al-Shabaab, which competes with state administrations over revenues and population control, both out-performing and pre-empting the fiscal efforts of the latter.

While tax revenue helps build the administrative and security capacities of prospective state(s) in the Somali territories, the ability of states to forge a social contract between themselves and communities is more speculative when taxes are primarily indirect, extracted from commodity flows. With few exceptions, traders in Somali East Africa perceive little reciprocity for their payments in terms of public services in markets or infrastructure development. But the provision of basic security in Somaliland, and protection—or at least avoidance of harassment—results in traders being willing to pay taxes, even in the case of al-Shabaab's coercive taxation. Beyond the simple question of tax compliance or non-compliance, we have argued that political subjectivity and everyday pragmatism are important factors to take into consideration. 'Tax games' illustrate the spectrum of existing relations between traders and taxing authorities, ranging from tax bargaining and negotiation to avoidance of heavily taxed routes. But these tax games are socially skewed. Local tax officers have discretionary powers, meaning fees and taxes are negotiable even for smaller trade operators, while big traders and businesses with political connections are much more successful in obtaining tax exemptions. Whereas a 'permissive' social contract (Nugent 2010) governs relations between big business and the state(s), the everyday taxation of stalls, shops, brokers, transporters and market vendors reaches a much larger segment of the population, which may reinforce the authority of public administrations. But, then again, many traders are subjected to multiple, competing taxing authorities as in Mogadishu or the contested areas of eastern Somaliland.

Capturing trade-based revenues is a main objective of Somali administrations in the regional politics of circulation, as they lack other revenue bases. These politics evolve around the control of trade corridors, ports and chokepoints and the competition over the routing of commodities, where lowering taxes is one strategy used by FGS, FMSs and Somaliland to lure commodities through 'their' ports (van den Boogaard and Isak forthcoming). This fiscal competition is rendered possible by the absence of centralised custom duties and a lack of political agreement over the distribution of revenue between FGS and the FMSs. But also the improvement of services, such as veterinary control in livestock export, port and road infrastructure, as well as smooth customs procedures, are tactics to increase the volume of commodity flows and associated tax revenues.[23] As argued in Chapter 1, taxing authorities must balance the revenue harvested from taxation with the friction that levying fees induces to commodity trading. Traders make use of their elbow room in the politics of circulation. If taxation becomes too onerous and time consuming, they opt for alternative routes to the extent that the dilapidated road infrastructure allows. Where no alternative route exists, the imperative of keeping up the circulation of goods forces traders to accept unlawful taxes by security forces and build working relations with them. Finally, our observations support Cantens and Raballand's (2021) suggestion that it would be better for stability to boost revenues from customs in conflict-torn areas instead of focusing on increasing conventional direct taxes. There is considerable potential for increasing fiscal revenues across the Somali territories by upgrading customs procedures and technologies in return for better services. However, this is not a technocratic exercise, but requires sustained political negotiations between competing administrations, including the FGS and FMSs.

8

TILLY IN THE TROPICS

TRADE AND SOMALI STATE-MAKING

Tobias Hagmann and *Finn Stepputat*

Introduction

Since the collapse of the Somali central state, commentators have
tended to consider Somali statehood as essentially dysfunctional or,
as *The Economist* phrased it, the 'most-failed state'.[1] But in reality,
and, as we will demonstrate in this chapter, political dynamics in
the Somali territories after 1991 very much conform with central
tenets of classic state formation theory. This becomes evident
when considering the politics of circulation that are at the centre
of our 'trade makes states' arguments spelled out in Chapter 1. In
this concluding chapter, we revisit Charles Tilly's (1985, 1992)
work to refine and expand our 'trade makes states' arguments. We
do so by identifying variegated post-1991 Somali state-building
trajectories and the relative mix of coercion and capital in these
processes, by drawing attention to the fiscal basis of aspiring states

and their implications for state formation, by highlighting how divergent configurations between political rulers and the mercantile class have shaped state making and by discussing the roles of revenue competition and international standards.

Tilly's dictum that 'war makes states' has gained almost folkloric status in Comparative Politics and International Relations (Leander 2004). Not least in the Africanist literature—including in academic debates on Somali state building (Balthasar 2013, 2017)—his observation that interstate warfare historically has contributed to creating fewer, but viable, European states has gained the attention of Africanists studying armed conflict and state formation (for example, Herbst 2000; Niemann 2007). But, as critics have argued, globalisation has undermined Tilly's historical argument, demonstrating that the key processes of war and state making he underscores not only fail to make states but rather may lead to the collapse of states (Sørensen 2001; Leander 2004; Taylor and Botea 2008).

We will not rehash this debate here, but instead pursue a different line of argumentation by Tilly, which has gained much less attention: the role of merchants and traders vis-à-vis an emerging state as well as the revenues that aspiring state-builders syphon off from commodity flows. Our contribution to Tilly and state-formation debates is thus, metaphorically speaking, to put Tilly 'in motion'. Building on Tilly's conceptual take on trade and the mercantile class, we explore some of the mechanisms of the politics of circulation by focusing on how nascent and aspiring state administrations in the Somali territories have sought to balance the capture and the facilitation of commodity flows.

In the following four sections, we first review different Somali state-formation trajectories with reference to Tilly's classic statebuilding activities: war-making, state making, protection and extraction. In the second section, we explore how one of the key fiscal strategies that Tilly identified in historical state-formation processes—'payments on flows'—has provided the predominant material basis of state projects in the Somali territories post-1991. The third section focuses on the relationship between the mercantile class—the Somali traders and merchants who pay for the many trade-derived taxes—the political rulers and aspiring state-builders, and the specialists in violence who provide protection (or fail to do so). The final section puts Tilly 'into motion' by pointing to how the politics of circulation impact on state-formation processes in Somali East Africa.

Coercion and capital: Somali state-building trajectories

Markedly different state-building trajectories have materialised across the Somali territories since 1991. The various sub-national and national state entities that have been established over the past three decades have differed for a long time, not only in terms of their legal and formal characteristics, but also in terms of their state capacity and ability to provide services (see UNDP 2001; Hagmann and Hoehne 2009). In other words, post-1991 Somali state-formation dynamics have varied considerably in regard to both their 'judicial' and 'empirical' stately features (Jackson and Rosberg 1982). Somali mini-states, proto states and more durable state entities—including the self-declared Republic of Somaliland and the Federal Member States that are part of the Somali Federal Republic with the capital Mogadishu—owe their existence to dissimilar state-building processes. This becomes evident when assessing the different politico-administrative bodies that sprang up after state collapse in 1991, in light of Tilly's (1985) four classic state-building activities: war-making, state making, protection and extraction.

As Tilly (1992) underscored, both 'capital' and 'coercion' have fashioned historical state formation in Europe. States engaged in warfare to get rid of external competitors ('war-making') as well as internal competitors ('state making'). For this purpose, they had to protect their clients and extract pecuniary and material means— through taxation or extortion—to fund state making activities. Tilly does not go into detail about 'traders' or 'mercantile groups' in his state-formation theory centred on the four above-mentioned state-building activities. But merchants and traders figure prominently in his *Coercion, Capital, and European States, AD 990–1992* (1992). As the previous chapters have demonstrated, in the Somali territories, merchants and traders—the Somali business class—have been main providers of capital to fund nascent administrations' state making endeavours. They have done so, and continue doing so, either directly through loans—as in the early stage of state building in Somaliland—or indirectly by paying indirect taxes, in particular taxes and fees derived from lucrative commodity trading. In return, they have benefited from state protection and preferential fiscal regimes, as has been the case in Somaliland (Phillips 2020; Elder 2021).

Tilly identifies three recurrent state-building trajectories, namely 'coercion-intensive', 'capital intensive', as well as a mixed form, 'capitalised coercion'. In the case of 'coercion-intensive' state building, political rulers appropriate resources from populations to finance war and state building. This incentivises them to build up a state bureaucracy capable of forced resource mobilisation (1992: 30). In the 'capital-intensive' variant of state formation, 'rulers relied on compacts with capitalists—whose interests they served with care—to rent or purchase military force, and thereby warred without building vast permanent state structures' (ibid.: 30). Tilly has a broad definition of 'capital' and 'capitalists'. They encompass traders, merchants, financiers—nearly everyone who is engaged in what he calls 'exploitation' (ibid.: 17). He reminds us that 'the relative presence or absence of commercial cities' within a state territory fashions the conditions under which political rulers can organise and finance war and security (ibid.: 86).

In Tilly's state-formation theory, the relation between 'extraction' and 'protection' is of particular significance. It prefigures debates in fiscal sociology that posit a contractual relationship between those who tax and those who are being taxed. Fiscality defines the boundaries and obligations of a political community and—in the case of collective bargaining—constitutes a social contract (Schumpeter 1991 [1918]; Moore 2004; Martin et al. 2009). In the case of 'capital-intensive' state building where political rulers—for example, a nascent Somali administration—rely on 'political finance' (de Waal 2015) to engage in basic state- and war-making, capitalists are in a strong negotiation position. They can choose to withhold funding from ruling elites if the latter fail or refuse to protect their commercial activities—namely the circulation of goods—or if they engage in too much extraction. Citing the economic historian Frederic C. Lane, Tilly identifies a crucial relation between 'protection', which citizens or merchants are afforded by the state, on the one hand, and on the other hand the payment of what he calls 'tribute', that is, the price citizens and merchants pay in taxes or other payments. Both past and present states thus had and have an interest to produce a 'protection rent' for their merchants and capitalists, protecting them against 'outside competitors' (Tilly 1985: 175).

Thirty years after state collapse in Somalia, Tilly's four basic state making activities prove analytically fruitful. A cursory review of war-making, state making, protection and extraction across subnational Somali political entities demonstrates a variety of both failed and successful state-formation dynamics after 1991 (see Table 8.1). While these processes are ongoing, and while few rigorous comparative studies or standardised data on these Somali state and state-like entities exist, available studies on Somaliland (Bradbury 2008; Hoehne 2009; Walls 2009; Eubank 2012; Renders 2012; Phillips 2020), Puntland (Reno 2003; ICG 2009; PDRC and Interpeace 2008, 2015; Albrecht 2018), the Federal Government of Somalia (Menkhaus 2014, 2018; Marchal and Yusuf 2017; Williams 2018; Majid et al. 2021; Isak and Wasuge 2021; Elder 2022), Jubbaland (ICG 2013; Saferworld 2016; Majid and Abdirahman 2021) and al-Shabaab[2] (Marchal 2011; Hansen 2013; ICG 2014; Ingiriis 2018; Ahmad et al. 2022) can be summarised as follows when using Tilly's taxonomy.[3]

In Somaliland, state building followed a 'capitalised coercion' pathway under President Mohamed Ibrahim Egal in the 1990s, which led to the re-establishment of commodity trading in the Berbera corridor, including Hargeisa Airport (Helling 2010; Balthasar 2013). It gradually evolved into a 'capital intensive' process as major trading and telecommunication companies gained a dominant position vis-à-vis the Somaliland administration. Issaq traders in control of imports with extensive networks to Saudi Arabia, Dubai and the Somaliland and Djiboutian gov-

Table 8.1: State-building trajectories of 'Somali states' according to Tilly

	War-making	State making	Protection	Extraction
Somaliland (1991–2021)	Civil war between Somali National Movement (SNM) and Somalia up to declaration of independence (1983–91). Territorial dispute with neighbouring Puntland (2007–18).	Elimination of internal competitors by Somaliland state following internal civil war (1992–94).	Basic protection established by Somaliland forces after 1994, with exception of Sool and Sanaag regions contested by Puntland.	Revenue extraction centred on Berbera Port and corridor, main trade routes and urban centres.
Puntland (1998–2021)	Territorial disputes with neighbouring Somaliland (2007–2018) and Galmudug (2015 [1991]–2017).	Mixed track record, including defeat of al Ittihad al-Islamiya in 1992 by SSDF, armed intra-elite conflict in 2001 and conflict with al-Shabaab and other Islamic militants since end of 2000s.	Limited protection provided by Puntland security forces. Ongoing insecurity from al-Shabaab, piracy and criminal groups.	Revenue extraction centred on Bosaso Port and corridor and main urban centres.

FGS (south-central Somalia) (2014–21)	Not applicable,[4] as federal government came into existence through internationally mediated and supported processes.	Internationalised conflict pitting Somali state forces and AMISOM against al-Shabaab. Conflicts with Federal Member States forces and various armed groups and clan militia.	Very limited protection by Somali security forces, AMISOM and private security companies focusing on key sites and towns.	Revenue extraction in government-controlled areas, namely Mogadishu Port, airport and checkpoints manned by pro-government forces.
Jubbaland (2013–21)	Not applicable.	Defeat of al-Shabaab by alliance of local militia and AMISOM in Kismayo in 2012. Ongoing conflict with al-Shabaab and FGS (2020).	Very limited protection by Jubbaland forces.	Revenue extraction in government-controlled areas, namely Kismayo Port and town.

Al-Shabaab (*ca. 2005–21*)	Conflict with AMISOM, Ethiopian, Kenyan, US and other international forces in Somalia and the region. With FGS/SNA, Puntland, other Federal Member States and AMISOM troops and allies.	Conflict with Somali security forces, Federal Member States, various clan militia and Islamic Sate.	Direct protection in al-Shabaab-controlled territory across south-central Somalia, indirect protection in main towns and marketplaces across the region.	Extensive resource extraction based on direct and remote governance of commodities and people in rural and urban areas in all Federal Member States.

ernments eventually replaced the traditional bourgeoisie—whose wealth was premised on livestock exports—as the dominant mercantile class in the breakaway republic. This led to what Elder (2021: 1752) describes as an 'oligopolistic state' in Somaliland, in which major companies 'colluded ... to limit competition and restrict the authority of the state'.[5] At the same time, Somaliland's multi-party democracy, established in 2002, allowed political elites to partly absorb popular discontent through elections and changes of governments.

State building in Puntland has veered between 'coercion' and 'capitalised coercion' over the years. Abdullahi Yusuf's leftist Somali Salvation Democratic Front (SSDF) struggled to win over local capitalists in the 1990s, and 'leader firms from the traditional business community and the bureaucratic bourgeoisie associated with the [Puntland] state' often ended up on opposite sides (Elder 2022: 412). State expansion saw the emergence of a new class of business elites made up of former civil servants and military officials, as well as traders from the southern parts of Puntland who encroached on the economic power previously held by the Majerteen bourgeoisie of the coastal areas (Hoffman et al. 2017). Contrary to Somaliland, Puntland often operated as a contracting state, outsourcing essential state tasks such as security provision to non-state actors (Reno 2003). As a result, state building in Puntland since 1998 has been much less effective when compared to Somaliland with regard to war-making, state making, protection and extraction. Internal conflict, domestic competitors like al-Shabaab and political tensions with the Federal Government of Somalia (FGS), of which Puntland is a Federal Member State, slowed and partly reversed some of Puntland's initial state-building gains.

The FGS and the various transitional governments preceding it have mostly relied on a 'capital intensive' strategy to finance state making, which here refers to its fight against al-Shabaab and other armed domestic competitors, with the local merchant class from the Hawiye clan family financing al-Shabaab's precursor, the Islamic Courts Union (ICU) (Ahmad 2014; Elder 2022).[6] Since 2007, international donors—including the European Union and the United Nations—have footed the bill for those AMISOM countries which have contributed troops—Burundi, Djibouti, Ethiopia, Kenya and Ethiopia—as well as the training of federal security forces (Williams 2017). If state building by the federal government has been coercive, it has largely relied on 'extraversion'. External finance and support has funded its internal 'state making', including the contested federalisation of the country and attempts to 'liberate' territories held by al-Shabaab (Hagmann 2016). In doing so, successive FGS leaders have reactivated an aid-dependent mode of state survival that characterised the Siyad Barre regime during the time between the Ogaden War of 1977–78 and the state's disintegration in 1991 (Lewis 2002 [1965]). Concomitantly, successive federal presidents have had to contend with an internationally funded humanitarian and logistics economy, whose rents based on logistics contracts have permeated Somali elite politics, destabilised political settlements and undermined political rulers' ability to generate revenue (Elder 2022).

If historic European state formation was a result of the interaction of 'war-making, extraction and capital accumulation' (Tilly 1985: 172), in the case of Somali federal state institutions—as with other post-colonial states—this interaction has been heavily internationalised. In contrast, Somaliland and Puntland were able to mobilise domestic capital from traders and merchants in their foundational state building phase. Resource mobilisation centred around the economic hubs of Hargeisa and Garowe and the inter-regional trade corridors of Berbera and Bosaso respectively, which allowed Somaliland and Puntland to fund 'state making' (that is, eliminate their internal competitors). The FGS, on the contrary, has struggled to emancipate itself from extraverted 'capital-intensive' state building reliant on foreign sources as both Mogadishu and its port have been fought over for decades. Only recently has the federal government managed to increase its fiscal revenues based on the extraction of domestic sources (Raballand and Knebelmann 2021).

Jubbaland evolved from a 'coercion intensive' to a 'capitalised coercion' type of state building, drawing on strong transnational business networks among Ogaadeen clan family members based in

Kenya and Ethiopia. The Jubbaland administration came into existence after an alliance of former Islamists, local clan militia and internationally sponsored Kenyan, Ethiopian and AMISOM troops defeated al-Shabaab in 2012. Jubbaland President and strongman Ahmed Madobe established a Federal Member State whose economy revolves around Kismayo Port—the main seaport connecting southern Somalia with north-eastern Kenya, and a main inlet and outlet for commodity trading—but with little remit or legitimacy beyond the port.

Al-Shabaab further illustrates the stark diversity of post-1991 state-building trajectories in Somalia. The Islamic militant group and al-Qaeda affiliate implemented the most coercive state making strategy of all the post-1991 Somali state-builders. Its operations have been predominantly locally funded through the systematic extortion of taxes, fees and contributions, which al-Shabaab has imposed on traders, businesses and local populations. Coercive taxation and a broad network of informers and sympathisers have allowed the group to survive militarily, to sustain operations against government forces and their international backers and to carry out terrorist attacks, both in Somalia and the wider region. Over the years, the Islamic insurgents built up their capacity to extract resources both for war-making and state making, providing protection and local justice—particularly by adjudicating land disputes—along the way (Ahmad et al. 2022). This has made al-Shabaab a 'shadow government' (Bandula-Irwin et al. 2022) and an efficient state-builder when applying Tilly's criteria, even though the group lacks a clearly defined territory or international recognition.

Payments on flows: The material basis of Somali states

As discussed in Chapter 7, the taxation of commodity flows, including livestock by state and other authorities, has constituted the main revenue extraction strategy in the Somali territories. Tilly's original taxonomy on the fiscal strategies employed by historical European governments—his concept of 'payments on flows' in particular—perfectly captures these taxes sustaining the politics of circulation in Somali East Africa. Five basic fiscal strategies were used by European states to extract resources for war making, state making and protection, namely 'tributes, rents, payments on flows, payments on stocks, and income taxes' (Tilly 1992: 87). Their routinisation over time was intricately interwoven with the need to fund wars or pay debts accumulated during wartime. Tributes consisted of 'arbitrary payments levied on individuals, groups, or localities' and included head taxes. Rents were 'direct payments for lands, goods, and services', which the state imposed on particular users. Payments on flows covered 'excise, customs, tolls, transaction charges, and other collections on transfers or movements', and payments on stock included both land and property taxes, while income taxes were levied on 'current revenues, especially salaries and other monetary revenues' (ibid.).

The creation of such payments on flows is a main motivation for Somali state and non-state actors to engage in the governance of internationalised, cross-border commodity trading. Seeking to extract resources for state building, district, regional or 'national' governments—here meaning both Somalia and Somaliland—have all pursued fiscal strategies targeting 'payments on flows' as described by Tilly.[7] The focus on taxing commodity flows rather than land or agricultural production reflects economic and historical legacies of mobile pastoralism, contested post-colonial Somali statehood and the lucrativeness of trading. Because many of these indirect taxes are either levied without a legal framework or remain unrecorded, their significance for state formation in the Somali territories after 1991 has been overlooked (Musa et al. 2021).

In principle, governments collect two main types of trade-derived taxes: tariffs on imports and exports as well as sales taxes when livestock or commodities are sold in markets. As Chapter 7 highlights, Somali administrations have levied a broad range of additional taxes and fees, including 'transit fees' for goods passing through main trade routes or crossing administrative boundaries and checkpoints. Tax collection takes place both formally and informally, meaning that state officials tax goods both in line with official and unofficial and unwritten rules, a practice that had existed even before Somali state collapse. Federal Somalia's provisional 2012 constitution recognises pre-existing tax and customs laws. This explains why outdated tax rates, valuation methods and tax categories partly continue to be applied.[8] In principle, Federal Member States have the right to formulate their own tax rates at main seaports while local governments collect municipal taxes (Raballand and Knebelmann 2021: 5).

Multiple taxes and fees of various degrees of legitimacy and legality are routinely solicited from commodity traders and merchants who buy, sell or transport goods. Many payments on flows collected along trade and transport routes lack a clearly defined legal basis, are partly arbitrary and are often applied inconsistently. But the way in which goods are taxed, the consistency—or lack thereof—of fees levied as well as the services that taxpayers obtain in return for their payments partly reflect the varying bureaucratic and fiscal capacities among taxing authorities.

From an evolutionary viewpoint, Schouten (2022) points out, 'payments on flows' is the most pragmatic and historically prevalent form of taxation, as it requires the least effort. More elaborate revenue extraction requires greater state capacity and legibility of populations and assets such as censuses, land cadastres and tax registries. Hence, to return to Tilly's vocabulary, 'payments on stocks' and 'income taxes' are the logical next steps for state administrations seeking to develop their extractive capacities. A first and most basic form of taxation occurs when truck drivers are stopped at a checkpoint, where they have to negotiate a fee to continue their journey (see, for example, Abdi 2021; Rasmussen 2017).[9] Interactions between drivers and traders on the one hand, and officials and militia posted at checkpoints on the other hand, remain essentially unregulated. They are rarely standardised, inviting both parties to bargain over tax duties in a personalised manner.[10] Various considerations—ranging from the value of the goods transported to the family ties of the trader, among other factors—influence this bargaining process.

A more consistent, but still crude, way of generating payments on flows is the application of a uniform fee to a given trade volume.

This is the second type of trade taxation practised across the Somali territories. For example, Puntland's Ministry of Finance applies a standardised sales tax per truck. Local checkpoint fees, which have to be paid for 'opening the rope' (i.e., letting trucks pass), also charge per vehicle. This type of transit fee does not take into account the actual value of commodities transported. But, when applied consistently, it at least has the advantage of predictability for traders (Musa 2021). A third type of payments on flows reflects goods' actual or estimated value: taxation *ad valorem*. This universal mode of taxing draws on customs valuation or value books, assigning a specific monetary value for both imports and exports. Somaliland, Puntland and the Federal Government of Somalia all make use of customs valuation books, with Somaliland having the longest track record of implementing and revising its customs tariffs.[11] To be effective, customs valuation books must be periodically updated to reflect price fluctuations and the entrance of new commodities on the market.

Finally, more complex customs and taxation regimes make use of differentiated tariffs and fees to strike a balance between the protection of local markets, state needs to extract revenue and the facilitation of international commodity flows. An example is the fiscal policy deployed by Somaliland in its eastern borderlands next to Puntland. Here, Somaliland officials implement a reduced tax rate for certain goods in order to appease borderland communities whose loyalty is divided between Somaliland and Puntland. At the same time, they ensure that valuable imported goods—namely electronics—entering Somaliland from Bosaso Port do not compete with those entering the self-declared republic from its main Berbera Port (ibid.).

While some Somali sub-national entities, including al-Shabaab, levy property and income taxes—particularly in urban centres—these taxes are far from systematic and remain of secondary financial importance when compared to taxes on commodity flows. For example, in Hargeisa, tax collectors determine business taxes based on estimates of retailers' and shop owners' earnings (Campos 2016). Income taxes are levied on government salaries and aid agency employees, which in the case of the FGS have often been paid, directly or indirectly, by foreign donors. Al-Shabaab's enforced collection of *zakat* taxes—which it collects from various groups, including government officials, traders, livestock producers and businesspeople—partly corresponds to an income tax (Hiraal Institute 2018). But *zakat* collections also bear similarity with what Tilly (1992: 87) describes as 'tributes'. In Somaliland, Puntland and the FGS, public financial management reforms have sought to improve financial planning, management, and transparency. Increasing fiscal revenues is a key component of these reforms, and the annual budgets of these political entities have increased over the years (Raballand and Knebelmann 2021). Still, in spite of attempts to formalise and professionalise Somali states' fiscal revenues, in many places taxation remains inconsistent and is the subject of both suspicion and negotiation (see Varming 2017). Although fiscal practices across the Somali territories are complex and vary, overall Somali administrations remain heavily dependent on 'payments on flows'. This particular type of revenue generation has implications for state building, a theme we will return to in the conclusion.

Protection for revenue: Mercantile class and political rulers

What then is the role of those who pay for the many trade-derived taxes to various Somali authorities? Traders, and the business sector more broadly, have occupied an important if ambivalent position with regards to state-(re-)making across the Somali territories. While they bore the brunt of extraction from aspiring state-builders, they have been far from passive bystanders in the establishment and, sometimes, erosion of state authority. The crucial role of the Somali post-civil war business class was noted early on by Marchal (1996). Somalia's war economy of the early 1990s allowed some merchants to engage in primitive accumulation. Yet, as a general rule, insecurity and lawlessness have not been conducive to business. Mubarak (1997: 2036) stressed that the economic boom after state collapse hinged on local communities' success in 'bringing law and order and external security to their locale' while 'economic activity remains suppressed' in situations of violence.

Hansen's (2007) research on Mogadishu-based companies highlighted how many businesspeople had lost their assets and property
during the peak of the civil war.

While there is agreement that insecurity and lawlessness hamper
business while security—whether provided by state or non-state
actors—enables it, the degree to which the Somali business community has been willing to finance, support and comply with state
authority has been much debated (Hagmann and Stepputat 2016).
Little (2003: 168) concluded that for many communities 'it does
not make a great deal of difference ... what kind of political configuration ... exists at the top ... as long as government does not
overly constrain local livelihoods ... and trading systems'. In the
early 2000s, the concomitance of statelessness and flourishing commodity trading raised the question of whether and to what degree
the increasingly powerful business class had an interest in the resur-
rection of a central Somali state. Menkhaus (2003: 414) argued
that protracted state collapse in southern and central Somalia was
also the consequence of 'certain ... economic interest groups' who
feared that a functioning state would diminish their profits.

Returning to Tilly and related state-formation theories allows
us to shed light on this puzzle, namely the relation between merchants and political rulers. Both Tilly (1992) and neo-institutional
economists like Douglass North (1981; 1990) emphasise the causal
relation between protection and revenue or, in the Somali case,
between protection and payments on (trade) flows. Spruyt (2011:
572) summarises Tilly's observation on this matter thus: '[c]entral
authority provided protection in exchange for revenue'. This
causal mechanism was historically positioned at the intersection of
a triangular power relation between kings, feudal groups and their
armed forces, and the mercantile class. In post-1991 Somali East
Africa, this triangular power relation encompasses political rulers
(leaders of various Somali state administrations), warlords and clan
militias (and other specialists in violence including government
security forces) and traders and major business owners.
Importantly, as Spruyt (ibid.: 573) points out, traders and merchants were indifferent to who provided protection to them, as
long as it was standardised across a given territory.[12]

This 'protection for revenue' dynamic has been at the core of evolving relations between the Somali private sector including major business conglomerates on the one hand, and (sub-)national governments and state-builders on the other hand. Once the Somali state and its security forces disintegrated in 1991, Somali mercantile groups—to use Spruyt's terminology—could no longer rely on the state for protection. During civil strife and inter-clan violence in the 1990s, Somali warlords and their clan-affiliated militias were the only actors who could provide basic security in return for payment, often operating like an extortion racket. As the following two examples illustrate, different and shifting relations have emerged across the Somali territories between, to put it simply, the Somali mercantile class and political rulers or governments. They have produced different configurations of the 'protection for revenue' dynamic across time and space.

Seeking standardised protection in Mogadishu

In Mogadishu and the adjacent Lower Shabelle region, a crucial shift in interactions between mercantile class and political rulers occurred when the capital's business class—which had been relying on warlord protection rackets since state collapse—began paying local *shari'a* courts for protection in the mid-2000s. The *shari'a* courts provided more reliable and standardised protection in local markets such as Bakara Market. They eventually scaled up into the Islamic Courts Union (ICU) and were able to pacify Mogadishu for the first time after 15 years of warlord rule and chronic lawlessness (Barnes and Harun Hassan 2007). The second half of the 1990s had been a 'period of re-establishment of businesses, and a change of structure of ... businesses' in Mogadishu (Hansen 2007: 52), even though the latter continued to rely on powerful local clan groups for protection.

Over time, the Somali business class—in particular big traders—trumped the politico-military dominance of the warlords and their foot soldiers. As the influence and geographical reach of armed clan factions shrank, businesspeople and larger companies increased their own security personnel between the middle and end of the 1990s. This eventually allowed them to ward off demands for protection payments (ibid.: 46–9). Menkhaus (2003: 417) points to 1999 as the year when 'leading Mogadishu businessmen broke with the warlords and refused to pay "taxes" at militia roadblocks', effectively ending their protection for revenue arrangement. Capitalising on the fact that many warlords were running out of cash, these businessmen 'bought the militiamen away from the warlords, and sub-contracted out management of the militia to sharia courts' (ibid.: 417). This move represented a qualitative change in Somalia's urban post-war protection economy, illustrating the growing emancipation of the business class from the warlords and their clan factions and, more broadly, their newly found political power (ibid.: 415). Many of these Mogadishu-based businessmen later became prominent backers and beneficiaries of the Transitional National Government (TNG) that emerged from the Djibouti (or Arta) peace process in 2000 (Webersik 2006) and which preceded the federal government and constitution of 2012.

Ahmad (2014) describes economic rather than religious or ideological motifs as the main reason why Mogadishu's business elite financed the *shari'a* courts and, later, the ICU. Islamic security providers were more advantageous for businesspeople who no longer had to rely on 'multiple warlord protection rackets' (ibid 95) or maintain their own permanent security detail. The *shari'a* courts had started out in the early 1990s as clan lineage jurisdictions at neighbourhood level before scaling up to transcend spatial and clan boundaries. They offered 'reputational benefits and social capital' (ibid.: 96) and provided a legal-religious normative order. But, most importantly, Islamic courts produced security across clan divides and territories. This made them a cheaper alternative to the fragmented clan-based protection of the warlords. This said, as Chapter 2 highlights, businesspeople's affinity to and relation with Islam cannot be reduced to economic interests only. Somali traders have long embraced Islam as a basis for social capital and trust, facilitating business transactions across clan and national boundaries (Musa 2019; see also Chapter 2).

While insecurity returned to Mogadishu following the Ethiopian military intervention in mid-2006 and fighting between al-Shabaab and the Somali government and AMISOM ensued, the shift in 'protection for revenue' from warlords to Islamic courts had long-standing state effects. It gave the Somali business class increased political autonomy and led to the creation of armed groups that cut across clan lineages. Most importantly it shaped al-Shabaab, which has mounted an effective protection racket in its areas of operation and beyond, taxing the mercantile class, but also government officials, and in exchange providing receipts that guarantee basic security (see Chapter 7). In so doing, al-Shabaab has proven an effective state-builder who managed to standardise, if not necessarily centralise, protection drawing on a mix of coercion and Islamic narratives.

Somaliland: Funding the state, but resisting its regulations

Somaliland reveals a different modality of the protection for revenue dynamic that expediates state formation. As noted in several chapters, the business community assumed an instrumental role in backing the creation and building of the Somaliland state (Musa and Horst 2019; Phillips 2020). Businessmen belonging to the Issaq clan family already played 'a leading role' during the formation of the rebel Somali National Movement (SNM) in the 1980s, which eventually defeated Somali government forces (Marchal 1996: 28). The peace and reconciliation conferences of the early 1990s that laid the political groundwork for the young Somaliland Republic benefited from financial contributions by the business community, the diaspora and the local population (Bradbury 2008: 70). Issaq traders based in Djibouti were instrumental in providing a major loan to President Egal's administration during a critical moment of Somaliland's contested state formation in the mid-1990s (Balthasar 2013: 223–4; Musa and Horst 2019; Elder 2021). Later, business elites 'covered budgetary shortfalls for both the Egal and Silanyo administrations', including a 3.5 million USD loan accorded to the Somaliland government between 2010 and 2012 (Phillips 2013: 64).

The mercantile class, to use Spruyt's (2011) terminology, also assumed a crucial role in funding Somaliland's increasingly costly electoral campaigns (Verjee et al. 2015). To this day, major business companies in Somaliland—in particular telecom and financial firms—enjoy considerable leverage over the political elite (Elder 2021; Hoffman et al. 2017). For example, in 2010, the company Telesom was able to block a proposed government regulation that sought to interconnect Telesom with its main competitor, Somtel (Musa and Horst 2019). Telesom knew that, if implemented, interconnection would increase competition in the telecommunication sector and reduce its profits.[13] Likewise, Dahabshiil, the *hawala* company, refused to open investment accounts for its customers so it could avoid paying depositors interest charges even though thousands of clients deposited their funds in its mobile money wallets (see Chapter 3).

Somaliland's major companies have diversified their business interests to reduce both transaction costs and competition. Hence, Dahabshiil is heavily invested in finance, telecommunication, energy, real estate, as well as imports and exports. Telesom is active in telecommunication, energy and finance. Omar and Deero companies are dominant both in import and export trading and in real estate. These powerful firms have enjoyed an oligopolistic position in the Somaliland economy thanks to de facto protectionist policies by the Somaliland government (Musa 2019; Musa and Horst 2019). They own warehouses, transport means and financial services, which increases their independence from state regulation. In return, powerful members of the Somaliland mercantile class—for example, members of the Habar Awal lineages—have helped stabilise Somaliland politically by resolving disputes and bankrolling the state.

These two vignettes demonstrate how Somali mercantile groups have sought to organise protection for revenue in their favour. In Mogadishu's case, the business class funded Islamic courts as it sought more reliable protection of its economic assets and investments. In Somaliland, the oligopolistic business elite bankrolled the government from early on, allowing it to eliminate local competitors—what Tilly refers to as 'state making'—thus achieving the basic security required to conduct business. Somaliland's dependence on the mercantile class—or, vice versa, the autonomy which the latter enjoys from the former—enabled it to resist efforts by the government to increase extraction. While the Somaliland business elite was ready to pay for peace and protection, it repeatedly resisted increased government regulation.[14]

Politics of circulation: Capturing and facilitating global flows

In the previous sections, we made sense of post-1991 Somali state-building trajectories regarding the respective roles of coercion and capital, payments on flows and the relation between merchant class, political rulers and specialists in violence. In this final section, we want to put Tilly 'in motion' by adding a politics of circulation perspective to state-formation dynamics in Somali East Africa. By this, we mean the struggles—in which domestic merchants, trade operators, political rulers and specialists in violence are all participants—over the power to influence the movement of commodities, finance and people, as well as the revenues that derive from these movements. As the chapters of this book demonstrate, commodity and financial flows in the greater Somali economy transcend local, national, regional and international scales and perimeters. They involve transregional Somali business networks, international investments in infrastructure and multiple stakes for local and state actors who govern and tax flows of value in their locality or 'territory'. Adopting a commodity-centric view on state formation thus leads us to consider, first, how revenue from trade flows is distributed among political rulers belonging to different polities; and, second, how international norms and standards bolster the external legitimacy of aspiring state-builders.

Competition for revenue

As argued in the introduction chapter, successful aspiring state entities need to do two things: capture economic and commodity flows, and at the same time facilitate their circulation by balancing between these two imperatives. Capture can be organised when flows are slowed down at choke- or checkpoints along roads or telecom networks; in larger market towns where commodities are transacted between smaller and bigger traders and between whole-salers and retailers; at gateways, including air-, sea- and dry-ports, where commodities are transferred from one means of transportation to another; or at border crossings (Carse et al. 2020; Schouten et al. 2019). Additionally, authorities indirectly capture revenue by licensing traders, exporters, truck owners, shipping agents, mobile money companies and other operators of circulation. Licensing also increases the scope for regulation by government authorities as licence holders are registered and therefore more easily subjected to taxation and law enforcement.

In the contiguous geographical areas where commodity flows transit between the Somali sea and its hinterlands, multiple routes and ports for the import and export of commodities exist. Since all major trade and transport corridors are fragmented by multiple—sometimes overlapping and often competing—polities and aspiring (sub-)state entities, the politics of circulation centre on the competition for the control over the flows, hubs and gateways from which political rulers can extract revenues. Public authorities have struggled to tax big businesses such as telecom and remittance companies and instead tax remittances indirectly by taxing imported goods, which are often paid for by diaspora remittances.

Examples of such politics of circulation abound. Djibouti, Somaliland and Puntland have been competing over livestock export revenues by means of different levels of taxation imposed on their export (Musa et al. 2021). Al-Shabaab has attacked government-controlled trade routes to Kenya in order to re-route traffic to roads under its control (Schouten 2022). When the Ethiopian government imposed stricter customs rules in its Somali Regional State, business on the Ethiopian side of the border in Tog'wajaale moved across the border to the Somaliland side where the marketplace was booming. Another example is the lucrative import of Ethiopian *khat* to Somaliland. Until 2016, import followed state-controlled routes. But when the Somaliland government increased taxes on *khat*, traders began to avoid the Berbera route and started using bush roads instead. They also armed themselves for confrontations with police forces at checkpoints. Finally, the Somaliland government reduced its taxes on *khat*, requesting importers return to main routes and transit their goods through state-controlled custom facilities.[15]

Politics of circulation have animated competition between state entities and major clan families who are rivals over the establishment, maintenance and scaling up of major trade and transport corridors. This competition has been most acute in corridors channeling imports to the Somali hinterland—including the Ethiopian and Kenyan markets—and exports, mostly livestock, to Arab Gulf states (Hagmann 2021). As discussed in Chapter 4, this strategic rivalry has led to the development of new and upgraded seaports and connecting roads, as well as programmes to reform customs procedures. Given the essential importance of customs—producing the payments on flows discussed in the previous section—both the Berbera and the Bosaso corridors have served as economic lifelines for, respectively, Somaliland and Puntland. The upgrading of Berbera Port and investments in the corridor to Ethiopia gives Somaliland an economic advantage. At the same time, increasing insecurity and a lack of standardised road taxation in Puntland have undermined the attractiveness of the Bosaso corridor (Musa 2021).

As described in Chapter 4, similar rivalries have been playing out between groups of businessmen and politicians in the south of Puntland as well as in revenue-strapped Gulmudug, where several port and corridor projects have been competing for investments. Competition already takes place between the ports of Mogadishu, Kismayo and partly Bosaso, as the FMSs of Jubbaland and Puntland—in the absence of an agreement on fiscal federalism—have lowered tariffs to attract more trade, much to the dissatisfaction of FSG and Mogadishu's traders (Raballand and Knebelmann 2021).

This competition between trade corridors and seaports reshapes the economic importance of particular trade hubs—often capital cities and commercial metropoles—as well as their political futures. Much of this struggle over gateways involves the construction of infrastructure to further state ambitions, a reminder that gatekeeping was always 'predicated on the state's infrastructure' (Dorman 2018: 315; see also Chapters 1 and 4). But, as the case of Mogadishu Port illustrates, there is no guarantee that the state in question will be able to monopolise the revenue streams deriving from it. Al-Shabaab has managed to obtain information from within this port about importers, goods and their destinations, enabling it to levy taxes from importers at the points of delivery (Majid et al. 2021).

State formation by global standards

The capture of revenue—or 'extraction', in Tillian parlance—is only one dimension of the politics of circulation underpinning state-formation dynamics in the Somali territories. Another is the compliance with, mimicking and selective appropriation of international norms and standards by both the Somali private sector and public authorities. To the extent that trade flows follow official channels in and out of Somali East Africa—Dobler's (2016) 'blue circuits'—their facilitation requires the adoption of the international norms and standards that underpin global transport networks, logistics, telecommunication and finance.[16] Neoliberal customs and trade reforms have promoted a series of travelling templates and technologies over the years. These include transport corridors that connect landlocked countries with the sea, transit and customs agreements, One-Stop Border-Posts, container scanners, port security systems, ASYCUDA-certified[17] systems for uniform and transparent online processing of customs data and public-private partnerships (Chalfin 2010; Kunaka and Carruthers 2014; Stepputat and Hagmann 2019).

When considering sovereignty from the vantage point of these reforms, as Sassen (2000: 28) suggested, state sovereignty becomes more preoccupied with facilitating transborder economic flows than protecting national populations and production. However, international standards and customs regimes can also have the effect of augmenting domestic sovereignty by bolstering the capacities and presence of national customs authorities (Chalfin 2010: 40). Hargeisa's Egal International Airport illustrates how the mobilisation of international security standards and technologies strengthened not only the everyday presence of an otherwise abstract 'state' when passengers enter or exit Somaliland territory through the airport, but also Somaliland's legitimacy and claim to international recognition (Gandrup 2016). As the then airport manager explained, 'we have to look like any other airport' (ibid.: 20) by living up to the technical and security standards applied in airports around the world and by moving up in the hierarchy of the International Civil Aviation Organization (ICAO) to the level of the airports in Addis Ababa and Nairobi. Indeed, by attracting international carriers such as Fly Dubai, Air Arabia and Ethiopian Airlines, Hargeisa's airport contributed to the piecemeal recognition of Somaliland's de facto statehood, not least in the eyes of Somalilanders (Tahir 2021). Even though the Berbera Port concession with DP World was met with some resistance (Ahmed and Stepputat 2019), Somaliland elites saw the huge investment and the prospect of having 'post-Panamax' cranes and containerships in Berbera Port as steps in the pursuit of international recognition 'the economic way' (see also Elder 2021).[18]

Another example of the selective adaptation of international standards is the mobile money sector. This business initially developed with very little state regulation or oversight, benefiting from low tax rates as telecommunication firms and mobile money operators enjoyed close relations with political rulers. But, as explained in Chapter 3, telecommunication, mobile money and remittance companies have contributed to state building with a sort of 'collateral tax', providing services, technical infrastructure and the protection thereof, which the Somali state(s) could otherwise have been expected to provide. In the 2010s, donors pressured Somalia to implement regulation that complies with international norms, such as the anti-money laundering and anti-terrorist financing standards for the strategically important mobile money sector. Somali companies, afraid of being blocked by the United States, adopted some of these regulations and made efforts to appease donor concerns of funding terrorist organisations in south-central Somalia. In the case of Somaliland, compliance with these regulations allowed the de facto state to pursue the quest for de jure statehood.

Because of Somali state institutions' limited reach and the region's deeply entrenched, and also effective, ways of conducting business informally, companies continue to rely on, for example, clan elders and religious leaders to mediate business disputes or engage in ad hoc agreements with local administrations in their areas of operation. These pragmatic business practices include protection payments to al-Shabaab for not attacking strategic private infrastructure such as telecommunication towers. Hence, Somali companies are straddling between international norms and standards on the one hand, and the messy, unregulated, dynamic local demands from various competing stakeholders on the other (see Chapter 3). Given these features of the Somali business context, many international companies operating in the African market abstain from investing or having a presence in the Somali territories, considering the Somali market to be impenetrable for outsiders. Hence, the way the Somali private sector straddles international norms and local realities amounts to a form of economic sovereignty that protects Somali businesses.

Finally, there are numerous examples of how international standards are ignored or mimicked with little or even adverse effect on state authority. Traders who import fake or substandard medicine to Somalia would be out of business if state administrations were more effective. In Eastleigh, Nairobi's Somali-dominated economic hub where large quantities of global commodities are sold, 'everyone' knows that the widely used stickers reading 'Kenya Bureau of Standards' (KEBS) are mostly fake. Rather than legitimising the Kenyan state, this practice undermines its authority, with the real quality assessment of a particular commodity occurring on the basis of trust relations between buyers and sellers.[19]

Conclusion

Much of the interdisciplinary literature on African statehood, both colonial and post-colonial, has been preoccupied with the governance of people and land (Kopytoff 1987; Herbst 2000; Boone 2014). *Trade Makes States* has argued that, to simplify, governing goods and their circulation is a key state-formation activity involving coercion and capital, logistics and infrastructure, power and profits. Both this chapter and our book underscore how the governance of commodities provides an analytically fertile vantage point to study state making. While the Somali territories are particular—but by no means exceptional—with regard to the economic, political and social importance of commodity trading, a 'governing goods' perspective expands our understanding of state-formation dynamics *tout court*. The Somali political experience thus not only challenges liberal Western conceptions of the relation between state and economy. Rather, it informs state-formation theory: not as an anomaly, but as a paradigmatic case of contemporary state making.

Applying Tilly to the metaphorical 'tropics' of Somali East Africa sheds light on important causal processes that have driven state-formation dynamics over the past 30 years. Somali state entities have 'wax[ed] and wane[d]' (Lund 2006: 697) over time, but their commercial foundations have consistently revolved around the facilitation, governance and capture of transnational commodity flows. Payments on flows, or indirect-derived taxes, reflect both the historical importance of entrepôts and transit routes and the least difficult way of introducing taxation. These payments on flows have constituted the material foundation of post-1991 Somali states. They are the predominant mode by which aspiring Somali administrations extract revenues. This has important consequences for state building. As political rulers seek to capture revenue along main trade and transport corridors, marketplaces, seaports and checkpoints, extending state presence essentially follows these key infrastructural networks and nodes. Territorial control and administration primarily serves the purpose of governing these economic hubs and flows to extract resources. Little revenue is to be made at the margins of major trading routes or urban centres, which are of limited strategic value for state entities in terms of extending territorial control.

Institutionalised states such as Somaliland or Federal Member States portray themselves as sovereign entities with a defined population and territory. But in the Somali areas actual existing or empirical statehood resembles much more a federation of bigger and smaller city-states. Some of these city-states are part of internationally recognised nation-states—whether (federal)

Somalia, (eastern) Ethiopia or (north-eastern) Kenya. Others belong to the unrecognised Republic of Somaliland or are contested between competing political entities. Internationally funded federal state building in Somalia is built on the assumption that, in the long run, a vertically differentiated Somali state with an even administration across its territory will emerge. But the prevailing politics of circulation, the prominence of payments on flows and the continued fragmentation of the Somali territories seriously call this approach into question. Instead, evidence highlighted in our book points towards a type of Somali statehood that is much more horizontal, organised around alliances between major trading states which will have to bargain resource and power-sharing between themselves in an attempt to maximise and pacify both protection and extraction.

As Chaudry (1997: 27) observed in her study on Yemen, in remittance economies private-sector elites have access to 'virtually unlimited amounts of foreign exchange for investment, imports, and hoarding, which enable them to thrive without the protection and supervision' of the state. This finding very much applies to the greater Somali economy, and there is thus a chance that state institutions will remain skeletal in the foreseeable future. In this sense, trade not only makes states, as this book has argued, but it also unmakes—or at least severely limits—the development of state capacity in Somali East Africa as public authorities have few incentives to expand territorial control beyond major trading routes and centres, play second fiddle to major companies and are unable to redistribute resources among populations. In this scenario, state institutions and fiscal social contracts remain weak, while social inequality thrives. In a more optimistic scenario, which might play out in the Somali territories, growing volumes of commodity flows do invite state-builders to, as Tilly (2010: 180) formulated it, initiate 'cycles of intervention, resistance, repression, and bargaining'. These not only create more revenues for states, but also increase citizens' ability to hold political rulers accountable.

What then will the future of Somali states look like? State-formation dynamics will not only depend on which political rulers prevail in the long-term with regard to war-making, state making, protection and extraction. Because of its distinctly transnational nature, the Somali economy—and, by extension, Somali state entities—will remain at the mercy of global terms of trade; of the security, trade and migration policies of states in the region and abroad; and of external aid flows (Reno 2003). Because most public revenues rely on the taxation of imported and exported goods that are often paid for with diaspora remittances, Somali states have very limited autonomy in their economic policies. The predominance of oligopolies in the telecommunication, finance and import-export sectors—as well as reliance on externally funded state building, in the case of the Federal Somali Government—are a reflection of this.

AFTERWORD

SOMALIA, AN ECONOMY WITH 'STATENESS'

Peter D. Little

Much has changed in Somalia and Somali East Africa since the publication of *Somalia: Economy Without State* almost two decades ago (Little 2003). Despite a dizzying pace of transition in certain economic sectors, especially in telecommunications and digital finance, there are certain processes and pursuits—such as pastoralism and migration—that have remained stubbornly consistent across the Somali territories. The chapters in this book, *Trade Makes States*, reflect the unstable equilibrium between 'economy' and 'state' in the region by treading familiar and enduring themes, such as trade and trust, as well as new subjects, such as the roles of infrastructure and taxation in state building.

Importantly, many of the contributors are scholars from the region whose stake in what happens in Somali East Africa goes well beyond academic goals. They breathe fresh emic perspectives on a research enterprise that, unfortunately, has been dominated by outside, mainly European and American, scholars. For those of us who care deeply about what happens in the region, the Somali story—particularly the theme of state making—has been an emotional roller coaster spanning more than 30 years, characterised by small advances followed by painful setbacks. It is not possible to write about the Somali inhabited territories in the post-1991 era without exposing both disappointments and achievements, and it is the latter that this book mainly addresses. There is much to celebrate with regards to the economy and local governance of Somali East Africa, which has demonstrated amazing innovation and resilience. The chapters in this book carefully document many examples of this.

This afterword discusses key findings of *Trade Makes States*, highlighting where it advances new or deepens current understandings of the region. I also suggest a few areas where additional research is needed to confirm or clarify key issues. Three interrelated themes from the book are addressed: (1) economy; (2) globalization and global networks; and (3) governance and state building. These topics overlap to a large extent, but they are central to the approach and argument elaborated in *Trade Makes States*.

The co-editors Tobias Hagmann and Finn Stepputat have framed the book with highly useful introductory and concluding chapters, laying out their materialist theory of state making based largely on Charles Tilly's (1992) lesser-known work on mercantile-political class alliances and their significance for state making in Europe. In doing so, the co-editors adapt Tilly's theory of state making to the Somali context. The book's other chapters serve integrative purposes and help to maintain theoretical and methodological consistency despite the multiple authors, topics and academic disciplines involved. The contribution by Neil Carrier and Hannah Elliott on trust in Somali culture, a common theme in writings on Somalia (Dalleo 1975; Little 2003; Samatar 1989), provides another entry point for fusing the book's different topics. Along with the fact that most of the research reported in the book derives from a single research project directed by the co-editors—titled 'Governing economic hubs and flows in Somali East Africa (GOVSEA)'—these three chapters make for a consistent and robust argument.

Although Hagmann and Stepputat lay out general theoretical parameters for the individual contributions, they allow for considerable flexibility in how this perspective is interpreted and supportive data analysed. Consider the corridor approach, for instance, that is proposed to address relationships among politics, infrastructure, logistics and the circulation of goods and finances—the politics of circulation—within key trade channels in the region (see also Stepputat and Hagmann 2019). In some contributions, it is treated as a relatively rigid territorial construct; in others, the corridor approach is considerably less apparent, serving more as a symbolic signpost for how Somalis organise their economic activities (for example, Chapter 5 by Fana Gebresenbet et al.). Importantly, the book argues that when political elites can derive enough resources from these trade and transport corridors to support personnel, services and systems of regulation, the evolution of state-like institutions begins.

Economy

The focus on commodity trade in the book is well suited to Somalia and Somali East Africa, where commerce has been prominent for centuries and has figured prominently in a number of studies (Cassanelli 1982; Lochery 2020; Samatar 1989; Thompson 2021). In Somalia itself, a lengthy coastline, good proximity to Middle Eastern markets and a string of natural harbours and seaports provide significant advantages for global trade. The empirical and analytical depth with which this book reveals new patterns and types of trade in Somali East Africa is among its great strengths. Another related contribution depicts how local governance bodies, both formal and informal, are able to tax trade and marketplaces to raise public revenues, mainly under conditions of informality, without overly constraining them or generating violent resistance. *Trade Makes States* provides considerable empirical depth and analytical sophistication on a topic—public revenue generation from 'informal' trade—that features prominently in recent studies of African state building and development (Moore et al. 2018; van den Boogaard and Santoro 2022a). In contrast to a common misperception about Somalia, the book shows that while tax extortion from traders and markets still exists and is widespread in some territories, tax structures on trade and other activities are considerably more systematic and predictable than previously acknowledged, including by myself (Little 2003, 2008). For instance, in Chpater 7 Musa and Varming describe how state building is in part financed by the existence of complex layers of fees on export and import commerce and local markets. In doing so, this and other chapters document a transition from the 'duty free' depiction of Somalia from the 1990s and 2000s to an economy where regulations and fees are governed both by informal and state-like bodies.

Trade Makes States demonstrates that while clan and kinship relations undergird many aspects of the economy there are sectors, such as finance and export trade, where acts of trusting move well beyond clan structures, thus solidifying positive inter-clan relations over expansive territories (see Chapter 2). Shareholders from different clans invest in some of the largest private companies in the region, especially in the telecommunications and finance sectors. The complexity of these firms and their need for global capital from diaspora and other sources complicate clan-privileged models of trade and other economic activities. Not only do the operations of these firms generate cooperation across clan and ethnicity, but they also often require state-like representation and authority to function, including for provision of security and contract enforcement.

Cross-border trade and investment is what essentially ties Somali East Africa together by binding different actors and institutions across multiple corridors and political spaces. As Chapter 5 and Chapter 6 show, cross-border trade in livestock from eastern Ethiopia accounts for a large percentage of Somaliland's valuable export trade, thus re-confirming what others have noted before about the importance of trans-border commerce (Eid 2014; Little et al. 2015). The Somali Regional State of Ethiopia also provides a key market for imports—often financed by revenues from livestock export trade—that circulate in the Berbera-based corridor discussed in the book. In a similar vein, trans-border commerce figures strongly in the southern corridor of Mogadishu/Kismayo-Garissa-Nairobi, where informal imports of sugar, livestock and electronics from southern Somalia fuel commerce and investment in Kenya, including the Eastleigh sub-area of Nairobi. As a

AFTERWORD

reminder that state capacity for enforcement differs widely in the region, Ethiopia's periodic assaults on cross-border trade between Somali Regional State and neighbouring Somaliland and Somalia corridors show that states can also 'un-make' trade. Moreover, while there is rich ethnographic evidence in the book on regional and local marketplaces and trade, the book leans heavily on export and import trade to support the 'trade makes states' argument. As will be discussed below, this privileges a certain segment of the population and model of state formation.

There are two other economic issues regarding the 'trade makes states' argument that are hinted at in the book but require additional consideration. First, export trade in valuable commodities, such as oil and metals or minerals, can occur without the evolution of state or state-like institutions or, in some cases, even inhibit them. Note the cases of the Central African Republic (CAR) and Democratic Republic of Congo (DRC), which both export valuable commodities without much—if any—state-like regulations or organisations (Lombard 2016; Raeymaekers 2014). Indeed, here one could turn the book's argument on its head and think about ways that trade un-makes states. In addition to the African examples mentioned, one might consider Latin American (Colombia and regions of Mexico) and Asian (Myanmar and Afghanistan) examples, where substantial high-value trade in illicit drugs, arms and gemstones has financed private militias and strongly challenged or unravelled state making (Carrol 2011; Meehan 2015; Pugh et al. 2004; Mansfield 2016).

To return to the Somalia case, large 'businessmen' and their trading activities performed very well for long periods in the post-1991 era by challenging the emergence of state-like institutions. The verdict is still out on whether large companies in Somalia will allow their federal government to impose additional restrictions and taxes on them, a policy point that the book also raises. Importantly, *Trade Makes States* helps us think through how a commodity's characteristics (high-value/low-value, perishable/non-perishable) and the physical corridors it traverses can help to explain why state-like institutions emerge in some trade corridors but not in others. The book highlights key export/import corridors centred on seaports that make it easier to govern imports, exports and state building. However, we might also use the same commodity- and corridor-based schema to explain why some export products—high-value metals, illicit drugs and gemstones that move across multiple borders—can constrain or even 'unmake' state institutions and governance in some political-economic contexts.

A second issue is what kind of state institutions and services, including infrastructure investments, are being established in these trade corridors and who they benefit. Do they mainly work for a small cadre of wealthy businessmen, export traders and urban-based money traders? Chapters 3, 6 and 7 hint at the unequal distribution of benefits from export/import trade and supporting financial networks and infrastructure, which is also confirmed by earlier publications (Samatar 1987; Little 1996). Chapter 3 by Iazzolino and Stremlau, for example, mentions the strong wealth differences and inequalities in Somaliland associated with digital finance, currency exchanges and internet access, often dividing along urban versus rural spaces. These class differences are implied elsewhere in the book, but the theme is not well developed despite its likelihood of impacting the nature of state making. Along these lines, questions to consider for future research include: (1) how does state making based on the politics of circulation impact wealth and class differences and patterns of inequality; and (2) how does state making in these corridors impact those who may not reside in key trade corridors and/or possess the material assets to participate in export/import trade, including pastoralists, agro-pastoralists and the urban poor?[1] I will return to these questions later in the chapter.

Globalisation and networks

The Somali economy's need for state-like institutions and global recognition was glaringly exposed during the 1990s and 2000s when lengthy bans on livestock exports due to outbreaks of Rift Valley Fever (RVF) were imposed by importing countries, especially Saudi Arabia. Along with these sanctions, restrictions on

AFTERWORD

money transfers from the UK in 2013 out of concern for possible financing of terrorism further exposed key difficulties for a country like Somalia, which despite being enmeshed in global trade and financial transfers lacked state-like institutions to represent its interests on the international stage. In fact, the campaign against punitive actions on remittance transfers to Somalia was led by NGOs and humanitarian organisations, further highlighting the challenges for a country without state-like representation (Oxfam 2013).

In the case of the RVF bans, Australia—one of Somalia's main competitors in the livestock business—pressured the World Organisation for Animal Health (OIE) to increase animal health regulations on global exports. The Australians were clearly aware that Somalia, with its weak veterinarian institutions and global status, would be strongly disadvantaged. Unsurprisingly, lengthy bans of up to six years on animal exports from Somalia to Saudi Arabia continued to threaten the export sector. Around 2006–08, Somaliland authorities negotiated agreements with Saudi firms to invest in and manage two quarantine facilities at Berbera. Soon after, in 2009, Saudi Arabia's ban on livestock exports from Somalia was lifted (The Cattle Site 2011; Musa et al. 2020: 3), and the presence of Saudi-owned quarantine yards even seemed to bolster exports to Saudi Arabia (ibid).

The global networks of shareholder companies, particularly in telecommunications, that have evolved in Somalia are carefully detailed in the book. With its premium geographic location, Somalia, including Somaliland, has become a potential frontier of global logistics in the region, attracting logistics-related investments from China, Turkey, Qatar and the United Arab Emirates (UAE) over the past decade or so. Somali businesses are striving to meet international standards and practices as they seek increased ties to global partners and markets. This transition toward improved logistics is most evident at key seaports where investments in mechanisation, worker training, connecting roads and modern scanning technologies have been implemented. Somali ports have attracted such investments to transform them to be more in line with global standards, an outcome that contributes to state making according to the authors of this book. Ports, such as Berbera and Mogadishu, have always played sizeable roles in state making in Somalia. Hence it is not surprising that the governance of ports and related infrastructures figures prominently in the book's 'trade makes states' argument. However, the book is relatively quiet on the Federal Government of Somalia's (FGS) position on port upgrades and infrastructure agreements with international partners in territories (e.g., Somaliland) that it considers still to be within its sovereign boundaries (International Crisis Group 2019). There is no doubt that certain geo-political and regional interests would like to see a politically and geographically fragmented rather than a united Somalia in the future.

The increased role of global companies, including international airlines, and their willingness to stake a presence in Somalia and Somaliland are implicit examples of the existence of state-like institutions and authorities, otherwise why would national carriers like Ethiopian Airlines or Turkish Airlines risk flying to Hargeisa or Mogadishu? In particular, the significance of contracts and public-private partnerships, including with the Ethiopian state, in the management of key infrastructures, such as ports, is a particularly germane case of 'stateness'. Moreover, by highlighting Somaliland's awarding a contract to Dubai Ports World (DPW) for the management of Berbera Port as a milestone in state making—in part because DPW cleaned up cronyism, corruption and clan-based partiality—the book shows how the DPW presence required Somaliland to perform formal state-like functions, such as empowering a port authority. DPW, in turn, rationalised port schedules, salary scales and cargo processing which increased public revenues for state making (see Chapter 4). Ports like Berbera generate the most revenues for state administrations, both in Somaliland and in other Federal Member States of Somalia. A state-like organisation is often needed to negotiate contracts with global actors to convert a port to an acceptable world-class facility. In the different infrastructure investments discussed in the book, the performance of state-like functions is shaped by the presence of a transnational firm or foreign country, rather than by demand from Somali citizens for improved governance and accountability. Context and circumstance matter, a reality that contributors to *Trade Makes States* skilfully address in their analyses.

Governance and state building

The volume shows how Somalia's ports are key gatekeepers and potential 'chokepoints' for public revenue generation and state making. They also are revealed to be sources of fierce contention, especially over control of Mogadishu and Kismayo Ports, because their command brings profits and tax collections. Although they have been targets of armed struggle in the past, once these ports are secured, they become visible fixtures in trade corridors. *Trade Makes States* highlights different structures of authority associated with port-based economic activities, particularly in Somaliland, and it avoids simplistic causality between trade and state making by hinting at the ambivalent nature of state building in the region. The authors attest to this by invoking terms like 'state-like', 'hybrid governance' and 'stateness', and by demonstrating the importance of context. For example, Hagmann and Stepputat show that 'state making' in Garissa County, Kenya and Somali Regional State, Ethiopia differed considerably from what was happening in Somaliland and Somalia. By focusing on corridors of commodity circulation and emphasising control of commodities and goods rather than people and territory, they are able to compare state making across different locations of Somali East Africa. The book's emphasis on flows of goods, peoples and finances mimics the mobility trope so central to Somali pastoralist culture, livelihoods and history.

As fixed spaces of commerce, town-based marketplaces figure prominently in the production of authority, revenues and state-like bodies. In comparison to rural borderland markets, they are relatively easy to tax and regulate. The chapters by Ahmed Musa and Varming and Asnake Kefale and Rasmussen highlight the ways in which marketplaces offer opportunities for state-like authorities to capture revenues through fees and taxes. Security and protection of goods at marketplaces, along with collection of revenues, are used as visible indicators of 'state making'. However, as the authors make clear, marketplace traders expect something in return for their taxes, and it is this demand for better services and infrastructure that motivates the formation of state-like bodies. Examples of individuals demanding services, such as security and waste removal, for fees are often more about accountability and the quality of services than to whom payments are made—whether it is a state or non-state entity.

Not surprisingly, the 'trade makes states' position holds up best in the Berbera trade corridor of Somaliland. By contrast, the southern corridor centred on Mogadishu and Kismayo Ports, where viable structures of governance have continued to be unstable and the presence of al-Shabaab is extensive, is probably the thinnest test case for the book's argument. In this space, the FGS interacts with international donors to generate capital and investment, not to mention resources to pay its employees, and its performance of 'stateness' is more related to aid and security dependency than to trade (Little 2021). In the northern corridor centred on Berbera, Somaliland, businessmen financed peace-making, government salaries and public institutions to support the establishment of Somaliland (Balthasar 2013). In this state and others, profits from trade clearly helped to build states. In Somaliland and elsewhere in the region, competition over infrastructure and investment—especially for ports and roads—is also highlighted as a positive sign that state-like bodies are needed to compete against other states. The negotiation of different state bodies with foreign investors has led to discussions about different port investments and healthy competition between state and private parties over the use of ports and associated infrastructures in the region (see Chapter 4 by Stepputat et al.). The book views evidence of this type of competition as positive for state making, including pending competitions between Lamu Port (Kenya) and Kismayo Port in the south, and Berbera Port and Djibouti Port in the north. The book borrows from Saskia Sassen (2000) to treat states as facilitators of transnational flows, which complements the politics of circulation theme, rather than as protectors of territory and its citizens.

Trade Makes States has taken on an important task by comparing state making across a vast territory of the Somali inhabited areas of the Horn of Africa, a monumental challenge in itself. However, controlling trade is an old story in African state making, dating back to the colonial and even the pre-colonial periods where companies such as the Imperial British East Africa Company violently opened the way for colonial state making. Since it was— and still is, in many respects—virtually impossible to collect incomes from individuals and informal firms, colonial and post-colonial African states built up revenues by taxing trade and markets via marketing boards for coffee, tea, sugar, cocoa and other key commodities (Bates 2014; Arhin et al. 1985). They also drew revenues from market traders, transporters and ports, all sources of state revenues addressed in *Trade Makes States*. Where this book differs from earlier studies and advances the argument is that unlike top-down, state-imposed marketing boards, 'stateness' and state-like authority is generated by the conditions and practice of trade itself. As Stepputat and Hagmann show in the book's introduction, 'state effects' and the 'production of stateness' derive from below through trade relationships and processes. Complex configurations of trade, they argue, have generated 'stateness' in the Somali territories after 1991 rather than their being imposed by states themselves.

Of course, a dichotomy between 'stateness' being generated from below as opposed to being imposed by a governing authority from 'above' is overly simplistic, and the book's empirics confirm this. Somaliland, once again, represents the best case for the book's main theme by showing how governance is about balancing the facilitation of trade in key corridors with the need to extract some resources from it to support state making. As the authors show, Somaliland has relatively high taxes and fees on trade, but also provides some level of security and infrastructure to assist it (see also Musa 2021).

Chapter 7 on taxation and fee collection by Musa and Varming is especially informative with regard to how to pay for state making. It shows that, regardless of the state's formal status in the region, Somali administrations in the region all pursue similar tax collection strategies based on government 'financial laws' from the 1960s. Thus, to paraphrase James C. Scott, they are performing like a state whether they are formal, informal or a mixture of both (Scott 1998). Much of the tax revenues stem from different levels of trade—local, regional cross-border and export/import—where there is a great deal of bargaining and gaming going on between taxpayers and collectors. As noted earlier, businessmen and women are willing to pay taxes to state and non-state actors as long as services are provided. In fact, Somali traders generally pay a range of different taxes across official and informal settings, but this does not mean extortion does not exist. There are overlapping levels of authority in most Somali regions, but even where informal and hybrid governance structures prevail, informal tax regimes are often highly standardised and regulated, thereby planting in these areas elements of 'stateness'.

Conclusion

Trade Make States is a very welcome addition to Somali and East African Studies, and more broadly to scholarship concerned with the political economy of state formation. The book moves away from the failed state narrative that still reverberates among policymakers and certain scholars of Somalia and the Horn of Africa by focusing on the emergence of formal and informal structures of governance and accountability. In addressing these political outcomes, the contributors emphasise the economy and its mercantile class of businessmen, highlighting their political alliances as key ingredients for state making in the region. What distinguishes this work from earlier studies of Somalia is not only its focus on trade and business networks in relation to governance and accountability, but also its regional perspective and robust empirics in a region where fieldwork has been particularly difficult in many locations. The book documents the evolution away from the militaristic 'warlord' dominated scenarios of the 1990s—where security, trade and aid flows were heavily dictated by violence and coercion—to the current period, where parts of the region are humming with export and import trade and transnational investment, as well as the security to counter violence. Each of the chapters in the book is supported by field research, and each asks how recent economic processes shape structures of governance and appearances of 'stateness'.

AFTERWORD

Trade Makes States is full of rich materials and theoretical insights into a region marked more by stereotypes and assumed wisdoms than careful study and analysis, and there is simply nothing equal to it in the field. Nonetheless, there are areas where *Trade Makes State* would have benefited from additional discussion, especially about the kind of future state(s) that should be generated. In fact, there is little in the book about the possibility of a unified Somalia state—the 'elephant in the room'—thus largely circumventing regional and geo-political forces that would prefer a politically fragmented landscape for Somalia, which would include an autonomous and internationally recognised Somaliland. Although it is sometimes difficult to ascertain in the book what labels are being applied to which territories and political entities—which may be disconcerting to some readers—this ambiguity often reflects on the ground realities in the region. This uncertainty captures the complex, ambiguous and incomplete nature of state making in Somali East Africa, but particularly in the territory claimed by the FGS.

Other important topics that are lacking in the book and call out for additional research include: (1) the relationship between trade and economic inequality, including careful consideration of class formations—that is, who benefits from commodity trading and state effects and who does not (see Samatar 2007); (2) gender analysis that examines the role of Somali women in urban and import/export trading and other important sectors (see Ali and Ali 2013; Lochery 2020); and (3) consideration of the quality and democratic depth of different governance structures—that is, whether there are autocratic, oligarchic and other undemocratic tendencies embedded in new governance structures which have evolved in Somali East Africa (see Elder 2021). These are important research issues that hopefully some of the book's contributors will take up in their future studies.

Trade Makes States does not claim to represent all views on 'state making' and economy in Somali East Africa. Rather, its approach is to emphasise how the circulation of material things and alliances between merchants and politicians can facilitate the development of governance and state-like bodies. One might ask: if a state is built on the interests of mercantile capitalists and the circulation of commodities from which they benefit, is this the kind of state that is beneficial? And, if so, for whom? Has this kind of neoliberal state not been shown to concentrate wealth among a small segment of the population while large segments of society remain disadvantaged? As this afterword has argued, these questions are not answered in the book, but nevertheless *Trade Makes States* offers a very promising and rich platform to begin to address them.

Trying to overlay politics and processes of state making across a region better defined by business and trade networks (the 'greater Somalia economy') is a monumental task for which the co-editors and authors should be applauded. In material terms, it is like pouring a fluid gel (politics) over a grid (economy) where in some places the substance solidifies, while in others it remains liquid-like. The book nicely captures both of these processes, although it shows that some territories—for example, Somaliland and perhaps Puntland—are easier to explain in terms of how trade and state making are enmeshed than in other parts of Somali East Africa. The co-editors admit in the concluding chapter that their theory is 'exploratory' with important gaps, and their thesis about the relationship between commodity trading and state making requires additional research. Some of these potential research areas have been indicated in this chapter. As I have also suggested, *Trade Makes States* may not explain the situation in all empirical contexts of Somali East Africa, but it represents a worthwhile start.

GLOSSARY OF SOMALI AND ARABIC WORDS

aammin	trustworthy (or *amana* in Arabic)
abbaan	a practice of protection, particularly accorded to traders, in exchange for money or goods, offered historically in Somali territories
amaan	security
aqil	a traditional leader in the customary Somali system who manages 'blood money' and settles conflicts between sub-clans
ardiya	daily market taxes
baad	extortion; it can be taken by soldiers, armed militias or even unarmed civilians
bacadjoog	'standing in the sand', used for naming corrupt practices
bir qaad	checkpoint opening fee
canshuur	taxation
cashuur dhaaf	tax exemptions
cashuur dhimid	tax reductions
cashuurta horumarinta degamada	district development tax (Puntland)
chat (or *khat*)	stimulant narcotic shrubs
dejin	unloading fee

dhaqan	tradition
dilaal	'deal', word used for broker
diya/diyo	Somalised Arabic for 'blood money' or 'compensation'; in Somali it is called *mag*.
franco valuta	import of commodities that do not involve foreign exchange expenditure from the domestic banking system nor official letters of credit
habesha	ethnonym referring to people from northern Ethiopian highlands
hajj	the annual pilgrimage to Mecca
halal/haram	'permitted' and 'forbidden' in accordance with the rulings of Islam
hawala	the Arabic word for a money-transfer system that does not move money (*xawaalad* in Somali)
kab	budget supplement
khat, qat (or *chat*)	stimulant narcotic shrubs
jilib	subclan or sub-lineage unit of a clan
liyu	a special police force (government-run militia) in Somali Regional State of Ethiopia
miraa	the word used for *khat* or *chat* in Kenya
musaalaha	Somali dispute-resolution institution
mu'amala	an Arabic term for good conduct evolving from economic transactions, linked to reputation
nabadgelyada	security allowance, not tax
qashin gur	garbage collection fee (Somaliland)
riba	interest, from Arabic
shari'a	rulings derived from the Islamic religion
shefagn	Somali replacement driver (in Ethiopia)
shirkaad	public company
somalinimo	Somalism, a political phrase signalling Somali unity and cooperation

GLOSSARY OF SOMALI AND ARABIC WORDS

taar	old two-way radio system with open frequency
tariff	import customs duty
wado maris	road tax (Somaliland)
woreda	(Amhara) a third-level administrative unit; a district
xawaalad	money-transfer agency or system (*hawala*, in Arabic)
xeer	Somali customary law
zakat	one of the pillars of Islam; a mandatory charitable contribution to those in need: this is a form of tax but is not enforceable by the state

NOTES

1. INTRODUCTION: TRADE AND STATE FORMATION IN SOMALI EAST AFRICA AND BEYOND

1. Interview with Ali Mohamed Omar, Berbera, 10 June 2015.
2. For the story about the beginnings of Somaliland and the Berbera corridor, see Bradbury (2008); Balthasar (2013); Stepputat and Hagmann (2019).
3. Loza Seleshie, 'Will Somaliland's Berbera Port be a threat to Djibouti's?', *The Africa Report*, 24 December 2020. Available at: https://www.theafricareport. com/54136/will-somalilands-berbera-port-be-a-threat-to-djiboutis/ (accessed 6 October 2021).
4. Somewhat parallel to us, Vigneswaran and Quirk (2015) argue that 'mobility makes states', but they are focusing on human mobility only.
5. See various annual editions of the Fragile States Index published by the Fund for Peace, available at: https://fragilestatesindex.org/ (accessed 6 October 2021).
6. Jeffrey Gettleman (2011), 'As an enemy retreats, clans carve up Somalia', *New York Times*, 9 September.
7. An example of this are repeat livestock bans imposed on Somalia by Arab Gulf states in 2000–09 and 2016–20.
8. Like economic or aid 'rents'.
9. Ethiopia published its first National Logistics Strategy for 2011–20, available at: https://etmaritime.com/wp-content/uploads/2019/04/Final-NLS-Disclosed-1.pdf (accessed 6 October 2021); a second strategy for 2018–28 is allegedly in place, according to a World Bank (2017) project, 'Ethiopia Trade Logistics Project', according to which the cost of exporting a container with clothes to Germany is 247% more expensive from Ethiopia than from Vietnam. Available at: http://documents1.worldbank.org/curated/en/888191486225 286967/pdf/PIDISDS-APR-Print-P156590-02-04-2017-1486225281150.pdf (accessed 6 October 2021).

10. See World Bank, 'Aggregated LPI 2012–2018', available at: https://lpi.world-bank.org/international/aggregated-ranking (accessed 8 February 2021).

11. Interview with Ali Ismael, Hargeisa, 6 June 2015.

12. The gate was typically a port. Mann (2008) notes that in colonial Africa, the capital city of a state in 70% of the cases was a port city.

13. However, the central government has kept control over 'the gate' for international aid.

14. GCR (2020), 'Anglo-Turkish consortium signs deal to build and operate Somalia's Hobyo Port', *Global Construction Review*, 5 November. Available at: https://www.globalconstructionreview.com/news/anglo-turkish-consortium-signs-deal-build-and-oper/ (accessed 12 July 2021).

15. See also Raeymaekers (2014).

16. Interview with Adam Ahmed Derie, Hargeisa, 7 June 2015.

17. IGAD is short for the Intergovernmental Authority for Development. Members of IGAD are Djibouti, Eritrea, Ethiopia, Kenya, Somalia, South Sudan, Sudan and Uganda.

18. IGAD Communique (2018), 'Meeting of ministers in charge of trade from IGAD member states on a draft regional policy framework on Informal Cross-border Trade (ICBT) and Cross-border Security Governance (CBSG)', 21 June, Mombasa, Kenya.

19. The following section draws on Hagmann and Stepputat (2016).

20. Nduru, M. (1996), 'No end in sight to banana war', Inter Press Service, posted 24 April at http://www.ipsnews.net/1996/04/somali-politics-no-end-in-sight-to-banana-war/ (accessed 2 November 2022).

2. TRUST AS SOCIAL INFRASTRUCTURE IN SOMALI TRADING NETWORKS

1. In this chapter, we focus primarily on relations between Somali traders. For more on how Somali trade in Eastleigh and elsewhere meshes with or circumvents state formations, see Carrier and Lochery (2013).

3. WAR, PEACE AND THE CIRCULATION OF MOBILE MONEY ACROSS THE SOMALI TERRITORIES

1. Reuters (2021), 'Somalia issues its first mobile money licence to Hormuud Telecom', 27 February. Available at: https://www.reuters.com/article/somalia-telecom-idUSL8N2KX07T (accessed 16 August 2022).

2. Global System for Mobile Communications Association.

3. BBC (2010), 'Al-Shabab bans mobile phone money transfers in Somalia', 18 October. Available at: https://www.bbc.com/news/world-africa-11566247 (accessed 6 September 2021). See also Abdi, S. (2010), 'Mobile transfers save money and lives in Somalia', Reuters, 3 March. Available at: https://www.

reuters.com/article/us-somalia-mobiles/mobile-transfers-save-money-and-lives-in-somalia-idUKTRE6222BY20100303 (accessed 6 September 2021).

4. See UN (2020), https://somalia.un.org/en/46669-aid-flows-somalia-2020; Federal Government of Somalia (2020), *Aid Flows in Somalia. Mogadishu: Ministry of Planning, Investment and Economic Development* (https://somalia.un.org/sites/default/files/2020–05/Aid%20Flows%20in%20Somalia%20-%202020.pdf).

5. Universities that have received funding from Dahabshiil are Hargeisa University, Amuud University and Mogadishu University; the '7 Hospitals' associated with Dahabshiil are Benadir Hospital, Burao Hospital, Garoowe Hospital, Hargeisa General, Las Anod Hospital, Kaysenay Hospital and Madina Hospital (Meester et al. 2019).

6. Following the terror attacks of 11 September 2001, Ali Ahmed Nur Jim'ale—then the main shareholder of BGC—was included in the Specially Designated Nationals and Blocked Persons List of the US Department of Treasury's Office of Foreign Assets Control. In 2008, the UN Security Council Committee pursuant to resolutions 751 (1992) and 1907 (2009) concerning Somalia and Eritrea included Ali Ahmed Nur Jim'ale's name in a list of individuals and entities 'subject to the travel ban, assets freeze and targeted arms embargo'. On 11 March 2014, the UNSC Committee approved the removal of Ali Ahmed Nur Jim'ale's name from the list. On 30 June 2016, Ali Ahmed Nur Jim'ale was removed from the US Office of Foreign Assets Control (OFAC) (UNSC 2020).

7. Reuters (2021), 'Somalia issues its first mobile money licence to Hormuud Telecom', 27 February.

8. In 2015, under pressure from the Somaliland Central Bank, Telesom started offering its customers the option to transfer Somaliland Shillings as well, but the transfer of USD remained most users' preferred option.

9. Reuters (2021), 'Somalia issues its first mobile money licence to Hormuud Telecom', 27 February.

10. For further information see the National Communications Authority (NCA) (https://nca.gov.so/), which was established through the Communications Act of 2017. The NCA is the regulatory authority for the communications sector in Somalia.

11. See also Chapter 7 on al-Shabaab's taxation practices.

12. See also Chapter 7.

4. THE REVIVAL AND RE-EMBEDDING OF SOMALI PORTS

1. See Pankhurst (1965); Abir (1965); Cassanelli (1982); Reese (1996); Dua (2017), (2019).

2. We thank Dennis Rodgers and Lars Buur for this take on Polanyi's concept.

3. Logistics Capacity Assessment (2018), 'Somalia port assessment' Available at: https://dlca.logcluster.org/display/public/DLCA/2.1+Somalia+Port+Assessment (accessed 13 January 2020).

4. Logistics Capacity Assessment (2018), 'Somalia Port of Kismayo' Available at:

https://dlca.logcluster.org/display/public/DLCA/2.1.4+Somalia+Port+of +Kismayo (accessed 13 January 2020).

5. *New York Times* (1984), 'U.S. will spend $38.6 million to refurbish port in Somalia', 20 September. Available at: https://www.nytimes.com/1984/09/20/world/us-will-spend-38.6-million-to-refurbish-port-in-somalia.html (accessed 16 September 2021).

6. Kismayo Port closed in September through December 1992 (World Bank 1996) and 1994–99 (Marchal 2002); Mogadishu Port in various periods in 1990–91, 1991–92 and 1995–2006; and Berbera Port in 1988–91 (Bradbury 2008).

7. In mid-1992, a ship with food aid was prevented from docking by mortar fire, making it clear that some merchants in the city still had food to sell at good prices and therefore didn't want food aid (Marchal 2002).

8. WFP (2006), 'First WFP food aid ship arrives in Somali Port of Mogadishu in more than a decade', *Reliefweb*, 4 September. Available at: https://reliefweb.int/report/somalia/first-wfp-food-aid-ship-arrives-somali-port-mogadishu-more-decade (accessed 13 January 2020); Logistics Capacity Assessment (2018), 'Somalia Port of Mogadishu'. Available at: https://dlca.logcluster.org/display/public/DLCA/2.1.1+Somalia+Port+of+Mogadishu (accessed 13 January 2020).

9. According to the Logistical Cluster, this committee was still operating the port in 2005. See https://logcluster.org/document/somali-ports-0 (accessed 20 January 2020).

10. See Logistical Cluster (2005) available at: https://logcluster.org/document/somali-ports-0 (accessed 20 January 2020).

11. WFP (2006), 'First WFP food aid ship arrives in Somali Port of Mogadishu in more than a decade', *Reliefweb*, 4 September 2006. Available at: https://reliefweb.int/report/somalia/first-wfp-food-aid-ship-arrives-somali-port-mogadishu-more-decade (accessed 13 January 2020).

12. Mainly Berbera, but since 2014 MSC and CMA-CGM have called at Mogadishu, as has Maersk from 2019 onwards. East Africa Business Week (2019), 'Maersk line begins operations in Mogadishu Port', *East Africa Business Week*, 8 January. Available at: https://www.busiweek.com/maersk-line-begins-operations-in-mogadishu-port/ (accessed 20 January 2020).

13. According to UNOPS' transport needs assessment (AfDB 2016).

14. Garowe Online (2018), 'Somalia, Ethiopia agree to deepen bilateral trade ties', 16 June. Available at: https://www.garoweonline.com/en/news/press-releases/somalia-ethiopia-agree-to-deepen-bilateral-trade-ties (accessed 16 June 2018).

15. Logistics Capacity Assessment, 'Somali port of Mogadishu'. Available at: https://dlca.logcluster.org/display/public/DLCA/2.1.1+Somalia+Port+of +Mogadishu (accessed 13 January 2020).

16. Financial Governance Committee (2019), 'Financial governance report July 2019'. Available at: https://mof.gov.so/sites/default/files/2019-10/2019%

20Financial%20Governance%20Report_EMAIL_0.pdf (accessed 16 September 2021).

17. In 2012, Puntland had launched the Bosaso Port renovation project and contracted Indian constructor KMC to upgrade the port.

18. Interview with Anthe Vrijlandt and Angus Miller, TMEA, Zoom, 21 March 2022. When the partnership was announced, BII was known as the Commonwealth Development Corporation (CDC).

19. Anderson, R. (2017), 'Dubai's P&O Ports wins 30-year concession in Somalia's Puntland', *Gulf Business*, 6 April. Available at: https://gulfbusiness.com/dubais-po-ports-wins-30-year-concession-somalias-puntland/ (accessed 16 September 2021).

20. Garowe Online (2017), 'Somalia: Puntland parliament endorses P&O Ports agreement', 27 July. Available at: https://www.garoweonline.com/en/news/puntland/somalia-puntland-parliament-endorses-dp-world-agreement (accessed 16 September 2021).

21. Al Jazeera (2019), 'Gunmen kill head of Dubai-owned port operation in Somalia', 4 February. Available at: https://www.aljazeera.com/news/2019/2/4/gunmen-kill-head-of-dubai-owned-port-operation-in-somalia (accessed 16 September 2021).

22. 'Puntland renegotiates DP World concession to manage Bosaso Port', *Puntland News*, 21 February 2022, at https://puntlandpost.net/2022/02/21/puntland-renegotiates-dp-world-concession-to-manage-bosaso-port/ (accessed 8 September 2022).

23. Interview with clearance agent, Berbera, 17 July 2018.

24. See Ahmed and Stepputat (2019).

25. Interview with an elder, Berbera, 8 December 2018.

26. We have yet to find out about dimensions of the labour contracts other than wage.

27. Interview with employee, Berbera Port, 8 December 2018.

28. Interview with employee, Berbera Port, 10 July 2017.

29. Interview with clearance agent, Berbera, 17 July 2018.

30. Interview with employee, Berbera Port, 8 December 2018.

31. Interview with an elder, Berbera, 8 December 2018.

32. The lack of this flexible workforce created many delays, according to the chairman of the stevedores' union. Interview with chairman of stevedores' union, Berbera, 9 July 2017.

33. Interview with chairman of stevedores' union, Berbera, 14 May 2018.

34. Interview with an elder, Berbera, 8 December 2018, our emphasis.

35. Interview with chairman of stevedores' union, Berbera, 14 May 2018.

36. Interview with chairman of stevedores' union, Berbera, 9 July 2017.

37. Interview with chairman of stevedores' union, Berbera, 14 May 2018.

38. See, for example, Taussig (1987).

39. 'It is We who have apportioned among them their livelihood in the life of this world and have raised some of them above others in degrees [of rank] that they

may make use of one another for service. But the mercy of your Lord is better than whatever they accumulate.' (Qur'an 43:32. Translation from https://quran.com/43/32-42?translations=20).

40. Interview with the chairman of stevedores' union, Berbera, 14 May 2018.
41. Interview with councillor and businessman, Berbera, 14 May 2018.
42. Interview with employee, Berbera Port, 8 December 2018.
43. Interview with Mayor of Berbera, 21 October 2019.
44. Interview with an elder, Berbera, 8 December 2018.
45. Ibid.
46. Interview with a real estate broker, Berbera, 14 May 2018.
47. Interview with a clearance agent, Berbera, 17 July 2018.
48. Ibid.
49. Interview with an elder, Berbera, 8 December 2018.
50. Corruption is known as *bacadjoog*—or 'standing in the sand'.
51. Somali trucks are in practice barred from entering Ethiopia because they would need Ethiopian registration at the cost of roughly 15,000 USD (compared to 400 USD for Ethiopian trucks to register in Somaliland), according to the chairman of the truckers' union in Berbera.
52. Interview with the chairman of truckers' union, Berbera, 8 July 2017.
53. Interview with shipping agent A, Berbera, 10 April 2017.
54. Interview with shipping agent B, Berbera, 10 April 2017; see also Wallisch (2018).
55. Interview with NGO (1), 27 September 2017.
56. Some clearing and forwarding companies in Berbera also operate without written contracts with importers from Somali and Oromo areas in Ethiopia; interview with shipping agent B, Berbera 10 April 2017.
57. Interview with logistical firm (C), 19 October 2017.
58. Interview with shipping agent B, 10 April 2017. DP World encouraged the formation of the union in order to have a single counterpart.
59. See, for example, Gilkes (1993); Bradbury (2008); Tahir (2021).
60. We do not have solid information on businesspeople's role in the trajectory of Kismayo Port.
61. 'Somali president inaugurates Gara'ad Port in Puntland's Mudug region', *Hiiraan Online*, 23 October 2022. Available at https://www.hiiraan.com/news4/2022/Oct/188378/somalia_president_inaugurates_gara_ad_port_in_puntland_s_mudug_region.aspx (accessed 25 October 2022).
62. 'China signs deal to build port in ancient Somalian town of Eyl', *Global Construction Review*, 3 June 2019. Available at: https://www.globalconstructionreview.com/china-signs-deal-build-port-ancient-somalian-town/ (accessed 10 September 2021).
63. 'Somalia: Government to build Hobyo Port in the coastal town', *Construction Review Online*, 14 August 2021. Available at: https://constructionreviewonline.com/news/somalia-government-to-build-hobyo-port-in-the-coastal-town/ (accessed 10 September 2021).

64. Interview with head of communications, DP World, 18 August 2021.
65. Interview in Hargeisa, 4 June 2015.
66. Interview with an elder, Berbera, 8 December 2017.
67. Interview with counsellor and businessman, Berbera, 14 May 2018.

5. GOVERNING MARKETPLACES: SELF-REGULATION, STATENESS AND MATERIALITIES

1. Unless otherwise mentioned, this chapter draws on studies by Fana Gebresenbet (2018), Varming (2017, 2020, 2021), Ng'asike (2019, 2021) and Ng'asike et al. (2020, 2021).
2. The TPLF-dominated EPRDF set up an ethnic-based federal government structure for Ethiopia.
3. The military-socialist government 1974–91. *Derg* means 'committee'.
4. We are indebted to Khalif Abdullahi for this observation.
5. FEWS NET has collected staple food prices in main Somali markets on a monthly basis since 1995. In 2022, the organisation monitored 39 markets of various sizes across Somalia and Somaliland. For each market, a different bundle of food items, including livestock, is covered by enumerators in function of local livelihood zones. FEWS NET data allows monitoring price developments over time, but it does not provide clues as to the financial volume of commodities traded, its evolution over time or the relative importance of particular commodities. There is an absence of comparable data on food prices in marketplaces in the Somali parts of Ethiopia and Kenya.
6. On Mogadishu's small neighbourhood markets, see Abukar Mursal (2018); on Jigjiga's central vegetable market, see Fana Gebresenbet (2018).
7. Such as the bridge over Tana River outside Garissa, which in terms of trade constitutes the de facto border between Somalia and Kenya.
8. In the case of livestock in Kenya, Ethiopia and Somaliland, local representatives of national state institutions are also involved.
9. In Ethiopia, it is widely believed that influential politicians—including from Addis Ababa—have been working with *khat* exporter Suhura Ismail, who in the 2010s faced strong competition from *khat* traders supported by the then regional president Abdi Mohamed Omar 'Iley'.
10. Interview by Varming, EBDA, Nairobi, 15 July 2015.
11. Interview with member of a market committee, July 2017, quoted by Abukar Mursal (2018: 19).
12. Garissa County, for example, earned 3 million USD from cattle sales in 2018, a below-average year.

6. GOVERNING COMMODITY FLOWS IN THE SOMALI BORDERLANDS

1. Where nothing else is noted, this chapter draws upon Rasmussen (2017); Asnake Kefale (2019).

2. Interview with Yusuf Hassan, MP for Kamukunji Constituency, Nairobi, February 2020.
3. Thomas, T. (2013), 'Jubbaland reborn: A look at Jubba and Somalia post-Addis Agreement', *Somalia Newsroom*, 3 September. Available at: http://somalianewsroom.com/2013/09/03/jubaland-reborn-a-look-at-jubba-and-somalia-post-addis-agreement (accessed 25 September 2021).
4. KTN, 17 February 2016, Live with Koinange.
5. Interview with former district commissioner, December 2014, Nairobi; interview with advisor to County Government in Northern Kenya, February 2020.
6. United Nations Security Council resolution no. 2036, S/RES/2036 (2012), 22 February 2012.
7. Quote from fieldnotes in Eastleigh 2015; the general characterisation of traders' focus on goods, handling and mobility is paraphrased from fieldnotes and interviews conducted in 2015, 2017 and 2019.
8. Asnake Kefale (2019), 'Shoes and clothes in Ethiopia: Why consumers prefer "old and trendy" over "new but fake"', *Governing Hubs and Flows, Somali East Africa*, Blog. Available at: https://govsea.tumblr.com/post/189625891339/shoes-and-clothes-in-ethiopia-why-consumers (accessed 11 October 2021).
9. Interview with independent policy researcher, Somalia-Kenya, February 2020; phone interview with a researcher at the Rift Valley Institute, August 2019.
10. Field assistants provided the second author with copies of receipts from 2019.
11. Interview with Kenyan police officer previously posted in northern Kenya, August 2019.
12. Interview with county bureaucrat, Garissa, November 2014.

7. RAISING FISCAL REVENUES: THE POLITICAL ECONOMY OF SOMALI TRADE TAXATION

1. See 'The recurrent costs and reform financing project', posted at https://www.worldbank.org/en/results/2021/01/14/helping-build-the-state-in-somalia-financing-financial-management-and-federalism (accessed 9 June 2022).
2. Where nothing else indicated, this chapter draws upon Varming (2017, 2019, 2021), Musa (2019, 2021), and Musa et al. (2021).
3. Somalilandlaw, 'Somaliland public finance laws'. Available at: http://www.somalilandlaw.com/somaliland_public_finance_law.html (accessed 4 October 2021); Ministry of Finance Puntland (2014), 'Puntland taxation framework' (Garowe: Ministry of Finance of Finance Puntland). Available at: https://mof.pl.so/wp-content/uploads/2020/01/Puntland-Taxation-Framework.pdf (accessed 8 October 2021).
4. See 'Tax on goods and services' in Table 7.1.
5. An IMF (2020: 12) document declares Somalia eligible for debt relief, noting that domestic revenue has increased by 70% from 2016–19, 'albeit from a very

low base', and that this reflects 'improvements in tax administration and new tax measures'.

6. Interview with customs clearance broker, Burao, 14 March 2021.
7. Interview with senior Somaliland customs officer, Lasanod, 10 March 2021.
8. Interview with employee, Lasanod, 12 March 2021.
9. Interview with municipal administrator, Garowe, 13 November 2014.
10. Interview with transporter, Garowe, 9 November 2014.
11. Field notes, Ahmed M. Musa, March 2021 and August 2018.
12. Interview with manager of general trading company, Lasanod, 8 March 2021.
13. Interview with senior Ministry of Finance official, Garowe, 25 April 2021. Numbers are approximations.
14. Hiraal Institute (2018) estimated that USD 3.5 million and 500,000 are collected annually from Mogadishu- and Bosaso-based businesspeople, respectively.
15. 'In Somalia, businesses face "taxation" by militants', *The Observer*, 4 December 2018. Available at: https://observer.ug/news/headlines/59387-in-somalia-businesses-face-taxation-by-militants (accessed 4 October 2021).
16. Interview with municipal administrator, Garowe, 13 November 2014.
17. Ibid.
18. Interview with fuel trader, Garowe, 17 November 2014.
19. Ibid.
20. Fifteen per cent of livestock exported through Berbera port originates from south-central Somalia.
21. Interview with member of investment company, Nairobi, 13 May 2015.
22. Interview with member of Eastleigh Hawkers' Association, Nairobi, 22 December 2016.
23. Berbera corridor is an obvious example, even though the transit agreement will exempt Ethiopia-bound commodities from custom duties. This is why tax reforms aim at 'moving tax revenues further inland' as a compensation.

8. TILLY IN THE TROPICS: TRADE AND SOMALI STATE-MAKING

1. *The Economist*, 'Most failed state: Twenty-five years of chaos in the Horn of Africa', 10 September 2016, https://www.economist.com/middle-east-and-africa/2016/09/10/most-failed-state.
2. Although al-Shabaab's creation date is disputed, the Islamic militants have existed for at least 15 years, pursuing a distinctive state-building strategy.
3. More recently created Federal Member States Hirshabelle, South West State and Galmudug are not included in this assessment, given their short state-building record. The capital Mogadishu, which is part of the Benadir Regional Administration, is indirectly governed by the federal government.
4. The federal government came into existence through an internationally mediated political process.
5. Already in 1996, Somaliland was described as a 'a profit-sharing agreement among the dominant livestock traders, with a constitution appended' (de Waal 1996).

6. Starting from the 1990s, business groups belonging to the Habar Gedir clan lineages have been able to convert control of trade corridors in southern Somalia into obtaining dominance in finance and telecommunication companies such as Hormud, Salaama or Juba Express. Meanwhile, Abgaal clan lineages in northern Mogadishu established dominance in import, export and the construction sector (Hoffman et al. 2017).

7. For a comparison of recent fiscal revenues by Somaliland, the Federal Government of Somalia and various Federal Member States, see Raballand and Knebelmann (2021: 9).

8. Federal Republic of Somalia, *Provisional Constitution*, 1 August 2012, Mogadishu: Federal Republic of Somalia.

9. The following paragraphs draw on Hagmann (2021).

10. Tax bargaining obviously also occurs in states with more bureaucratic capacities, including in OECD countries. A case in point are tax exemptions on imports, which the Ethiopian government accords to politically savvy businesspeople.

11. See Republic of Somaliland (2020), 'Customs valuation book 2020' (Hargeisa: Ministry of Finance Development). Available at: https://slmof.org/wp-content/uploads/2021/04/2020-Customs-Valuation-Book-A4.pdf (accessed 15 October 2021); Ministry of Finance Puntland (2014), 'Puntland taxation framework' (Garoowe: Ministry of Finance Puntland). Available at: https://mof.pl.so/wp-content/uploads/2020/01/Puntland-Taxation-Framework.pdf (accessed 15 October 2021); the Somali federal parliament passed a revenue act in 2019, but custom duties continue to be based on pre-1991 legislation and directives. For an overview of Ethiopia custom duties, see Ethiopian Revenues and Customs Authority (2017), 'Ethiopia customs guide' (Addis Ababa: Ethiopian Revenues and Customs Authority). Available at: https://admin.theiguides.org/Media/Documents/Ethiopia_Customs_Guide.pdf (accessed 15 October 2021).

12. 'As far as military protection goes mercantile groups would be indifferent between who provided protection. However, kings were more attractive as contracting parties than local feudal lords, given efficiencies of scale' (Spruyt 2011: 573).

13. The Somaliland government instituted an embryonic tax regime in 1996 with the adoption of the Somaliland Direct Tax Law and a series of tax laws governing indirect taxation (World Bank and IFC 2012: 44).

14. Musa and Horst (2019: 42) cite a key informant who speculated that if Somaliland's five major companies paid full taxes, the government's budget would have doubled from 500 million to 1 billion USD.

15. Ahmed Musa, personal communication, 19 June 2021.

16. A different set of norms and standards guides what Dua (2017) calls the 'underbelly' of globalization; Bosaso Port, for example, is used by many dhows that operate ports that many larger vessels and shipping companies cannot serve because of security, insurance issues or technical problems.

17. UNCTAD's Automated System for Customs Data.

18. Interview with Mohamed Behi Yonis, Somaliland Minister of Foreign Affairs, Hargeisa, June 2015. 'Post-Panamax' refers to a standard size of containerships that are bigger than the ones that could enter the original Panama Canal.

19. Interviews with KEBS officers, Nairobi, November 2014 and February 2020; conversations and observations among wholesalers in Eastleigh, March 2015, August 2019 and February 2020. Jacob Rasmussen, personal communication.

9. AFTERWORD: SOMALIA, AN ECONOMY WITH 'STATENESS'

1. In the introduction, Stepputat and Hagmann acknowledge the difficulty of conducting field research among pastoralists and agro-pastoralists in central and southern Somalia due to insecurity. They acknowledge, in turn, that these sub-populations are not well represented in the book. However, their absence is noteworthy because they produce the product (livestock) that fuels the region's main export industry and comprise about 50% of the region's population.

BIBLIOGRAPHY

Abdi, C. M. (2015), *Elusive Jannah: The Somali Diaspora and a Borderless Muslim Identity* (Minneapolis, MN: University of Minnesota Press).

Abdi, S. (2010), 'Mobile transfers save money and lives in Somalia', Reuters, 3 March. Available at: https://www.reuters.com/article/us-somalia-mobiles/mobile-transfers-save-money-and-lives-in-somalia-idUKTRE6222BY20100303 (accessed 6 September 2021).

Abdirahman, K. (2021), 'Contested commerce: Revenue and state-making in the Galkayo borderlands'. Rift Valley Institute, London and Nairobi. Available at: https://riftvalley.net/publication/contested-commerce-revenue-and-state-making-galkayo-borderlands (accessed 3 November 2022).

Abir, M. (1965), 'Brokerage and brokers in Ethiopia in the first half of the 19th century', *Journal of Ethiopian Studies*, 3(1), pp. 1–5.

Abrams, P. (1988 [1977]), 'Notes on the difficulty of studying the state', *Journal of Historical Sociology*, 1(1), pp. 58–89.

Abshir, S., K. Abdirahman and H. Stogdon (2020), 'Tax and the state in Somalia: Understanding domestic revenue mobilisation'. Rift Valley Institute Briefing Paper, London and Nairobi, May. Available at: https://riftvalley.net/sites/default/files/publication-documents/Tax%20and%20the%20State%20in%20Somalia%20by%20Sagal%20Abshir%2C%20Khalif%20Abdirahman%20and%20Hannah%20Stogdon%20-%20RVI%20%282020%29.pdf (accessed 3 November 2022).

Abukar Mursal, F. (2018), '"Elders among traders": Market committees and everyday state formation in Mogadishu'. Danish Institute for International Studies Working Paper 2018: 5, Copenhagen.

AfDB (2016), 'Somalia. transport sector needs assessment and investment programme', African Development Group, Abidjan. Available at: https://www.afdb.org/fileadmin/uploads/afdb/Documents/

BIBLIOGRAPHY

Publications/Somalia_Transport_Sector_Needs_Assessment_and_Investment_Programme.pdf (accessed 2 November 2022).

Ahmad, A. S. (2012), 'Between the Mosque and the Market: An Economic Explanation of State Failure and State Formation in the Modern Muslim World', PhD Dissertation, Department of Political Science, McGill University.

Ahmad, A., T. Bandula-Irwin and M. Ibrahim (2022), 'Who governs? State versus jihadist political order in Somalia', *Journal of Eastern African Studies*, 16(1), pp. 68–91.

————— (2014), 'The security bazaar: Business interests and Islamic power in civil war Somalia', *International Security*, 9(3), pp. 89–117.

Ahmed, W. M. and F. Stepputat (2019), 'Berbera Port: Geopolitics and state-making in Somaliland'. Rift Valley Institute Briefing paper, Nairobi, August. Available at: https://pure.diis.dk/ws/files/3006484/RVI_Briefing_2019_Ahmed_and_Stepputat_Berbera.pdf (accessed 3 November 2022).

Albrecht, P. (2018), 'The interplay of interventions and hybridisation in Puntland's security sector', *Cooperation and Conflict*, 53(2), pp. 216–36.

Ali, A. H., and Ali, A. S. (2013), 'Challenges and constraints faced by Somali women entrepreneurs in Benadir region', *Interdisciplinary Journal of Contemporary Research in Business*, 5(2), pp. 436–41.

Anand, N., A. Gupta and H. Appel (eds) (2018), *The Promise of Infrastructure* (Durham, NC: Duke University Press).

Anderson, B. (1983), *Imagined Communities: Reflections on the Origin and Spread of Nationalism* (London and New York: Verso).

Anderson, D. M. and J. McKnight (2015), 'Kenya at war: Al-Shabaab and its enemies in eastern Africa', *African Affairs*, 114 (454), pp. 1–27.

Anderson, J. and L. O'Dowd (1999), 'Borders, border regions and territoriality: Contradictory meanings, changing significance', *Regional Studies*, 33(7), pp. 593–604.

Appadurai, A. (1986), 'Introduction: Commodities and the politics of value', in A. Appadurai (ed.), *The Social Life of Things: Commodities in Cultural Perspective* (Cambridge: Cambridge University Press), pp. 3–62.

Arhin, K. P. Hesp and L. van der Laan (eds) (1985), *Marketing Boards in Tropical Africa* (London: Keegan Paul).

Asiwaju, A. I. (1993), 'Borderlands in Africa: A comparative research perspective with particular reference to western Europe', *Journal of Borderland Studies*, 8(2), pp. 1–12.

Asnake Kefale (2019), 'Shoats and smart phones: Cross-border trading in the Ethio-Somaliland corridor'. Danish Institute for International Studies (DIIS) Working Paper 7, Copenhagen.

BIBLIOGRAPHY

Bakonyi, J. (2013), 'Authority and administration beyond the state: Local governance in southern Somalia, 1995–2006', *Journal of Eastern African Studies*, 7(2), pp. 272–90.

Balthasar, D. (2013), 'Somaliland's best kept secret: Shrewd politics and war projects as means of state-making', *Journal of Eastern African Studies*, 7(2), pp. 218–38.

Bandula-Irwin, T., M. Gallien, A. Jackson, V. van den Boogaard and F. Weigand (2022), 'Beyond greed: Why armed groups tax', *Studies in Conflict & Terrorism*. DOI: 10.1080/1057610X.2022.2038409.

Banks, N., M. Lombard and D. Mitlin (2019), 'Urban informality as a site of critical analysis', *Journal of Development Studies*, 56(2), pp. 223–38.

———— (2017), 'State-making at gunpoint: The role of violent conflict in Somaliland's march to statehood', *Civil Wars*, 19(1), pp. 65–86.

Barnes, C. and Harun Hassan (2007), 'The rise and fall of Mogadishu's Islamic courts', *Journal of Eastern African Studies*, 1(2), pp. 151–60.

Barth, F. (2000), 'Boundaries and connections', in A. Cohen (ed.), *Signifying Identities: Anthropological Perspectives on Boundaries and Contested Identities* (London: Routledge), pp. 17–36.

Bates, R. (2014), *Markets and States in Tropical Africa: The Political Basis of Agricultural Policies* (Berkeley: University of California Press).

Baud, M. and W. van Schendel (1997), 'Toward a comparative history of borderlands', *Journal of World History*, 8(2), pp. 211–42.

BBC (2010), 'Al-Shabab bans mobile phone money transfers in Somalia', BBC, 18 October. Available at: https://www.bbc.com/news/world-africa-11566247 (accessed 6 September 2021).

Bertazzini, M. C. (2018), 'The long-term impact of Italian colonial roads in the Horn of Africa, 1935–2000', Economic History Working Paper No. 272, LSE, London.

Bjork, S. R. (2007), 'Modernity meets clan: Cultural intimacy in the Somali diaspora', in A. M. Kusow and S. R. Bjork (eds), *From Mogadishu to Dixon: The Somali Diaspora in a Global Context* (Trenton, NJ: Red Sea Press), pp. 135–58.

Bøås, M. (2014), *The Politics of Conflict Economies: Miners, Merchants and Warriors in the African Borderland* (London: Routledge).

Bonacich, E. and J. B. Wilson (2008), *Getting the Goods: Ports, Labor, and the Logistics Revolution* (New York: Cornell University Press).

Boone, C. (2014), *Property and Political Order in Africa: Land Rights and the Structure of Politics* (New York: Cambridge University Press).

Bradbury, M. (2008), *Becoming Somaliland* (Oxford: James Currey).

Bräutigam, D. (2008), 'Introduction: Taxation and state-building in developing countries', in D. Bräutigam, O. H. Fjeldstad and M. Moore (eds), *Taxation and State-building in Developing Countries: Capacity and Consent*. (Cambridge: Cambridge University Press), pp. 1–33.

Broch-Due, V. and M. Ystanes (2016), 'Introduction: Introducing ethnographies of trusting', in V. Broch-Due and M. Ystanes, eds, *Trusting and Its Tribulations: Interdisciplinary Engagements with Intimacy, Sociality and Trust* (New York: Berghahn Books), pp. 1–36.

Brons, M. H. (2001), *Society, Security, Sovereignty and the State in Somalia: From Statelessness to Statelessness?* (Utrecht: International Books).

Bruzzone, A. (2019), 'Territorial Appropriation, Trade, and Politics in the Somalia-Kenya Borderlands (c.1925–1963): State Formation in Transnational Perspective', PhD Dissertation, University of Warwick.

Burton, R. F. (1943 [1856]), *First Footsteps in East Africa* (London and New York: Dent & Sons and Dutton & Co.).

Campos, J. A. (2016), 'On taxes and suspicion: Ambivalences of rule and the politically possible in contemporary Hargeisa, Somaliland'. Danish Institute for International Studies (DIIS) Working Paper 2016: 5, Copenhagen.

Cantens, T. and G. Raballand (2021), 'Taxation and customs reforms in fragile states: Between bargaining and enforcement'. Working Paper 120, International Centre for Tax and Development, Brighton.

Carey, M. (2017), *Mistrust: An Ethnographic Theory* (London: Hau Books).

Carrier, N. (ed.) (2007), *Kenyan Khat: The Social Life of a Stimulant* (Leiden: Brill).

——— (2017), *Little Mogadishu: Eastleigh, Nairobi's Global Somali Hub* (London: Hurst).

Carrier, N. and E. Lochery (2013), 'Missing states? Somali trade networks and the Eastleigh transformation', *Journal of Eastern African Studies*, 7(2), pp. 334–52.

Carrier, N. and H. Elliott (2019), 'Demanding and commanding goods: The Eastleigh transformation told through the "lives" of its commodities', in N. Carrier and T. Scharrer (eds), *Mobile Urbanity: Somali Presence in Urban East Africa* (New York: Berghahn Books), pp. 97–117.

Carrier, N. and H. H. Kochore (2014), 'Navigating ethnicity and electoral politics in northern Kenya: The case of the 2013 election', *Journal of Eastern African Studies*, 8(1), pp. 135–52.

Carroll, L. A. (2011), *Violent Democratization: Social Movements, Elites, and Politics in Colombia's Rural War Zones, 1984–2008* (Notre Dame, IN: University of Notre Dame Press).

Carse, A., T. Middleton, J. Cons, J. Dua, G. Valdivia and E. C. Dunn (2020), 'Chokepoints: Anthropologies of the constricted contemporary', *Ethnos*. DOI: 10.1080/00141844.2019.1696862.

Cassanelli, L. V. (1982), *The Shaping of Somali Society: Reconstructing the History of a Pastoral People, 1600–1900* (Philadelphia: University of Pennsylvania Press).

Chalfin, B. (2001a), 'Border zone trade and the economic boundaries of the state in north-east Ghana', *Africa*, 71(2), pp. 202–24.

———— (2001b), 'Working the border: Constructing sovereignty in the context of liberalisation', *Political and Legal Anthropology Review*, 24(1), pp. 129–48.

———— (2010), *Neoliberal Frontiers: An Ethnography of Sovereignty in West Africa* (Chicago, IL: University of Chicago Press).

Chatham House (2013), 'Somalia's future: Building a unified regional state: British government consultation with the Somali diaspora'. Chatham House, London, 18 April. Available at https://www.chathamhouse.org/sites/default/files/field/field_document/20130418SomaliasFuture.pdf (accessed 2 November 2022).

Chaudhuri, K. N. (1985), *Trade and Civilisation in the Indian Ocean: An Economic History from the Rise of Islam to 1750* (Cambridge: Cambridge University Press).

Chaudry, K. A. (1997), *The Price of Wealth: Economies and Institutions in the Middle East* (Ithaca, NY: Cornell University Press).

Cheeseman, N. G. Lynch and J. Willis (2016), 'Decentralisation in Kenya: The governance of governors', *Journal of Modern African Studies*, 54(1), pp. 1–35.

Chome, N. (2016), 'Violent extremism and clan dynamics in Kenya', Peaceworks 123, SAHAN and United States Institute of Peace, Washington, DC. Available at: https://www.usip.org/publications/2016/10/violent-extremism-and-clan-dynamics-kenya (accessed 3 November 2022).

Chua, C., M. Danyluk, D. Cowen and L. Khalili, L. (2018), 'Introduction: Turbulent circulation: Building a critical engagement with logistics', *Environment and Planning D: Society and Space*, 36(4), pp. 617–29.

Ciabarri, L. (2017), 'Biographies of roads, Biographies of nations: History, territory and the road effect in post-conflict Somaliland', in K. Beck, G. Klaeger and M. Stasik (eds), *The Making of the African Road* (Leiden and Boston: Brill), pp. 116–40.

Cissokho, S. (2022), 'Infrastructure, development and neoliberalism in Africa: The concept of transport corridors', in Lamarque and Nugent (eds), *Transport Corridors in Africa* (Woodbridge: James Currey), pp. 35–56.

Clapham, C. (2017), *The Horn of Africa: State Formation and Decay* (London: Hurst).

BIBLIOGRAPHY

Cockayne, J. and Shetret, L. (2012), 'Capitalizing on trust: Harnessing Somali remittances for counterterrorism, human rights and state building'. Center on Global Counterterrorism Cooperation, Washington, DC. Available at: https://www.globalcenter.org/wp-content/uploads/2012/07/CapitalizingOnTrust.pdf (accessed 6 September 2021).

Coe, N. M. (2012), 'Missing links: Logistics, governance and upgrading in a shifting global economy', *Review of International Political Economy*, 21(1), pp. 224–56.

Cohen, A. (1969), *Custom and Politics in Urban Africa* (London: Routledge & Kegan Paul).

Collins, T. (2022), 'Somalis changed the face of money transfers worldwide', *Quartz Africa*, 8 April, https://qz.com/africa/2152271/somalia-changed-the-face-of-money-transfers-worldwide/ (accessed 18 March 2021).

Cooper, F. (2002), *Africa Since 1940: The Past of the Present* (Cambridge: Cambridge University Press).

——— (2018), 'Gatekeeping practices, gatekeeper states and beyond', *Third World Thematics*, 3(3), pp. 455–68.

Cowen, D. (2014), *The Deadly Life of Logistics: Mapping Violence in Global Trade* (Minneapolis: University of Minnesota Press).

CSSF (2019), 'Charcoal case study, 2019'. Conflict, Stability and Security Fund, Eastern Africa, March.

D'Arcy, M. (2020), 'Devolution and the county government', in N. Cheeseman, K. Kanyinga and G. Lynch (eds), *The Oxford Handbook of Kenyan Politics* (Oxford: Oxford University Press), p. 251.

D'Arcy, M. and A. Cornell (2016), 'Devolution and corruption in Kenya: Everyone's turn to eat?', *African Affairs*, 115(459), pp. 246–73.

Dahou, T. and B. Chalfin (2019), 'Governing Africa's seas in the neoliberal era', in N. Cheseman (ed.), *Oxford Research Encyclopedia of Politics*. DOI: 10.1093/acrefore/9780190228637.013.904.

Dalleo, P. T. (1975), 'Trade and Pastoralism: Economic Factors in the History of the Somali of Northeastern Kenya, 1892–1948', PhD Dissertation, Syracuse University, New York.

De Waal, A. (1996), 'Class and power in a stateless Somalia: A discussion paper', Justice Africa, London.

——— (2015). *The Real Politics of the Horn of Africa: Money, War and the Business of Power* (Cambridge: Polity Press).

Dereje Feyissa and M. V. Hoehne (2010), 'State borders and borderlands as resources. An analytical framework', in D. Feyissa and M. V. Hoehne (eds), *Borders and Borderlands as Resources in the Horn of Africa*. (Rochester, NY: James Currey), pp. 1–25.

BIBLIOGRAPHY

Devereux, S. (2006), *Vulnerable Livelihoods in Somali Region, Ethiopia* (Brighton: Institute of Development Studies).

Dobler, G. (2016), 'The green, the grey and the blue: A typology of cross-border trade in Africa', *Journal of Modern African Studies*, 54(1), pp. 145–69.

Dorman, S. R. (2018), 'Beyond the gatekeeper state? Studying Africa's states and state systems in the twenty-first century', *Third World Thematics*, 3(3), pp. 311–24.

Dorussen, H. and H. Ward (2010), 'Trade networks and the Kantian peace', *Journal of Peace Research*, 47(1), pp. 29–42.

Dua, J. (2017), 'From pirate ports to special economic zones: Violence, regulation and port-making in the Somali peninsula'. Danish Institute for International Studies Working Paper No. 12, Copenhagen.

———— (2018), 'Chokepoint sovereignty', in A. Carse, J. Cons and T. Middleton (eds), *Limn* 10, pp. 35–8.

———— (2019), *Captured at Sea. Piracy and Protection in the Indian Ocean* (Oakland: California University Press).

Dua, J. with A. Warsame and A. Shire (2020), 'Bosaso and the Gulf of Aden Changing dynamics of a land-sea network'. Rift Valley Institute, Nairobi. Available at: https://riftvalley.net/sites/default/files/publication-documents/Bosaso%20and%20the%20Gulf%20of%20Aden%20by%20Jatin%20Dua%2C%20Abdideeq%20Warsame%20and%20Ahmed%20Shire%20-%20RVI%20X-Border%20Project%20%282020%29_0.pdf (accessed 02 November 2022).

Eid, A. (2014), 'Jostling for trade: The politics of livestock marketing on the Ethiopia-Somaliland border'. Future Agricultures Project Working Paper 75, Institute of Development Studies, Brighton.

Elder, C. (2021), 'Somaliland's authoritarian turn: Oligarchic–corporate power and the political economy of de facto states', *International Affairs*, 97(6), pp. 1749–65.

———— (2022), 'Logistics contracts and the political economy of state failure: Evidence from Somalia', *African Affairs*, 121(484), pp. 395–417.

Elliott, H. (2014), 'Somali displacements and shifting markets: Camel milk in Nairobi's Eastleigh estate', in A. Hammar (ed.), *Displacement Economies in Africa: Paradoxes of Crisis and Creativity* (London and New York: Zed Books), pp. 127–44.

———— (2018), 'Anticipating Plots: (Re)Making Property, Futures and Town at the Gateway to Kenya's "New Frontier"', PhD Dissertation, Department of Theology, University of Copenhagen.

Elwert, G. (1997), 'Markets of violence', in G. Elwert, S. Feuchtwang and D. Neubert (eds), *Dynamics of Violence. Processes of Escalation and De-escalation in Violent Group Conflicts* (Berlin: Duncker & Humbolt), pp. 85–102.

Emmenegger, R. (2013), 'Entre pouvoir et autorité. Propriété urbaine et production de l'État à Jigjiga, Éthiopie', *Politique Africaine*, 132(4), pp. 115–37.

Enns, C. (2019), 'Infrastructure projects and rural politics in northern Kenya: The use of divergent expertise to negotiate the terms of land deals for transport infrastructure', *Journal of Peasant Studies*, 46(2), pp. 358–76.

Eubank, N. (2012), 'Taxation, political accountability and foreign aid: Lessons from Somaliland', *Journal of Development Studies*, 48(4), pp. 465–80.

Ezekiel Gebissa (2004), *Leaf of Allah: Khat and Agricultural Transformation in Harerge, Ethiopia 1875–1991* (Oxford, Addis Ababa, Hargeisa and Athens: James Currey, Addis Ababa University Press, Btec Books and Ohio University Press).

Fana Gebresenbet (2018), 'Perishable state-making: Vegetable trade between self-governance and ethnic entitlement in Jigjiga, Ethiopia'. Danish Institute for International Studies (DIIS) Working Paper 2018: 1, Copenhagen.

Fantu Cheru, C. Cramer and A. Oqubay (eds), (2019), *The Oxford Handbook of the Ethiopian Economy* (Oxford: Oxford University Press).

Fanusie, Y. and A. Entz (2017), 'Al Shabaab financial assessment', in *Terror Finance Briefing Book* (Washington, DC: Foundation for Defense of Democracies, Center on Sanctions and Illicit Finance).

Fau, N. (2019), 'Comment étudier les corridors de développement?', *EchoGéo*, 49. DOI: 10.4000/echogeo.18066.

Feyissa, D. and M. V. Hoehne (eds) (2010), *Borders and Borderlands as Resources in the Horn of Africa* (Woodbridge: James Currey).

Forrest, I. and A. Haour (2018), 'Trust in long-distance relationships, 1000–1600 CE', *Past and Present*, 238(13), pp. 190–213.

Gallien, M. and F. Weigand (2021), 'Channelling contraband: How states shape international smuggling routes', *Security Studies*, 30(1), pp. 79–106.

Gallien, M. and V. van den Boogaard (2021), 'Rethinking formalisation: A conceptual critique and research agenda', ICTD Working Paper 127, Institute of Development Studies, Brighton.

Gandrup, T. (2016), 'Enter and exit: Everyday state practices at Somaliland's Hargeisa Egal International Airport'. Danish Institute for International Studies Working Paper 2016: 3, Copenhagen.

BIBLIOGRAPHY

Geertz, C. (1978), 'The bazaar economy: Information and search in peasant marketing', *American Economic Review*, 68(2), pp. 28–32.

Gettleman, J. (2011), 'As an enemy retreats, clans carve up Somalia', *New York Times*, 9 September. Available at: https://www.nytimes. com/2011/09/10/world/africa/10somalia.html (accessed 11 December 2022).

Gilkes, P. S. (1993), 'Two wasted years. The republic of Somaliland, 1991–1993' (Unpublished manuscript, Biggleswade, Bedfordshire).

Goldsmith, P. (1997), 'The Somali impact on Kenya, 1990–1993: The view from the camps', in H. M. Adam and R. Ford (eds), *Mending Rips in the Sky: Options for Somali Communities in the 21st Century* (Lawrenceville, NJ: Red Sea Press), pp. 461–84.

González-Ruibal, A., J. de Torres, M. A. Franco, M. A. Ali, A. M. Shabelle, C. M. Barrio and K. A. Aideed (2017), 'Exploring long distance trade in Somaliland (AD 1000–1900): Preliminary results from the 2015–2016 field seasons', *Azania: Archaeological Research in Africa*, 52(2), pp. 135–72.

Goodhand, J. (2009), 'Bandits, borderlands and opium wars: Afghan statebuilding viewed from the margins'. DIIS Working Paper 2009: 26, Copenhagen, DIIS.

Gregson, N. (2017), 'Logistics at work: Trucks, containers and the friction of circulation in the UK', *Mobilities*, 12(3), pp. 343–64.

Grossman, S. (2021), *The Politics of Order in Informal Markets* (Cambridge: Cambridge University Press).

Haas, A. (2017), 'An overview of municipal finance in Hargeisa, Somaliland'. International Growth Centre, 1 December. Available at: https://www.theigc.org/wpcontent/uploads/2018/01/201712Har geisaMunicipalFinanceWP_Final2.pdf (accessed 24 September 2019).

Haas, P. (2016), 'Trusting the untrustworthy: A Mongolian challenge to Western notions of trust', in V. Broch-Due and M. Ystanes (eds), *Trusting and Its Tribulations: Interdisciplinary Engagements with Intimacy, Sociality and Trust* (New York: Berghahn Books), pp. 84–104.

Hagmann, T. (2005), 'From state-collapse to duty-free shop: Somalia's path to modernity', *African Affairs*, 104(416), pp. 525–35.

——— (2014), 'Punishing the periphery: Legacies of state repression in the Ethiopian Ogaden', *Journal of Eastern African Studies*, 8(4), pp. 725–39.

——— (2016), 'Stabilization, extraversion and political settlements in Somalia'. Rift Valley Institute, London and Nairobi. Available at: https://www.politicalsettlements.org/wp-content/uploads/2015/10/PSRP-RVI-Report-7-Stabilization-Extraversion-and-

239

Political-Settlements-in-Somalia-Tobias-Hagmann-2016.pdf (accessed 2 November 2022).

——— (2021), 'Trade, taxes and tensions in the Somali borderlands'. Rift Valley Institute, London and Nairobi. Available at: https://riftvalley.net/sites/default/files/publication-documents/RVI%20 2021.11.24%20Trade%20taxes%20%26%20tensions.pdf (accessed 3 November 2022).

Hagmann, T. and B. Korf (2012), 'Agamben in the Ogaden: Violence and sovereignty in the Ethiopian-Somali frontier', *Political Geography*, 31(4), pp. 205–14.

Hagmann, T. and F. Stepputat (2016), 'Corridors of trade and power: Economy and state formation in Somali East Africa'. Danish Institute for International Studies (DIIS) Working Paper 2016: 8, Copenhagen.

Hagmann, T. and M. V. Hoehne (2009), 'Failures of the state failure debate: Evidence from the Somali territories', *Journal of International Development*, 21(1), pp. 42–57.

Hagmann, T., A. N. Mohamed, A. E. Ali, J. Mohamed, M. Wasuge, M. H. Ibrahim, S. Koshin, Y. Mohamed and H. Stogdon (2022), 'Commodified cities: Urbanization and public goods in Somalia'. Rift Valley Institute, London and Nairobi. Available at: https://riftvalley. net/sites/default/files/publication-documents/rvi-commodified-cities-report-2022-en.pdf (accessed 2 November 2022).

Halderman, M. (2004), 'The political economy of pro-poor livestock policy making in Ethiopia'. Pro-Poor Livestock Policy Initiative Working Paper 19, Food and Agriculture Organization of the United Nations.

Hammond, L. (2014), 'History, overview, trends and issues in major Somali refugee displacements in the near region. New Issues in Refugee Research'. Research Paper No. 268, UNHCR, Geneva.

Hammond, L., M. Awad, A. I. Dagane, P. Hansen, C. Horst, K. Menkhaus and L. Obare (2011), 'Cash and compassion: The role of the Somali diaspora in relief, development and peace-building'. UNDP, New York and Nairobi, December. Available at: file:///C:/Users/ruko/ Downloads/Cash%20and%20Compassion_%20The%20Role%20 of%20the%20Somali%20Diaspora%20in%20Relief,%20 Development%20and%20Peacebuilding.pdf (accessed 3 November 2022).

Hann, C. and K. Hart (2009), 'Introduction: Learning from Polanyi', in C. Hann and K. Hart (eds), *Market and Society: 'The Great Transformation' Today*. (Cambridge: Cambridge University Press), pp. 1–16.

Hansen, S. J. (2007), 'Civil war economies, the hunt for profit and the incentives for peace: The case of Somalia', 'Big Business' in Peacemaking and Disarmament Working Paper 1, Department of Economics and International Development, University of Bath.

———— (2013), *Al-Shabaab in Somalia: The History and Ideology of a Militant Islamist Group, 2005–2012* (New York: Columbia University Press).

Hansen, T. B. and F. Stepputat (eds) (2001), *States of Imagination: Ethnographic Explorations of the Postcolonial State* (Durham, NC: Duke University Press).

———— (2005), *Sovereign Bodies: Citizens, Migrants, and States in the Postcolonial World* (Princeton, NJ: Princeton University Press).

Haour, A. (2017), 'What made Islamic trade distinctive—as compared to pre-Islamic trade?', in D. Mattingly et al. (eds), *Trade in the Ancient Sahara and Beyond* (Cambridge: Cambridge University Press), pp. 80–100.

Harding, A. (2015), 'Somalia outrage at remittance ban', BBC, 21 May. Available at: http://www.bbc.com/news/world-africa-32796857 (accessed 6 September 2021).

Harper, M. (2020), 'Somalia conflict: Al-Shabab "collects more revenue than government"', BBC News, 26 October. Available at: https://www.bbc.com/news/world-africa-54690561 (accessed 4 October 2021).

Hart, K. (1973), 'Informal income opportunities and urban employment in Ghana', *Journal of Modern African Studies*, 11(1), pp. 61–89.

Hassan, Y. (2019), 'Being and becoming mobile', in N. Carrier and T. Scharrer (eds), *Mobile Urbanity: Somali Presence in Urban East Africa* (Oxford and New York: Berghahn Books), pp. 26–32.

Hedemann, P. (2011), 'Drug trade in Africa: How the queen of Khat got so rich', *Worldcrunch*, 30 August. Available at: https://worldcrunch.com/world-affairs/drug-trade-in-africa-how-the-queen-of-khat-got-so-rich (accessed 4 October 2021).

Helling, D. (2010), 'Tillyan footprints beyond Europe: War-making and state-making in the case of Somaliland', *St Antony's International Review*, 6(1), pp. 103–23.

Herbst, J. (2000), *States and Power in Africa: Comparative Lessons in Authority and Control* (Princeton, NJ: Princeton University Press).

Hesse, B. (2010), 'Where Somalia works', *Journal of Contemporary African Studies*, 28(3), pp. 343–62.

Hibou, B. (2004), 'From privatizing the economy to privatizing the state: An analysis of the continual formation of the state', in B. Hibou (ed.), *Privatizing the State* (London: Hurst & Co.), pp. 1–46.

Hiraal Institute (2018), 'The AS Finance System'. Hiraal Institute paper, Mogadishu. Available at: https://hiraalinstitute.org/wp-content/uploads/2018/07/AS-Finance-System.pdf (accessed 11 November 2021).

———— (2020), 'A losing game: Countering al-Shabab's financial system', October. Available at: https://hiraalinstitute.org/a-losing-game-countering-al-shababs-financial-system/ (accessed 27 September 2021).

Hoehne, M. V. (2009), 'Mimesis and mimicry in the dynamics of state and identity formation in Northern Somalia', *Africa*, 79(2), pp. 252–81.

———— (2015a), 'Between Somaliland and Puntland'. Rift Valley Institute, London and Nairobi. Available at: https://riftvalley.net/sites/default/files/publication-documents/Between%20Somaliland%20and%20Puntland%20by%20Markus%20Hoehne%20-%20RVI%20Contested%20Borderlands%20%282015%29.pdf (accessed 3 November 2022).

———— (2015b), 'Continuities and changes regarding minorities in Somalia', *Ethnic and Racial Studies*, 38(5), pp. 792–807.

———— (2016), 'The rupture of territoriality and the diminishing relevance of cross-cutting ties in Somalia after 1990', *Development and Change*, 47(6), pp. 1379–411.

Hoffman, A. and Lange, P. (2016), 'Growing or coping? Evidence from small and medium sized enterprises in fragile settings', The Hague: Clingendael (Netherlands Institute of International Relations).

Hoffmann, K., K. Vlassenroot and G. Marchais (2016), 'Taxation, stateness and armed groups: Public authority and resource extraction in eastern Congo', *Development and Change*, 47(6), pp. 1434–56.

Hoffman, A., C. Elder, J. Meester and W. van den Berg (2017), 'Somalia's business elites: Political power and economic stakes across the Somali territories and in four key economic sectors'. The Hague: Clingendael CRU Report.

Hönke, J. (2018), 'Beyond the gatekeeper state: African infrastructure hubs as sites of experimentation', *Third World Thematics: A TWQ Journal*, 3(3), pp. 347–63.

Horst, C. (2006), *Transnational Nomads: How Somalis Cope With Refugee Life in the Dadaab Camps of Kenya* (New York and Oxford: Berghahn Books).

Humphreys, M., A. Stokenberga, M. Herrera Dappe, A. Iimi and O. Hartmann (2019), 'Port development and competition in east and southern Africa: Prospects and challenges'. World Bank, Washington

DC, 18 June. Available at: https://openknowledge.worldbank.org/bitstream/handle/10986/31897/9781464814105.pdf?sequence=2&isAllowed=y (accessed 02 November 2022).

Iazzolino, G. (2015), 'Following mobile money in Somaliland'. Rift Valley Institute Research Paper 4, London and Nairobi. Available at: https://riftvalley.net/sites/default/files/publication-documents/Following%20Mobile%20Money%20in%20Somaliland%20by%20Gianluca%20Iazzolino%20-%20RVI%20Rift%20Valley%20Forum%20Research%20Paper%204%20%282015%29_0.pdf (accessed 3 November 2022).

Ibrahim Shire, M. (2020), 'How do leadership decapitation and targeting error affect suicide bombings? The case of al-Shabaab', *Studies in Conflict and Terrorism*, DOI: 10.1080/1057610X.2020.1780021.

ICG (International Crisis Group) (2009), 'Somalia: The trouble with Puntland', 12 August, Africa Briefing No. 64, Nairobi/Brussels.

———— (2012), 'The Kenyan military intervention in Somalia'. Crisis Group Africa Report No. 184, 15 February. Available at: https://d2071andvip0wj.cloudfront.net/184%20The%20Kenyan%20Military%20Intervention%20in%20Somalia.pdf (accessed 6 September 2021).

———— (2013), 'Jubaland in jeopardy: The uneasy path to state-building in Somalia', 21 May, Commentary, Nairobi/Brussels.

———— (2014), 'Somalia: Al-Shabaab—It will be a long war', 26 June, Africa Briefing No. 99, Nairobi/Brussels.

———— (2019), 'Somalia-Somaliland: The perils of delaying new talks', Report No. 280, 12 July. Available at: https://www.crisisgroup.org/africa/horn-africa/somalia/280-somalia-somaliland-perils-delaying-new-talks (accessed 10 February 2022).

ILO (1972), 'Employment, incomes and equality: A strategy for increasing productive employment in Kenya'. International Labour Office, Geneva.

IMF (2020), 'Somalia: Enhanced heavily indebted poor countries (HIPC) initiative—decision point document'. IMF Country Report No. 20/86, 26 March. Available at: https://www.imf.org/en/Publications/CR/Issues/2020/03/26/Somalia-Enhanced-Heavily-Indebted-Poor-Countries-HIPC-Initiative-Decision-Point-Document-49290 (accessed 2 November 2022).

Indimuli, R. (2022), 'Access to social protection in Kenya: The role of micro-traders' associations', in L. Riisgaard, W. Mitullah and N. Torm (eds), *Social Protection and Informal Workers in Sub-Saharan Africa: Lived Realities and Associational Experiences From Kenya and Tanzania* (London: Routledge), pp. 147–71.

Ingiriis, M. H. (2018), 'The invention of al-Shabaab in Somalia: Emulating the anti-colonial dervishes movement', *African Affairs*, 117(467), pp. 217–37.

International Telecommunication Union (2018), 'Measuring the information society report, Vol. 2'. Available at: https://www.itu.int/en/ITU-D/LDCs/Documents/2017/Country%20Profiles/Country%20Profile_Somalia.pdf (accessed 6 September 2021).

IOM (2016), 'Somalia—Displacement Report 2'. DTM Somalia, 31 July. Available at: https://dtm.iom.int/reports/somalia-——-displacement-report-2-july-2016 (accessed 18 March 2021).

Isak, F. and M. Wasuge (2021), 'Fiscal federalism in Somalia: Constitutional ambiguity, political economy and options for a workable arrangement'. Somali Public Agenda, Mogadishu, July. Available at: https://somalipublicagenda.org/wp-content/uploads/2022/03/Fiscal-Federalism-in-Somalia.pdf (accessed 25 October 2022).

Jackson, R. H. and C. G. Rosberg (1982), 'Why Africa's weak states persist: The empirical and the juridical in statehood', *World Politics*, 35(1), pp. 1–24.

Jamal, V. (1988), 'Somalia: Understanding an unconventional economy', *Development and Change*, 19(2), pp. 203–65.

Jaspars, S., G. M. Adan and N. Majid (2020), 'Food and power in Somalia: Business as usual? A scoping study on the political economy of food following shifts in food assistance and in governance'. Conflict Research Programme, LSE, London. Available at: https://eprints.lse.ac.uk/103138/7/Food_and_Power_in_Somalia_business_as_usual_v5.pdf (accessed 3 November 2022).

JFJ (Journalists for Justice) (2015), *Black and White: Kenya's Criminal Racket in Somalia*. Nairobi, International Commission of Jurists, Kenya Chapter, 2015.

Jones, K. (1996), 'Trust as an affective attitude', *Ethics*, 107(1), pp. 4–25.

Juul, K. (2006), 'Decentralization, local taxation and citizenship in Senegal', *Development and Change*, 37(4), pp. 821–46.

Khalif Abdurahman (2021), 'Contested commerce: Revenue and state-making in the Galkayo borderlands'. Rift Valley Institute, London and Nairobi. Available at https://riftvalley.net/sites/default/files/publication-documents/RVI%202021.11.23%20Contested%20Commerce_0.pdf (accessed 28 August 2022).

Khan, M. and Casswell, J. (2019), 'Telesom ZAAD: Pushing the mobile money CVA frontier', GSMA, 19 June. Available at: https://www.gsma.com/mobilefordevelopment/resources/telesom-zaad-pushing-the-mobile-money-cva-frontier/ (accessed 6 September 2021).

KHRC (2009), 'Foreigners at home: The dilemma of citizenship in northern Kenya'. Report for the Kenya Human Rights Commission, 31 October. Available at: https://www.khrc.or.ke/mobile-publications/equality-and-anti-discrimination/66-foreigners-at-home-the-dilemma-of-citizenship-in-northern-kenya/file.html (accessed 6 September 2021).

Kopytoff, I. (1987), *The African Frontier. The Reproduction of Traditional African Societies* (Bloomington and Indianapolis: Indiana University Press).

Korf, B., T. Hagmann and M. Doevenspeck (2013), 'Geographies of violence and sovereignty: the African frontier revisited', in B. Korf and T. Raeymaekers (eds), *Violence on the Margins: States, Conflict and Borderlands* (New York: Palgrave), pp. 29–54.

Koshin, S. A. (2021), 'Galkayo's khat economy: The role of women traders in Puntland, Somalia'. Rift Valley Institute, London and Nairobi. Available at: https://riftvalley.net/sites/default/files/publication-documents/RVI%202022.03.23%20Galkayo%27s%20Khat%20Economy.pdf%20.pdf (accessed 02 November 2022).

Koster, M. and Y. van Leynseele (2018), 'Brokers as assemblers: Studying development through the lens of brokerage', *Ethnos*, 83(5), pp. 803–13.

Krupa, C. and D. Nugent (eds) (2015), *State Theory and Andean Politics: New Approaches to the Study of Rule* (Philadelphia: University of Pennsylvania Press).

Kunaka, C. and R. Carruthers (2014), *Trade and Transport Corridor Management Toolkit* (Washington, DC: World Bank).

Lakshmanan, T. R., U. Subramanian, W. P. Anderson and A. F. Léautier (2001), *Integration of Transportation and Trade Facilitation: Selected Regional Case Studies* (Washington, DC: World Bank).

Leander, A. (2004), 'Wars and the un-making of states: Taking Tilly seriously in the contemporary world', in S. Guzzini and D. Jung (eds), *Contemporary Security Analysis and Copenhagen Peace Research* (London: Routledge), pp. 69–80.

Leeson, P. T. (2007), 'Better off stateless: Somalia before and after government collapse', *Journal of Comparative Economics*, 36(4), pp. 689–710.

Lewis, I. M. (1989), 'The Ogaden and the fragility of Somali segmentary nationalism', *African Affairs*, 88(353), pp. 573–79.

————— (1994), *Blood and Bone: The Call of Kinship in Somali Society* (Lawrenceville, NJ: Red Sea Press).

————— (1999 [1961]), *A Pastoral Democracy: A Study of Pastoralism and Politics Among the Northern Somali of the Horn of Africa* (London: Oxford University Press).

————— (2002 [1965]), *A Modern History of the Somali: Nation and State in the Horn of Africa* (Oxford, Hargeisa and Athens: James Currey, Btec Books and Ohio University Press).

Lind, J., P. Mutahi and M. Oosterom (2017), '"Killing a mosquito with a hammer": Al-Shabaab violence and state security responses in Kenya', *Peacebuilding*, 5(2), pp. 118–35.

Lindley, A. (2007), 'Protracted displacement and remittances: The view from Eastleigh, Nairobi'. Research Paper No. 143, UNHCR, Geneva.

————— (2009). 'Between "dirty money" and "development capital": Somali money transfer infrastructure under global scrutiny', *African Affairs*, 108(433), pp. 519–39.

Little, P. D. (1996), 'Conflictive trade, contested identity: The effects of export markets on pastoralists of southern Somalia', *African Studies Review*, 39(1), pp. 25–53.

————— (2003), *Somalia: Economy Without State* (Bloomington and Oxford: Indiana University Press and James Currey).

————— (2005), 'Unofficial trade when states are weak: The case of cross-border commerce in the Horn of Africa'. UNU-WIDER Working Paper 13, United Nations University World Institute for Development Economics Research, Helsinki.

————— (2008), 'Livelihoods, assets and food security in a protracted political crisis: The case of the Jubba region, southern Somalia', in L. Alinovi, G. Heimrich and L. Russo (eds), *Beyond Relief: Food Security in Protracted Crises* (Rugby: ITDG Publications/Practical Action Publishing), pp. 107–26.

————— (2014), *Economic and Political Reform in Africa: Anthropological Perspectives* (Bloomington and Indianapolis: Indiana University Press).

————— (2021), 'Trusting in Somalia's stateless money: The persistence of the Somali shilling', *African Affairs*, 120(478), pp. 103–22.

Little, P. D., W. Tiki and D. N. Debsu (2015), 'Formal or informal, legal or illegal: The ambiguous nature of cross-border livestock trade in the Horn of Africa', *Journal of Borderlands Studies*, 30(3), pp. 405–21.

Lochery, E. (2015), 'Generating Power: Electricity Provision and State Formation in Somaliland', PhD Dissertation, Department of Politics and International Relations, University of Oxford.

————— (2020), 'Somali ventures in China: Trade and mobility in a transnational economy', *African Studies Review*, 631, pp. 93–116.

Lombard, L. (2016), *State of Rebellion: Violence and Intervention in the Central African Republic* (London: Zed Books).

Lund, C. (2006), 'Twilight institutions: Public authority and local politics in Africa', *Development and Change*, 37(4), pp. 685–705.

———— (2011), 'Property and citizenship: Conceptually connecting land rights and belonging in Africa', *Africa Spectrum*, 46(3), pp. 71–5.

———— (2016), 'Rule and rupture: State formation through the production of property and citizenship', *Development and Change*, 47(6), pp. 1199–228.

Luther, W. (2012), 'Money Without a State'. PhD Dissertation, George Mason University. Available at: https://historyarthistory.gmu.edu/defenses/591 (accessed 6 September 2021).

Lydon, G. (2009), *On Trans-Saharan Trails: Islamic Law, Trade Networks, and Cross-Cultural Exchange in Nineteenth-Century Western Africa* (Cambridge: Cambridge University Press).

Mahmoud, H. A. (2008), 'Risky trade, resilient traders: Trust and livestock marketing in Northern Kenya', *Africa*, 78(4), pp. 561–81.

———— (2010), 'Livestock trade in the Kenyan, Somali and Ethiopian borderlands'. Chatham House Briefing Paper, Africa Programme, London, September. Available at: https://www.chathamhouse.org/sites/default/files/field/field_document/0910mahmoud.pdf (accessed 3 November 2022).

Majid, N. and K. Abdirahman (2021), 'The Jubbaland project and the transborder Ogadeen: Identity politics and regional reconfigurations in the Ethiopia-Kenya-Somalia borderlands', Conflict Research Programme Research Memo, 23 February, London School of Economics and Political Science, Conflict Research Programme.

Majid, N., Abdirahman, K. and Hassan, S. (2018), 'Remittances and vulnerability in Somalia'. Rift Valley Institute Briefing Paper, London and Nairobi, September. Available at: https://riftvalley.net/sites/default/files/publication-documents/Remittances%20and%20Vulnerability%20in%20Somalia%20by%20Nisar%20Majid%20-%20RVI%20Briefing%20%282018%29.pdf (accessed 3 November 2022).

Majid, N., A. Sarkar, C. Elder, K. Abdirahman, S. Detzner, J. Miller and A. de Waal (2021), 'Somalia's politics: The usual business? A synthesis paper of the conflict research programme'. Conflict Research Programme, London School of Economics and Political Science.

Mampilly, Z. (2021), 'Rebel taxation: Between the moral and market economy', in N. Di Cosmo, D. Fassin and C. Pinaud (eds), *Rebel Economies: Warlords, Insurgents, Humanitarians* (Lanham, MD: Lexington Books), pp. 77–100.

Mann, M. (1984), 'The autonomous power of the state: Its origins, mechanisms and results', *European Journal of Sociology*, 25(2), pp. 185–213.

———— (2008), 'Infrastructural power revisited', *Studies in Comparative International Development*, 43(3), pp. 355–65.

247

BIBLIOGRAPHY

Mansfield, D. (2016), *A State Built on Sand: How Opium Undermined Afghanistan* (Oxford: Oxford University Press).

Marchal, R. (1996), *The Post Civil War Somali Business Class* (Nairobi: European Commission/Somalia Unit).

——— (2002), *A Survey of Mogadishu's Economy* (Nairobi: European Commission/Somalia Unit). Available at: http://www.eeas.europa.eu/archives/delegations/somalia/documents/more_info/mogadishu_economic_survey_en.pdf (accessed 20 January 2020).

——— (2011), 'The rise of a jihadi movement in a country at war: Harakat Al-Shabaab Al-Mujaheddin in Somalia'. CNRS, Paris, March. Available at: https://www.sciencespo.fr/ceri/sites/sciencespo.fr.ceri/files/art_RM2.pdf (accessed 3 November 2022).

Marchal, R. and Z. M. Sheikh (2015), 'Salafism in Somalia: Coping with coercion, civil war and its own contradictions', *Islamic Africa*, 6(1–2), pp. 135–63.

Marchal, R. and Z. Yussuf (2017), 'Power politics in Somalis: A political economy analysis'. European Union and NIS Foundation.

Marchal, R., Mubarak, J. A., Del Buono, M. and Manzolillo, D. L. (2000), 'Globalization and its impact on Somalia'. UNDP/UNDOS, Nairobi, 28 January. Available at: https://reliefweb.int/report/somalia/globalization-and-its-impact-somalia (accessed 6 September 2021).

Martin, I. W., Mehrotra, A. K. and M. Prasad (eds) (2009), *The New Fiscal Sociology: Taxation in Comparative and Historical Perspective* (Cambridge: Cambridge University Press).

Martinez, O. (1994), *Border People: Life and Society in the U.S.-Mexico Borderlands* (Tuscon: University of Arizona Press).

Maruf, H. and D. Joseph (2018), *Inside al-Shabaab—The Secret History of Al-Qaeda's Most Powerful Ally* (Bloomington: Indiana University Press).

Masese, W. (2013), 'Trust: The driving force behind many Somali traders' success', *The Standard*, 29 December. Available at: https://www.standardmedia.co.ke/business/business/article/2000101023/trust-the-driving-force-behind-many-somali-traders-success (accessed 16 August 2022).

Mattelart, A. (2000), *Networking the World, 1794–2000* (Minneapolis: University of Minnesota Press).

Mauss, M. (2001 [1923]), *The Gift: The Form and Reason for Exchange in Archaic Societies* (London and New York: Routledge, 2nd edition).

Mboya, T. (2002), 'State and Agriculture in Kenya: The Case of Sugar Industry', PhD Dissertation, University of Nairobi, Nairobi.

Meagher, K. (2014), 'Smuggling ideologies: From criminalization to hybrid governance in African clandestine economies', *African Affairs*, 113(453), pp. 497–517.

Medhane Tadesse (2015), 'Making sense of Ethiopia's regional influence', in G. Prunier and É. Ficquet (eds), *Understanding Contemporary Ethiopia. Monarchy, Revolution and the Legacy of Meles Zenawi* (London: Hurst), pp. 257–82.

Meehan, P. (2015). 'Fortifying or fragmenting the state? The political economy of the drug trade in Shan State, Myanmar, 1988–2012', *Critical Asian Studies*, 47(2), pp. 253–82.

Meehan, P. and S. Plonsky (2017), 'Brokering the margins: A review of concepts and methods'. Working Paper, SOAS and University of Bath.

Meester, J., A. Uzelac and C. Elder (2019), 'Transnational capital in Somalia: Blue desert strategy'. The Hague: Clingendael, CRU Report, June. Available at: https://www.clingendael.org/sites/default/files/2020–02/transnational-capital-in-somalia.pdf (accessed 01 November 2022).

Menkhaus, K. (2003), 'State collapse in Somalia: Second thoughts', *Review of African Political Economy*, 39(97), pp. 405–22.

———— (2004a), 'Somalia: State collapse and the threat of terrorism'. Adelphi Paper 363, International Institute for Security Studies, London.

———— (2004b), *Somalia: State Collapse and the Threat of Terrorism* (London: Routledge).

———— (2006), 'Governance without government in Somalia: Spoilers, state building, and the politics of coping', *International Security*, 31(3), pp. 74–106.

———— (2014), 'State failure, state-building and prospects for a "functional failed state" in Somalia', *The ANNALS of the American Academy of Political and Social Science*, 656(1), 154–72.

———— (2018), 'Elite bargains and political deals project: Somalia case study', Stabilisation Unit, Foreign and Commonwealth Office, London, February. Available at: https://assets.publishing.service.gov.uk/government/uploads/system/uploads/attachment_data/file/766049/Somalia_case_study.pdf (accessed 2 November 2022).

Migdal, J. S. and K. Schlichte (2005), 'Rethinking the state', in K. Schlichte (ed.), *The Dynamics of States: The Formation and Crises of State Domination* (Aldershot: Ashgate), pp. 1–40.

Miller, N. N. (1981), 'The other Somalia, part I. Illicit trade and the hidden economy'. American Universities' Fieldstaff Reports. Available at https://normanmillerarchive.com/wp/wp-content/uploads/2019/01/The_Other_Somalia_Part_I1.pdf (accessed 6 July 2022).

Mitchell, T. (1999), 'Society, economy and state effect', in G. Steinmetz (ed.), *State/Culture: State-formation and the Cultural Turn* (Ithaca, NY and London: Cornell University Press), pp. 76–97.

Mohamed, A. (2015), 'Hawala's closure hits Somalis hard', *The Star*, 10 April. Available at: https://www.the-star.co.ke/news/2015/04/10/hawalas-closure-hits-somalis-hard_c1116544 (accessed 6 September 2021).

Montclos, M. P. and P. Kagwanja (2000), 'Refugee camps or cities? The socio-economic dynamics of the Dadaab and Kakuma camps in northern Kenya', *Journal of Refugee Studies*, 13(2), pp. 2015–222.

Moore, M. (2004), 'Revenues, state formation, and the quality of governance in developing countries', *International Political Science Review*, 25(3), pp. 297–319.

———— (2021), 'Glimpses of fiscal states in sub-Saharan Africa', WIDER Working Paper, UNU-WIDER, Helsinki.

Moore, M., W. Prichard and O. Fjeldstad (2018), *Taxing Africa: Coercion, Reform and Development* (London: Zed Books).

Mubarak, J. A. (1996), *From Bad Policy to Chaos in Somalia: How an Economy Fell Apart* (Westport, CT and London: Praeger).

———— (1997), 'The "hidden hand" behind the resilience of the stateless economy of Somalia', *World Development*, 25(12), pp. 2027–41.

Muhumed, M. M. (2016), 'Somaliland trade, exports and imports: An overview', *Developing Country Studies*, 6(8), pp. 138–43.

Mukhtar, M. H. (2003), *Historical Dictionary of Somalia* (Lanham, MD and Oxford: The Scarecrow Press, Inc.).

Muñoz, José-María (2018), *Doing Business in Cameroon. An Anatomy of Economic Governance* (Cambridge: Cambridge University Press).

Murunga, G. (2005), 'Conflict in Somalia and crime in Kenya: Understanding the trans-territoriality of crime', *African and Asian Studies*, 4(1–2), pp. 137–61.

Musa, A. M. (2019), 'From trust to oligopoly: Institutional change in livestock trade in Somaliland after 1991'. Danish Institute for International Studies (DIIS) Working Paper 8, Copenhagen.

———— (2021), 'Lasanod: City at the margins. The politics of borderland trade between Somaliland and Puntland'. Rift Valley Institute, London and Nairobi. Available at: https://riftvalley.net/sites/default/files/publication-documents/RVI%202021.10.01%20Lasanod_City%20at%20the%20Margins_0.pdf (accessed 3 November 2022).

Musa, A. M. and C. Horst (2019), 'State formation and economic development in post-war Somaliland: The impact of the private sector in an unrecognised state', *Conflict, Security and Development*, 19(1), pp. 35–53.

BIBLIOGRAPHY

Musa, A. M. and R. Schwere (2019), 'The hidden tactile negotiation sign language in Somaliland's livestock markets', *Bildhaan: An International Journal of Somali Studies*, 18(7), pp. 50–69.

Musa, A. M., F. Stepputat and T. Hagmann (2021), 'Revenues on the hoof: Livestock trade, taxation and state-making in the Somali territories', *Journal of Eastern African Studies*, 15(1), pp. 108–27.

Musa, A. M., O. Wasonga and N. Mtimet (2020), 'Factors influencing livestock export in Somaliland's terminal markets', *Pastoralism: Research, Policy and Practice*, 10(1), pp. 1–13.

Mustafe M. Abdi (2021), 'Regularly irregular: Varieties of informal trading in the Ethiopia-Somaliland borderlands'. Rift Valley Institute, London and Nairobi. Available at: https://riftvalley.net/sites/default/files/publication-documents/RVI%202021.10.18%20Regularly%20Irregular.pdf (accessed 2 November 2022).

Nenova, T. (2004), 'Private sector response to the absence of government institutions in Somalia', World Bank, Washington, DC, 30 July. Available at: https://documents1.worldbank.org/curated/en/248811468302977154/pdf/802300WP0Somal0Box0379802B00PUBLIC0.pdf (accessed 3 November 2022).

Ng'askie, P. O. (2019), 'Fusing formal and informal trading: Emerging practices in the livestock value chains between Kenya and Somalia'. Danish Institute for International Studies (DIIS) Working Paper No. 2019: 12, Copenhagen.

———— (2021), 'Governance of Value Chains in Cross Border Livestock Trade between Kenya and Somalia', PhD Dissertation, University of Nairobi, Nairobi.

Ng'asike, P. O., T. Hagmann and O. V. Wasonga (2021), 'Brokerage in the borderlands: The political economy of livestock intermediaries in northern Kenya', *Journal of Eastern African Studies*, 15(1), pp. 168–88.

Ng'asike, P. O., F. Stepputat and J. T. Njoka (2020), 'Livestock trade and devolution in the Somali-Kenya transboundary corridor', *Pastoralism*, 10(1), pp. 1–14.

Niemann, M. (2007), 'War making and state making in Central Africa', *Africa Today*, 53(3), pp. 21–39.

Njiru, N., N. Mtimet, F. Wanyoike, A. Kutu, A. Songolo, I. Dahir and G. Jillo (2017), 'Assessment of livestock marketing associations in arid and semi-arid lands in northern Kenya'. International Livestock Research Institute and USAID, Nairobi.

Nori, M. (2009), 'Milking Drylands: Gender Networks, Pastoral Markets and Food Security in Stateless Somalia'. PhD Dissertation, University of Wageningen, the Netherlands.

Nori, M., M. B. Kenyanjui, M. A. Yusuf and F. H. Mohamed (2006),

'Milking Drylands: The Emergence of Camel Milk Markets in Stateless Somali Areas', *Nomadic Peoples*, 10(1), pp. 9–28.

North, D. (1981), *Structure and Change in Economic History* (New York: W. W. Norton).

———— (1990), *Institutions, Institutional Change and Economic Performance* (Cambridge: Cambridge University Press).

Nugent, P. (2010), 'States and social contracts in Africa', *New Left Review*, 63, pp. 35–68.

Nugent, P. and H. Lamarque (2022), 'Introduction. Transport corridors in Africa: Synergy, slippage and sustainability', in H. Lamarque and P. Nugent (eds), *Transport Corridors in Africa* (Woodbridge: James Currey), pp. 1–34.

Olson, M. (1993), 'Dictatorship, democracy, and development', *American Political Science Review*, 87(3), pp. 567–76.

Oxfam (2013), 'Briefing note on strengthening and maintaining remittance transfers to Somalia', August. Available at: https://oxfamilibrary.openrepository.com/bitstream/handle/10546/301322/bn-keeping-lifeline-open-somalia-uk-remittances-060913-en.pdf;jsessionid=7908F84DDCEBDE5704ADA9363D262028?sequence=1 (accessed 6 October 2022).

Pankhurst, R. (1965), 'The trade of the Gulf of Aden ports of Africa in the nineteenth and early twentieth centuries', *Journal of Ethiopian Studies*, 3(1), pp. 36–81.

———— (1974), 'Indian trade with Ethiopia, the Gulf of Aden, and the Horn of Africa in the nineteenth and early twentieth centuries', *Cahiers d'Études Africaines*, XIV(3), pp. 453–97.

Pasquale, F. (2017), 'From territorial to functional sovereignty: The case of Amazon', Law and Political Economy Project, 12 June. Available at: https://lpeproject.org/blog/from-territorial-to-functional-sovereignty-the-case-of-amazon/ (accessed 16 August 2022).

PDRC (Puntland Development Research Center) and Interpeace (2008), 'The Puntland experience: A bottom-up approach to peace and statebuilding. Peace initiatives in Puntland 1991–2007'. PDRC, Garowe. Available at: https://www.interpeace.org/wp-content/uploads/2008/07/2008_SomP_PDRC_Interpeace_A_Bottom_Up_Approach_To_Peace_And_Statebuilding_EN.pdf (accessed 3 November 2022).

———— (2015), 'Peace in Puntland: Mapping the progress. Democratization, decentralization, and security and rule of law'. PDRC, Garowe. Available at: https://www.interpeace.org/wp-content/uploads/2016/01/2015_1_5_peace_in_puntland_english.pdf (accessed 2 November 2022).

BIBLIOGRAPHY

Peebles, G. (2010), 'The anthropology of credit and debt', *Annual Review of Anthropology*, 39, pp. 225–40.

Pénicaud, C. and McGrath, F. (2013), 'Innovative inclusion: How Telesom ZAAD brought mobile money to Somaliland'. GSMA, 3 July. Available at: https://www.gsma.com/mobilefordevelopment/resources/innovative-inclusion-how-telesom-zaad-brought-mobile-money-to-somaliland/ (accessed 6 September 2021).

Phillips, S. (2013), 'Political settlements and state formation: The case of Somaliland'. DLP Research Paper 23, University of Birmingham.

Phillips, S. G. (2020), *When There Was No Aid: War and Peace in Somaliland* (Ithaca, NY and London: Cornell University Press).

Polanyi, K. (2001 [1944]), *The Great Transformation: The Political and Economic Origins of Our Time* (Boston, MA: Beacon Press).

Portes, A. and J. Sensenbrenner (1993), 'Embeddedness and immigration: Notes on the social determinants of economic action', *American Journal of Sociology*, 98(6), pp. 1320–50.

Pugh, M., N. Cooper and J. Goodhand (2004), *War Economies in a Regional Context. Challenges for Transformation* (London: Lynne Rienner).

Qassim, A. (2004), 'The collapse of the Somali banking system' in A. M. Kusow (ed.), *Putting the Cart Before the Horse: Contested Nationalism and the Crisis of the Nation-State in Somalia* (Trenton, NJ: Red Sea Press), pp. 185–6.

Raballand, G. J. and J. S. C. Knebelmann (2021), 'Domestic resource mobilization in Somalia'. World Bank, Washington, DC, February. Available at https://documents1.worldbank.org/curated/en/121391596804622057/pdf/Domestic-Resource-Mobilization-in-Somalia.pdf (accessed 19 May 2022).

Raeymaekers, T. (2014), *Violent Capitalism and Political Power on the Congo-Uganda Border* (Cambridge: Cambridge University Press).

Rahman, K. (2017), 'Somalia: Overview of corruption and anti-corruption'. Chr. Michelsen Institute (CMI) & Transparency International, 7 December. Available at: https://www.u4.no/publications/somalia-overview-corruption-and-anticorruption (accessed 27 September 2021).

Rasmussen, J. (2017), 'Sweet secrets: Sugar smuggling and state formation in the Kenya-Somalia borderlands'. Danish Institute for International Studies (DIIS) Working Paper 11, Copenhagen.

——— (2020), 'Raw sugar, raw power: Illicitness and contamination in the Somali-Kenyan sugar trade'. Unpublished manuscript, Roskilde University, Denmark.

Rasmussen, J. and A. Wafer (2019), 'Documentary evidence: Proving identity and credibility in Africa's urban estuaries', *African Studies*, 78(1), pp. 74–90.

Rasmussen, M. B. and C. Lund (2018), 'Reconfiguring frontier spaces: The territorialization of resource control', *World Development*, 101, pp. 388–99.

Reese S. S. (1996), 'Patricians of the Benaadir: Islamic Learning, Commerce and Somali Urban Identity in the Nineteenth Century', PhD Dissertation, University of Pennsylvania, Philadelphia.

Reid, R. J. (2011), *Frontiers of Violence in North-East Africa: Genealogies of Conflict Since c. 1800* (Oxford: Oxford University Press).

Renders, M. (2012). *Consider Somaliland. State-Building With Traditional Leaders and Institutions* (Leiden and Boston: Brill).

Reno, W. (2003), 'Somalia and survival in the shadow of the global economy', *QEH Working Paper Series* 100, Queen Elizabeth House, University of Oxford.

Reuters (2021), 'Somalia issues its first mobile money licence to Hormuud Telecom', Reuters, 27 February. Available at: https://www.reuters.com/article/somalia-telecom-idUSL8N2KX07T (accessed 16 August 2022).

Roitman, J. (2005), *Fiscal Disobedience: An Anthropology of Economic Regulation in Central Africa* (Princeton, NJ: Princeton University Press).

Rosenfeld, M. (2012), 'Mobility and social capital among Lebanese and Beninese entrepreneurs engaged in transnational trade', *International Review of Sociology*, 22(2), pp. 211–28.

Roth, J., D. Greenburg and S. Wille (2004), 'National commission on terrorist attacks upon the United States: Monograph on terrorist financing'. Staff Report to the Commission. Available at: https://www.hsdl.org/?view&did=449287 (accessed 27 September 2021).

RVI (2013), 'Somalia's Jubbaland: Past, present and potential futures'. Rift Valley Institute Meeting Report Nairobi Forum, London and Nairobi, 22 February. Available at: https://riftvalley.net/sites/default/files/publication-documents/RVI%20-%20Nairobi%20Forum%20-%20Somalia%27s%20Jubaland%20Report.pdf (accessed 2 November 2022).

Sabahi (2014), 'Al-Shabaab closes Hormud Telecom in Jilib, detains staff', *allAfrica*, 3 February. Available at: https://allafrica.com/stories/201402040594.html (accessed 16 August 2022).

Saferworld (2016), *Forging Jubaland: Community Perspectives on Federalism, Governance and Reconciliation* (Nairobi: Saferworld).

Sahlins, P. (1989), *Boundaries: The Making of France and Spain in the Pyrenees* (Los Angeles: University of California Press).

BIBLIOGRAPHY

Samatar, A. (1987), 'Merchant capital, international livestock trade and pastoral development in Somalia', *Canadian Journal of African Studies*, 21, pp. 355–74.

——— (1989), *The State and Rural Transformation in Northern Somalia, 1884–1986* (Madison: University of Wisconsin Press).

Samatar, A. I. (1988). *Socialist Somalia: Rhetoric and Reality* (London and New Jersey: Institute for African Alternatives and Zed Books).

——— (2007), 'Somalia's post-conflict economy: A political economy approach', *Bildhaan: International Journal of Somali Studies*, 7, pp. 126–68.

——— (2021), 'The making of Dahabshiil: A brief interview', *Bildhaan*, 21, pp. 26–63.

Samatar, H. M. (2008), 'Experiences of Somali entrepreneurs in the twin cities', *Bildhaan: An International Journal of Somali Studies*, 4, pp. 78–91.

Sassen, S. (2000), 'Spatialities and temporalities of the global: Elements for a theorization', *Public Culture*, 12(1), pp. 215–32.

Sayer, A. (2001), 'For a cultural critical political economy', *Antipode* 33, pp. 687–708.

Scheele, J. (2012), *Smugglers and Saints of the Sahara: Regional Connectivity in the Twentieth Century* (Cambridge: Cambridge University Press).

Schlee, G. (2013), 'Customary law and the joys of statelessness: Idealised traditions versus Somali realities', *Journal of Eastern African Studies*, 7(2), pp. 258–71.

Schouten, P. (2022), *Roadblock Politics: The Origins of Violence in Central Africa* (Cambridge: Cambridge University Press).

Schouten, P., F. Stepputat and J. Bachmann (2019), 'States of circulation: Logistics off the beaten path', *Environment and Planning D: Society and Space*, 37(5), pp. 779–93.

Schumpeter, J. A. (1991 [1918]), 'The crisis of the tax state', in R. Swedberg (ed.), *The Economics and Sociology of Capitalism* (Princeton, NJ: Princeton University Press), pp. 99–140.

Scott, J. C. (1985). *Weapons of the Weak: Everyday Forms of Peasant Resistance* (New Haven, CT and London: Yale University Press).

——— (1998), *Seeing Like a State. How Certain Schemes to Improve the Human Condition Have Failed* (New Haven, CT and London: Yale University Press).

Shell, J. (2015), *Transportation and Revolt: Pigeons, Mules, Canals, and the Vanishing Geographies of Subversive Mobility* (Cambridge, MA: MIT Press).

Shipton, P. (2007), *The Nature of Entrustment: Intimacy, Exchange and the Sacred in Africa* (New Haven, CT and London: Yale University Press).

Simons, A. (1995), *Networks of Dissolution: Somalia Undone* (Boulder, CO: Westview Press).

Sørensen, G. (2001), 'War and state-making: Why doesn't it work in the third world?', *Security Dialogue*, 32(3), pp. 341–54.

Spruyt, H. (2011), 'War, trade, and state formation', in R. E. Goodin, ed., *Oxford Handbook of Political Science* (Oxford: Oxford University Press), pp. 568–92.

Stenmanns, J. (2019), 'Logistics from the margins', *Environment and Planning D: Society and Space*, 37(5), pp. 850–67.

Stepputat, F. and T. Hagmann (2019), 'Politics of circulation: The makings of the Berbera corridor in Somali East Africa', *Environment and Planning D: Society and Space*, 37(5), pp. 794–813.

Stremlau, N. (2012), 'Somalia: Media law in the absence of a state', *International Journal of Media and Cultural Politics*, 8(2–3), pp. 159–74.

———— (2018), 'Law and innovation in the Somali territories', in B. Mutsvairo (ed.), *The Palgrave Handbook of Media and Communication Research in Africa*. (Cham: Palgrave Macmillan), pp. 297–309.

Stremlau, N. and Osman, R. (2015), 'Courts, clans and companies: Mobile money and dispute resolution in Somaliland', *Stability: International Journal of Security and Development*, 4(1), pp. 1–15.

Sztompka, P. (1999), *Trust: A Sociological Theory* (Cambridge: Cambridge University Press).

Tahir, A. I. (2021), 'Critical infrastructures as sites of conflict over state legitimacy: The case of Hargeisa Airport in Somaliland, Northern Somalia', *Geoforum*, 125, pp. 110–19.

Taussig, M. T. (1987), *The Devil and Commodity Fetishism in South America* (Chapel Hill: University of North Carolina Press).

———— (1997), *The Magic of the State* (New York and London: Routledge).

Taylor, B. D and R. Botea (2008), 'Tilly tally: War-making and state-making in the contemporary third world', *International Studies Review*, 10(1), pp. 27–56.

Tegegne Teka and Alemayehu Azeze (2002), 'Cross-border trade and food security in the Ethiopia-Djibouti and Ethiopia-Somali borderlands'. Organization for Social Science Research in Eastern and Southern Africa Development Research Report Series 4, Addis Ababa, December. Available at: http://crsps.net/wp-content/downloads/BASIS/Inventoried%2010.19/13–2002–7–384.pdf (accessed 3 November 2022).

Tendler, J. (2002), 'Small firms, the informal sector, and the Devil's deal', *IDS Bulletin*, 33(3), pp. 1–15.

BIBLIOGRAPHY

Tezera Tazebew and Asnake Kefale (2021), 'Governing the economy: Rule and resistance in the Ethiopia-Somaliland borderlands', *Journal of Eastern African Studies*, 15(1), pp. 147–67.

The Cattle Site (2011), 'Horn of Africa to double livestock exports to Saudi', *The Cattle Site*, 4 April. Available at: https://www.thecattle-site.com/news/34125/horn-of-africa-to-double-livestock-exports-to-saudi/ (accessed 16 August 2022).

Thompson, D. K. (2021), 'Respatializing federalism in the Horn's borderlands: From contraband control to transnational governmentality', *Journal of Borderlands Studies*, 37(2), pp. 295–316.

Thrift, N. (2004), 'Movement-space: The changing domain of thinking resulting from the development of new kinds of spatial awareness', *Economy and Society*, 33, pp. 582–604.

Tibebe Eshete (2014), *Jijiga: The History of a Strategic Town in the Horn of Africa* (Los Angeles, CA: Tsehai Publishers).

Tiilikainen, M. (2003), 'Somali women and daily Islam in the diaspora', *Social Compass*, 50(1), pp. 59–69.

Tilly, C. (1975), *The Formation of National States in Western Europe* (Princeton, NJ: Princeton University Press).

———— (1985), 'War making and state making as organized crime', in P. Evans, D. Rueschemeyer and T. Skocpol (eds), *Bringing the State Back in* (New York: Cambridge University Press), pp. 169–91.

———— (1992), *Coercion, Capital, and European States, AD 990–1992* (Malden: Blackwell Publishing).

———— (2010), 'Extraction and democracy', in Martin, I. W., Mehrotra, A. K. and M. Prasad (eds), *The New Fiscal Sociology: Taxation in Comparative and Historical Perspective* (Cambridge: Cambridge University Press), pp. 173–82.

Titeca, K. and T. De Herdt (2011), 'Real governance beyond the "failed state": Negotiating education in the Democratic Republic of the Congo', *African Affairs*, 110(439), pp. 213–31.

Toscano, A. (2014), 'Lineaments of the logistical state', *Viewpoint Magazine*, 28 September. Available at: www.viewpointmag.com/2014/09/28/lineaments-of-the-logistical-state/ (accessed 19 February 2020).

Trujillo, L., M. M. González and J. L. Jiménez (2013), 'An overview on the reform process of African ports', *Utilities Policy*, 25(C), pp. 12–22.

Tsing, A. L. (2005), *Friction. An Ethnography of Global Connection* (Princeton, NJ: Princeton University Press).

———— (2009), 'Supply chains and the human condition', *Rethinking Marxism*, 21(2), pp. 148–76.

——— (2015), *The Mushroom at the End of the World* (Princeton, NJ: Princeton University Press).

——— (2016), 'What is emerging? Supply chains and the remaking of Asia', *The Professional Geographer*, 68(2), pp. 330–37.

UN (202), 'Aid flows in Somalia 2020', 4 January. Available at: https://somalia.un.org/en/46669-aid-flows-somalia-2020 (accessed 27 September 2020).

UNCTAD (2000), 'Transport Newsletter', No. 20, 20 November. Available at: https://unctad.org/webflyer/transport-newsletter-no-20-nov-2000 (accessed 27 September 2021).

UNDP (United Nations Development Programme) (2001), 'National Human Development Report Somalia 2001'. UNDP, New York, NY. Available at: https://hdr.undp.org/system/files/documents//somalia2001enpdf.pdf (accessed 02 November 2022).

UNSC (United Nations Security Council) (2018), 'Letter dated 2 October 2018 from the Monitoring Group on Somalia and Eritrea addressed to the Chair of the Security Council Committee pursuant to Resolutions 751 (1992) and 1907 (2009) concerning Somalia and Eritrea (S/2018/1002)', New York, United Nations Security Council.

——— (2020), 'Letter from the Chair of the Security Council Committee pursuant to resolution 751 (1992) concerning Somalia addressed to the President of the Security Council', 28 September. Available at: https://www.securitycouncilreport.org/atf/cf/%7B6 5BFCF9B-6D27–4E9C-8CD3-CF6E4FF96FF9%7D/S_2020_949.pdf (accessed 6 September 2021).

van Brabant, K. (1994), 'Bad borders make bad neighbours: The political economy of relief and rehabilitation in the Somali Region 5, eastern Ethiopia'. Overseas Development Institute, London, September. Available at https://odihpn.org/wp-content/uploads/1994/09/networkpaper04.pdf (accessed 2 November 2022).

van den Boogaard, V. (2018), 'Gender and the formal and informal systems of local public finance in Sierra Leone'. International Center for Tax and Development Working Paper 87. Institute of Development Studies, Brighton.

——— (2020), 'Informal Revenue Generation and the State: Evidence From Sierra Leone', PhD Dissertation, University of Toronto.

van den Boogaard, V. and N. N. Isak (forthcoming), 'The political economy of taxation in Somalia: Historical legacies, informal institutions, and political settlements'. ICTD Working Paper, Institute of Development Studies, Brighton.

van den Boogaard, V. and F. Santoro (2022a), 'Co-financing community-driven development through informal taxation: Evidence from south-central Somalia', *Governance*. DOI: 10.1111/gove.12678.

———— (2022b), 'Financing governance beyond the state: Informal revenue generation in south-central Somalia', *African Affairs*, 121(485), pp. 569–94.

van Schendel, W. and I. Abraham (2005), 'Introduction: The making of illicitness' in W. Van Schendel and I. Abraham (eds), *Illicit Flows and Criminal Things: States, Borders, and the Other Side of Globalization* (Bloomington and Indianapolis: Indiana University Press), pp. 1–36.

Varming, K. S. (2017), 'The experiential limits of the state: Territory and taxation in Garoowe, Puntland'. Danish Institute for International Studies (DIIS) Working Paper 2017: 7, Copenhagen.

———— (2019), 'Ideological taxation: Hybridity and images of state in Puntland, Somalia', *Bildhaan*, 19(1), pp. 1–23.

———— (2020), 'Urban subjects: Somali claims to recognition and urban belonging in Eastleigh, Nairobi', *African Studies* 79(1), pp. 1–20.

———— (2021), 'Contested practices of trade and taxation: (In)formalization and (il)legitimization in Eastleigh, Nairobi', *Journal of Eastern African Studies*, 15(1), pp. 128–46.

Verjee, A., A. Y. Abokar, Y. A. Haroon, A. M. Warsame, M. A. Farah and M. F. Hersi (2015), 'The economics of elections in Somaliland: The financing of political parties and candidates'. Rift Valley Institute Research Paper 3, London and Nairobi. Available at: https://riftvalley.net/publication/economics-elections-somaliland (available 3 November 2022).

Vigneswaran, D. and J. Quirk (2015), *Mobility Makes States: Migration and Power in Africa* (Philadelphia: University of Pennsylvania Press).

Wallisch, S. (2018), 'Logistical challenges to relief aid: An explorative study on Somaliland's transport sector and the emergence of logistics service providers', MA Thesis, Aarhus University.

Walls, M. (2009), 'The emergence of a Somali state: Building peace from civil war in Somaliland', *African Affairs*, 108(432), pp. 371–89.

Wasuge, M. (2016), 'Turkey's assistance model in Somalia: Achieving much with little'. Heritage Institute for Policy Studies, Mogadishu. Available at http://www.heritageinstitute.org/wp-content/uploads/2016/02/Turkeys-Assistance-Model-in-Somalia-Achieving-Much-With-Little1-1.pdf (accessed 25 October 2022).

Webersik, C. (2006), 'Mogadishu: An economy without a state', *Third World Quarterly*, 27(8), pp. 1463–80.

Weitzberg, K. (2017), *We Do Not Have Borders: Greater Somalia and the Predicaments of Belonging in Kenya* (Athens: Ohio University Press).

WFP (World Food Programme) (2018), 'Emergency rehabilitation work and capacity building at the Port of Kismayo: Standard project report 2018'. World Food Programme in Somalia. Available at: https://docs.wfp.org/api/documents/WFP-0000103933/download/?_ga=2.44457255.2036574073.1579087473–1013100212.157623 0855 (accessed 13 January 2020).

Whitehouse, B. (2012), *Migrants and Strangers in an African City: Exile, Dignity, Belonging* (Bloomington: Indiana University Press).

Williams, P. (2018), *Fighting for Peace in Somalia. A History and Analysis of the African Union Mission (AMISOM), 2007–2017* (Oxford: Oxford University Press).

Williams, P. D. (2017), 'Paying for AMISOM: Are politics and bureaucracy undermining the AU's largest peace operation?', *The Global Observatory*, 11 January. Available at: https://theglobalobservatory.org/2017/01/amisom-african-union-peacekeeping-financing/ (accessed 15 October 2021).

World Bank (1995), 'Implementation completion report, special assistance grant, Somalia. Report no. 14299'. World Bank, Washington, DC. 5 April. Available at: http://documents.worldbank.org/curated/pt/798281468335359742/pdf/multi0page.pdf (accessed 13 January 2020).

——— (2017), 'Somali poverty profile, June 2017: Findings from Wave 1 of the Somali High Frequency Survey'. World Bank, Washington, DC. June. Available at: https://openknowledge.worldbank.org/handle/10986/28470 (accessed 18 March 2021).

——— (2020), 'Somalia urbanization review. Fostering cities as anchors of development'. World Bank, Washington, DC. Available at: https://openknowledge.worldbank.org/handle/10986/35059 (accessed 2 November 2022).

World Bank and IFC (International Finance Corporation) (2012), *Doing Business in Hargeisa* (Washington, DC: World Bank).

Young, C. (1994), *The African Colonial State in Comparative Perspective* (New Haven, CT and London: Yale University Press).

INDEX

INDEX

INDEX

person-to-business payments, 69

political economy of, 60, 68–70

private telecom companies, 60, 64

socio-legal dimensions, 60

Somali digital financial ecosystem, emergence of, 66–8

Somali remittances, birth of, 61–6

Somali telecom sector, 64–70

state and non-state regulation and taxation, 60, 70–5

state formation and, 59–60

mobile network operator (MNO), 66–8, 75–6

Mogadishu market committees, 115–16, 119–20

Mogadishu Port, 14, 20, 78, 80–1, 82, *83*, 194, 208, 209

closure of, 82

gatekeeping practices, 99

relations to state making, 97

reopening of, 27, 85

revenues, 86, 87

revival and upgrading, 87

violence in, 84–5

Mogadishu

Islam and trade in, 50

local government and al-Shabaab partial incorporation, 121

markets governance, 118

Mohamed, Prophet, 48

Moi, Daniel arap, 133–5

M-Pesa, 40, 41

MSC, 86

Mu'salaha, 41

Mubarak, J. A., 185

multi-clan ownership, 44–5

Muñoz, José-María, 103

Mursal, Abukar, 114, 115–16, 120, 122

Nairobi City County (NCC), 115, 121, 165–6

National Communications Act, 71

NGOs, 96, 207

9/11 terror attacks, 60, 65–6

non-Somali truck drivers, 109

North Eastern Province, 22, 23

Northern Frontier District (NFD), 22

Ogaadeen clan, 129, 180–1

Ogaden War (1977–78), 24, 180

Ogaden, 22, 42

Ogadeni clan, 133–4

'oligopolistic state', 179

Olson, M., 9, 10

Omar, 190

One-Stop Border-Posts, 194

ONLF, 21

'Operation Linda Duka', 52

Osman Mohamud Majeerteen, 85

Overseas Development Assistance (ODA), 61

P&O Ports, 87, 88

'parking tax', 161

Polanyi, K., 80

political authorities, multiplication of, 10–11

'political-military entrepreneurship', 25

politics of circulation, 5–6, 146–7

Port of Sudan, 97, 100

porters, 91–2

private-public 'landlord model', 79

INDEX